Colonial Australian Fiction

SYDNEY STUDIES IN AUSTRALIAN LITERATURE

Robert Dixon, Series Editor

The **Sydney Studies in Australian Literature** series publishes original, peer-reviewed research in the field of Australian literary studies. It offers well-researched and engagingly written re-evaluations of the nature and importance of Australian literature, and aims to reinvigorate its study both locally and internationally. It will be of interest to those researching, studying and teaching in the diverse fields of Australian literary studies.

Alex Miller: The Ruin of Time
Robert Dixon

Contemporary Australian Literature: A World Not Yet Dead
Nicholas Birns

The Fiction of Tim Winton: Earthed and Sacred
Lyn McCredden

Shirley Hazzard: New Critical Essays
Ed. Brigitta Olubas

Colonial Australian Fiction

Character Types, Social Formations and the Colonial Economy

Ken Gelder and Rachael Weaver

SYDNEY UNIVERSITY PRESS

First published by Sydney University Press
© Ken Gelder and Rachael Weaver 2017
© Sydney University Press 2017

Reproduction and Communication for other purposes
Except as permitted under the Act, no part of this edition may be reproduced, stored in a retrieval system, or communicated in any form or by any means without prior written permission. All requests for reproduction or communication should be made to Sydney University Press at the address below:

Sydney University Press
Fisher Library F03
University of Sydney NSW 2006
AUSTRALIA
sup.info@sydney.edu.au
sydney.edu.au/sup

National Library of Australia Cataloguing-in-Publication Data

Creators:	Gelder, Kenneth and Weaver, Rachael, authors.
Title:	Colonial Australian fiction : character types, social formations and the colonial economy / Kenneth Gelder and Rachael Weaver.
ISBNs:	9781743324615 (pbk)
	9781743324622 (ebook: epub)
	9781743324639 (ebook: mobi)
	9781743325209 (ebook: PDF)
Series:	Sydney studies in Australian literature.
Notes:	Includes bibliographical references and index.
Subjects:	Literature and society—Australia.
	Australian fiction—19th century—History and criticism.
	Australian literature—19th century—History and criticism
	Authors, Australian—19th century—History and criticism.

Cover image: Detail from William Strutt, *Bushrangers, Victoria, Australia 1852* (1887), oil on canvas, 75.7cm x 156.6cm (sight), The University of Melbourne Art Collection. Gift of the Russell and Mab Grimwade Bequest 1973. 1973.0038.
Cover design by Miguel Yamin

Contents

Acknowledgements   vii

Introduction: The Colonial Economy and the Production of Colonial Character Types   1

1   The Reign of the Squatter   29

2   Bushrangers   53

3   Colonial Australian Detectives   73

4   Bush Types and Metropolitan Types   91

5   The Australian Girl   117

Works Cited   139

Index   149

Acknowledgements

This book was produced with the assistance of an Australian Research Council Discovery Grant (DP140102288) and we are grateful to the ARC for its generous support of the project. We want to thank Rachel Fensham, head of the School of Culture and Communication at the University of Melbourne, for her encouragement and sponsorship, especially over the last year or so. Thanks also go to the dean of the Faculty of Arts at the University of Melbourne, Mark Considine, for the faculty's ongoing support of the Australian Centre where this book was researched and written. We would like to thank Denise O'Dea and Agata Mrva-Montoya for their production work on our manuscript and cover design. Our thanks especially go to Robert Dixon and Susan Murray for welcoming this book into their Sydney Studies in Australian Literature series at Sydney University Press, and for providing such thoughtful feedback and assistance.

We are grateful to the Ian Potter Museum of Art at the University of Melbourne for permission to reproduce on the cover a section of William Strutt's painting *Bushrangers, Victoria, Australia 1852* (1887).

Introduction
The Colonial Economy and the Production of Colonial Character Types

This book is about character types in colonial Australian fiction and their relationship to a rapidly developing colonial economy, which we understand in broad terms as an entire network of transactions and investments to do with land purchase and infrastructure, financial speculation and enterprise, labour, manufacturing and productivity, the accumulation of wealth and the circulation of capital.[1] One of our arguments is that colonial Australia generated a multiplicity of character types, each of which engaged with the economy in a particular way. We can think of character types as models of social identity, or what Elizabeth Fowler calls "social persons".[2] An identity defined by nation or colony provided one obvious way of invoking such a model, deployed in order both to generalise and to stabilise character in social terms: for example, as an "Australian", a "Queenslander", a "Vandemonian" (after Van Diemen's Land), and so on. In colonial Australia, "settler" and "Aboriginal" also provided two definitive categories of social identification, generally understood in opposition to each other, that is, antagonistically. But these *macro* forms of identification in turn accommodated a remarkable range of character types, each of which enunciated a colonial predicament that was unique in so far as it projected the values, dispositions and desires that were specific to it. Nationally identified character types can certainly do this, but they are difficult to sustain; they soon break down into component parts that are animated and put into play, quickly developing traits of their own. Whenever types speak, other types are invariably invoked, and frequently talk back. In colonial Australian fiction, this might happen as much around a camp fire as it does around a dining table or on the street in a city or a country town. And

---

1   We draw the term "colonial economy" from the work of economic historians such as Philip McMichael, *Settlers and the Agrarian Question: Foundations of Capitalism in Colonial Australia* (Cambridge: Cambridge University Press, 1984); Noel Butlin, *Forming a Colonial Economy: Australia 1810–1850* (Cambridge: Cambridge University Press, 1994); and Ian W. McLean, *Why Australia Prospered: The Shifting Sources of Economic Growth* (Princeton, NJ: Princeton University Press, 2013). These historians trace a range of phases in Australia's early economic development, from pre-1788 Aboriginal economies to "convict economies", the pastoral economy, the growth of colonial cities and increasing levels of commercial independence.
2   See Elizabeth Fowler, *Literary Character: The Human Figure in Early English Writing* (Ithaca, NY: Cornell University Press, 2003), 2: "Social persons are models of the person, familiar concepts of the social being that attain currency through common use".

as encounters and exchanges take place, narratives develop that are littered with types and are even driven by types: a new chum's experience, a squatter's story, a hut shepherd's tale, a colonial detective's investigations, the chronicles of an "Australian girl" in the colonies.

In fact, colonial Australian fiction emerged at the very moment that European literature turned its attention to character types, under the influence of work in disciplines such as ethnology (e.g. James C. Pritchard), physiognomy (Johann Lavatar, Franz Gall) and evolutionary zoology (Carl Linnaeus, Comte de Buffon, Georges Cuvier). In the foreword ("Avant Propos") to his *La Comédie Humaine* – the extraordinarily wide-ranging series of novels and stories he published through the 1830s and early 1840s – Honoré de Balzac made the link between zoological species and character types explicit:

> Does not Society make man, according to the environment in which he lives and acts, into as many different men as there are species in zoology? The differences between a solider, a worker, an administrator, a lawyer, a vagrant, an academic, a statesman, a businessman, a sailor, a poet, a pauper, and a priest are as great, although more difficult to define, than those between the wolf, the lion, the ass, the crow, the shark, the seal, the ewe, etc. Thus, there have always existed, and will always exist, social species just as there have always existed zoological species. If Buffon could produce a magnificent work by attempting to represent in a single book the whole realm of zoology, is there not a work in this genre to complete for the social realm?[3]

The view that a city like Paris – a "social realm" – was full of differentiated human "species" or "types" soon became commonplace. Albert Smith, who had spent time in Paris as a medical student, was an early contributor to *Punch* and went on to become a popular novelist and theatrical entertainer; Charles Dickens and William Thackeray were among his literary acquaintances. He was also the author of a series of light-hearted but detailed "natural histories" of English character types, published in 1847 and 1848: the "gent" ("We trust the day will come . . . when the Gent will be an extinct species"),[4] the "idler upon town", the ballet-girl, and others. Paying tribute to "the unceasing labours of Cuvier, Linnaeus, Buffon . . . and other animal-fanciers on a large scale", Smith used the evocative phrase "social zoology" to describe his studies of the "different varieties of the human race".[5] Later on we shall see Albert Smith mentioned, along with Dickens, in a passage written in Sydney by Frank Fowler in the late 1850s that describes the colonial-born "Australian boy". This is important to note, because Balzac's sense of character-as-species and Smith's notion of "social zoology" – among other prevailing pseudo-scientific ways of configuring literary characters – did indeed travel out to the Australian colonies to influence representations

---

3 Honoré de Balzac, foreword to *The Human Comedy*, in *European Literature from Romanticism to Postmodernism: A Reader in Aesthetic Practice*, ed. Martin Travers (London: Bloomsbury, 2001), 87.
4 Albert Smith, *The Natural History of the Gent* (London: David Bogue, 1847), 104.
5 Albert Smith, *The Natural History of the Ballet-Girl* (London: David Bogue, 1847), 7–8. Jo Briggs has argued that Smith's natural histories were directly influenced by Louis Huart's *Physiologie du flâneur*, published in Paris in 1841, a book that has subdivided the figure of the city stroller into various component parts – for example, the *musard* (or "idler"), the *gamin de Paris* (or "Parisian street urchin"), and so on. See Jo Briggs, "Flâneurs, Commodities, and the Working Body in Louis Huart's *Physiologie du flâneur* and Albert Smith's *Natural History of the Idler Upon Town*", in *The Flâneur Abroad: Historical and International Perspectives*, ed. Richard Wrigley (Newcastle upon Tyne, UK: Cambridge Scholars Publishing, 2014).

and understandings of colonial life. To give just one brief example from around this time: Thomas McCombie's novel *Adventures of a Colonist* (1845), is subtitled *Godfrey Arabin, the Settler*. But it soon breaks the "settler" down into a series of more specific character types, one of which is the "squatter" (the subject of Chapter 1 of our book). This type is then itself broken down into a variety of "species", and in fact the novel pauses at one point precisely to describe "the numerous samples of the 'squatter' species who crowded about the room".[6] It repeats this colonial version of "social zoology" later on when a party of squatters and settlers come together to tell each other stories:

> The persons assembled were all settlers or squatters, and excellent specimens of the squatting interest. There was the outlandish settler, a rough, half-civilised (in manner) kind of fellow. There was a more dandified settler, whose station was just across the river; and a stock-owner and jobber, who had stations in different parts of the country. (240)

The "outlandish settler", we should note, is momentarily mistaken for another colonial Australian character type, the bushranger – but he distinguishes himself from the latter by sourly noting (rather like Albert Smith on the extinction of the "gent") that "bushranging will soon be out of date" (240).

The zoological mapping of social realms in terms of species and specimens – or types – flowed naturally enough into literary frameworks, providing a pseudo-scientific basis for the production (and recognition) of character. The words *species* and *specimen* are etymologically derived from the Latin *specere*, "to see" or "to look (at)": they are "spectacular" things, soliciting the writer's attention, asking to be apprehended and examined. It was the task of capturing the essence of these types and species that gave literature its ethnographic imperative. Balzac's contemporary, the journalist and critic Jules Janin, had turned to the question of the social type in his book *The American in Paris* (1843), insisting that character could *only* be understood ethnographically: for example, by an urban spectator sufficiently familiar with street life, or by novelists. Here, the type is not a fixed or solid entity but something more fleeting or chimerical. And yet, paradoxically, it is also already fully formed, and properly representative:

> The French writers of the modern school very often use a word, which is quite new, the word *type*. Whoever speaks of *type*, speaks of a complete character, a model man, a curious thing. Paris is full of types, or rather of singular minds, of original characters, out of which a good book might easily be made. The passing stranger is not very ready, in seizing these shadows, these differences, these eccentric singularities. It is necessary to walk the street of the great city, for some time, to be able to trace with a sure hand, one of these brilliant meteors; they appear and disappear, like the cloud or the smoke . . .[7]

For Mary Gluck, Janin's commentary expresses "the unprecedented nature of modernity"; the social realist novel at this time therefore becomes an increasingly inclusive, analytical form, providing space for an emerging and ever-widening array of distinct "social and occupational groups" whose essential nature has to be properly conveyed. Gluck writes:

---

6 Thomas McCombie, *Adventures of a Colonist; or, Godfrey Arabin, the Settler* (London: John & Daniel A. Darling, 1845), 110. All subsequent references are to this edition and appear in parentheses in the text.
7 Jules Janin, *An American in Paris* (London: Longman, Brown, Green & Longmans, 1843), 162.

"Creating types and classifying them according to social categories represented a kind of modern ethnography, whose purpose was to achieve a comprehensive picture of contemporary humanity".[8] In our book, however, we want to suggest that social types also frustrate this purpose, unravelling the possibility of being "comprehensive" by the sheer fact of their proliferation. The more one focuses on a particular type or species, the more one analyses and dissects it, the more prominent it then becomes – to the extent that it can completely override the aspiration to be all-inclusive. Types can take control of a narrative, determining its priorities and ideological direction. We shall see this happen over and over in the following chapters: for example, in the "squatter novel" or in bushranger fiction, or in narratives about hut shepherds or swagmen or "currency lasses". But types also change, they come and go, they interrupt, they mutate. To return to Janin, above, they "appear and disappear, like the cloud or the smoke": this is another reason why comprehensiveness is difficult to sustain.

Heads of the People

A few years after Balzac and Janin's commentaries on species and types, the Sydney journalist and printer William Baker launched a weekly magazine called *Heads of the People*, with lithographic illustrations by the well-known local portrait painter, William Nicholas. It ran from April 1847 to March 1848: the same years that saw the publication of Albert Smith's English "natural histories". *Heads of the People* was a quasi-literary magazine that, among other things, serialised Charles Dickens' *Dombey and Son* just a few months after that novel's serialisation commenced in England. Its main purpose, however, was to represent or model colonial character types, in a way that combined close ethnographic observation with the literary sketch. "The conductors of this journal", an early editorial announced, "have chosen to depict the heads of the people – and to find them we must look into the classes whose habits and customs and mode of life most extensively influence the prevailing manners of the times".[9] The striking thing about this Sydney weekly is that the various character types it presents to its readers – the mayor, the inspector of nuisances, the night auctioneer, the pieman, the editor's wife – seem to have been selected almost at random, many of them going against the expected sense of what "heads of the people" might conventionally imply, that is, leaders or people of high rank. Baker's weekly took its title – and its project – from a series of sketches published in England in 1840-41, assembled by a network of well-known writers that included Thackeray, Leigh Hunt, William Howitt (who visited Australia in the early 1850s), Richard Brinsley Peake and Douglas Jerrold. The preface to *Heads of the People: or, Portraits of the English* talks initially about national identity, invoking the figure of John Bull. But it soon divides this nationally representative figure into a "family" of character types that continues to multiply: "We here give some thirty of his children: we shall present the world with at least as many more".[10] Again, these types seem almost randomly strung together: "the cockney", "the diner-out", "the young squire", "the sporting gentleman", "the basket-woman", and so

---

8   Mary Gluck, *Popular Bohemia: Modernism and Urban Culture in Nineteenth-Century Paris* (Cambridge, Mass.: Harvard University Press, 2005), 93.
9   "The Night Auctioneer", *Heads of the People: An Illustrated Journal of Literature, Whims, and Oddities*, 8 May 1847, 1.

on. Some types immediately call up others, expressing small-scale economic or social dependencies: "the debtor and creditor", for example, or "the chaperon and the debutante". There is no overall coherence to these character sketches, however, and no apparent hierarchy of importance. This English *Heads of the People* reads a bit like an anthology, a multi-authored conglomeration of literary sketches of social types who occupy the same time and place but do not necessarily connect to each other. We could draw on the term *parataxis* here to describe the way this mid-nineteenth-century series strings social types together, one after the other, without investing in any sort of comprehensive, unified image of "society". Its social fracturing is in fact what makes it modern: "Parataxis is the dominant mode of postindustrial experience. It is difficult to escape from atomized subject areas, projects, and errands into longer, connected stretches of subjectively meaningful narrative – not to mention life".[11]

Baker's Sydney-based *Heads of the People* came in the wake of these English character sketches and took its cue from them, especially in terms of its light satirical mode. But by making its character types emphatically colonial – and, in particular, by situating them in the framework of a fledgling colonial economy – it gave these otherwise atomised settler figures a larger role to play. In her important book *The Economy of Character* (1998), Deirdre Shauna Lynch talks about how readers, by the mid-eighteenth century, increasingly "used characters ... to renegotiate social relations in their changed, commercialized world".[12] Under its newer ethnological imperative, literature ushered in a range of novel character types, each of which needed to be made "legible" to readers not just in terms of professional/social identity but through a connotative set of dispositions, foibles, sensibilities, habits, strengths and weaknesses, hopes and longings. In fact, it is the very multiplicity of types that made a character's definition and legibility all the more necessary. The categorisation and classification of multiple character types might very well have fractured the social realm, but these things could also work as markers to orient readers and help them adjust to a rapidly transforming modern world. "What changes as the eighteenth century unfolds", Lynch argues, "are the pacts that certain ways of writing character establish ... with other, adjacent discourses – discourses on the relations that instruct people in how to imagine themselves as participants in a nation or in a marketplace or as leaders or followers of fashion".[13] Baker's *Heads of the People* put readers and character types into a sort of dialogue with each other, orienting/instructing the former and reconfiguring the social status and economic function of the latter. Some of these types might seem peripheral or minor; but we want to suggest that this colonial weekly insisted on their potential as structuring mechanisms in the successful functioning of an emerging colonial social world.

As we have noted, one of the early "heads of the people" this journal singles out for attention is the night auctioneer: "a member of the community", the editorial tells us, "with whom numbers of our Sydney population are on terms of intimate acquaintance".[14]

---

10   Preface to *Heads of the People: or, Portraits of the English*, illus. by Kenny Meadows (Philadelphia: Carey & Hart, 1841), vi.
11   Bob Perelman, "Parataxis and Narrative: The New Sentence in Theory and Practice", in *The Ends of Theory*, ed. Jerry Herron et al. (Detroit: Wayne State University Press, 1996), 246.
12   Deirdre Shauna Lynch, *The Economy of Character: Novels, Market Culture, and the Business of Inner Meaning* (Chicago: University of Chicago Press, 1998), 4.
13   Lynch, *The Economy of Character*, 11.
14   "The Night Auctioneer", 1.

This character type was usually associated with stolen goods, thieves and criminals, and the night auctions themselves were hidden away, secretive and illicit. Nevertheless, the night auctioneer is given an instrumental role in the fluid circulation of goods through the marketplace. More importantly, he invests those goods with enabling narratives that lend them the legitimacy needed to make transactions possible. "The half-dozen of silver spoons that you brought with you from home", the journal tells us, "are described as the remnant of the family plate of a person of distinction, who is about to proceed to India. The Cashmere shawl and silk dress, which he pronounces unrivalled in the Colony, were the property of a lady remarkable for taste and fashion, who had perished at sea". The night auctioneer's stories make these goods exotic and desirable by putting them into an aristocratic register (with overtones of tragedy) and connecting them to the global/colonial circulation of luxury commodities. He reminds the colony that the goods that flow into it have what Arjun Appadurai had called "social lives" (fictional or otherwise) that lend them new value.[15] In doing so, this otherwise fraudulent, self-interested character type plays out a public, even pastoral role that contributes to the colony's wellbeing:

> Assuredly in the operation of such a system, the night auctioneer is a "head of the people" . . . [He] ought then to be respectable; but a man cannot be respectable whose profession is misrepresented and despised. He cannot in such a position feel his respectability; and it is to this end – the true appreciation of his situation and importance – that we have devoted this article, and as long as the class can boast of such members as the one whose portrait adorns our present pages, we are sure that its pursuits, however at times perverted, must be compatible with every duty of good citizenship.[16]

Instead of being excluded from the colonial social fabric, the night auctioneer is brought back in as a binding, regulatory – and unexpectedly compassionate – force. His role arguably resembles that of the "civic-republican", which Nancy Fraser invokes in her essay "Rethinking the Public Sphere". Engaging with the work of Jurgen Habermas, Fraser offers a sense of the public sphere as a "plurality of competing publics", each "situated in a single 'structured setting' that advantages some and disadvantages others".[17] The night auctioneer in colonial Sydney is folded into this "structured setting", bringing publics together, advantaging some and disadvantaging others as the exchange of goods takes place. But as a minor or marginal character type he is also distanced from all this: he can never fully inhabit the role of "good citizenship". Operating at the illicit, peripheral end of commercial activity, his pastoral role both co-exists and contrasts with the "perverted" nature of his "pursuits". *Heads of the People* therefore asks its readers to entertain contradictory aspects of the colonial economy through this distinctive figure: publicity versus secrecy, legitimacy versus illicitness, fraudulence versus honesty, and the common good versus self-interest.

---

15   Arjun Appadurai, "Introduction: Commodities and the Politics of Value", in *The Social Life of Things: Commodities in Cultural Perspective*, ed. Arjun Appadurai (New York: Cambridge University Press, 1986), 5.
16   "The Night Auctioneer", 1.
17   Nancy Fraser, "Rethinking the Public Sphere: A Contribution to the Critique of Actually Existing Democracy", in *Habermas and the Public Sphere*, ed. Craig Calhoun (Cambridge, Mass.: MIT Press, 1992), 125.

Introduction

The August 1847 issue of *Heads of the People* introduced a Sydney pieman, William Francis King, who by this time was a kind of local celebrity. King's story begins in London where, as the son of a government paymaster, he works at first for a company of stockbrokers and traders and then as a clerk in the Treasury. His circumstances in England look promising; but the journal goes on to note that King's "restless disposition did not allow him to hold long", and in 1829 he leaves for the colonies. He becomes a provincial school master at Bong Bong in the Southern Highlands of New South Wales, and then a children's tutor; later, he wants to return to England but his "unsettled temper" makes this impossible. Finding work as a barman in Sydney, he then – as *Heads of the People* puts it – "commenced performing a series of feats of pedestrianism, in which he seems to have taken great delight":

> One of his earliest feats was walking one thousand six hundred and thirty-four miles in five weeks and four days, out of which period he had only nine days of fair weather. It was at the time of the flood on the Hawkesbury. Some heavy bets were made on this feat; but it did not appear that the poor pieman reaped any advantage beyond his self-gratification at having acquitted himself so well . . . He walked from Sydney to Parramatta and back, twice a day for six consecutive days. He undertook on one occasion to carry a dog, weighing upwards of seventy lbs, from Campbelltown to Sydney, between the hours of half-past twelve at night and twenty minutes to nine the next morning; which he accomplished twenty minutes within the given time. He was backed to carry a live goat, weighing ninety-two lbs, with twelve lbs dead weight besides, from the Old Talbot Inn, on Brickfield Hill, to Mr Nash's, at Parramatta, in seven hours; which he performed, having twelve minutes to spare.[18]

King literally enacts his "restless disposition" in the colonies here, moving relentlessly from place to place, carrying increasingly ludicrous burdens. Transactions happen (through a gambling economy), but nothing productive occurs; on the other hand, King's reputation spreads and he gains self-esteem from "having acquitted himself so well". This is a narrative that transforms colonial failure into a certain sort of heroic achievement. Henry Kingsley mentioned "the immortal 'flying pieman'" in *The Recollections of Geoffry Hamlyn* (1859); and in fact, King's remarkable pedestrian feats are remembered even today: "In an age of eccentrics, William King stands out as a true original".[19]

The point at which King becomes a "head of the people", however, is when these walking circuits are put to use as delivery routes, when he becomes a pieman: that is, when this "pass-time" becomes an occupation. Selling hot pies on the street, his voice is now "among the most prominent of the Sydney 'cries'". Street criers in colonial Sydney were themselves notable types, performing a civic function by disseminating information, making public announcements, selling goods, and so on. Anne Doggett has written about town criers in colonial Australian towns and cities along exactly these lines: "Underlying much of the community response to bellmen was the impact of the personalities themselves, with their distinctive public presence and their relationship with the people".[20] The Flying Pieman had already appeared as a character in *Life in Sydney; or, The Ran*

---

18 "The Pieman", *Heads of the People*, 7 August 1847, 1.
19 Edwin Barnard, "The Ladies' Walking Flying Sporting Pieman, All Hot as Love", in *Emporium: Selling the Dream in Colonial Australia* (Canberra: National Library of Australia, 2015), 150.

Dan Club (1843), a colonial play modelled on Pierce Egan's immensely popular series of sketches, *Life in London* (1820-22). When he walks onto the stage, surrounded by cheering boys and girls, another character announces, "Why, Jerry, this fellow is by profession a pieman, his voice may be heard all up and down Pitt Street every night singing All Hot".[21] King's occupation turns out to have a regulatory, binding force for the colony. "The piemen are . . . a useful class", *Heads of the People* tells us. Their pies are consumed by "jurors, witnesses and spectators at the Darlinghurst Court House". The editor himself consumes them, and goes on to note how often "the lonely bachelor, on leaving the theatre between 11 and 12 o'clock, [has] paused at the corner of the street, and partaken of these pasties of sweet smelling savour, who might otherwise have gone supperless to his solitary pallet".[22] The pieman helps to reintegrate "solitary" individuals into the social life of the colony here; and he also – linking his pedestrian feats with the delivery of pies – brings continuity to otherwise distant parts of the city. In her 2010 book about Sydney, Delia Falconer invokes this figure in exactly these terms:

> the city has always loved its public "characters", like . . . the "peculiar and vivacious" Flying Pieman, William King, who, top hat decorated with streamers, would sell his home-made pastries to passengers boarding the Parramatta steamer at Circular Quay, then sprint 18 miles overland to sell them the remainder as they disembarked.[23]

It is as if the pieman and his pies are everywhere at once: places of departure and arrival, the courthouse, the theatre, the editor's offices, and so on.

Like the night auctioneer, then, the Sydney pieman was a minor or peripheral colonial character type who nevertheless performed a kind of socially binding civic duty. What was previously a "past-time" of manic proportions – his pedestrianism – now becomes a part of the "structured setting" of Sydney's colonial economy: not central to anything in particular, but no less important to its successful operation. An 1889 article about the history of Parramatta in the *Illustrated Sydney News* fondly remembered King and cast him as fully representative of his social type: "Such . . . pie-vendors were once very familiar sights in the streets of Sydney, but King, who, from his occupation and rapid gait, had received the popular *soubriquet* of 'The Flying Pieman', was far and away the most noted specimen of the whole *genus*".[24] This sense of King as a representative type sits alongside accounts of his eccentricity, just as his role in binding different aspects of the colony together sits alongside his peripheral or minor social status.

It is worth briefly comparing this account of a colonial Sydney pieman to Henry Mayhew's description of street piemen in *London Labour and the London Poor*, a popular and influential series of ethnographic studies of itinerant London street folk that was gathered together as a four-volume publication in 1861. The London piemen, Mayhew notes, "are seldom stationary" – although there are no remarkable feats of pedestrianism worth mentioning.[25] What Mayhew finds most interesting about the piemen are the

---

20 Anne Doggett, "Crying in the Colonies: The Bellmen of Early Australia", *Journal of Australian Colonial History* 14 (2012), 63.
21 See Richard Fotheringham, ed. *Australian Plays for the Colonial Stage, 1834–1899* (St Lucia: University of Queensland Press, 2006), 67.
22 "The Pieman", 1.
23 Delia Falconer, *Sydney* (Sydney: NewSouth Books, 2010), 169.
24 "Parramatta – Past and Present", *Illustrated Sydney News*, 22 August 1889, 17.

everyday details of their trade: what the pies consist of, who the customers are, and what kinds of transactions take place. There is no sense here that London piemen have any kind of larger, socially binding role to play. Quite the opposite, in fact: the growth in "penny pie-shops" meant that street piemen were an endangered species, facing extinction. *London Labour and the London Poor* works by atomising its street folk, subdividing them into discrete units ("Of Street Piemen", "Of Water-Carriers", "Watercress Girl", and so on) that are then minutely analysed as "specimens" or character types. What prevents this ethnographic study from becoming paratactic – an arbitrarily arranged string of microscopic case studies, like the English and Sydney-based *Heads of the People* – is Mayhew's overarching moral perspective, which (however sympathetically) registered itinerant street folk as essentially deviant or degenerate, and perpetually struggling to survive. Daniel Bivona and Roger B. Henkle note that, for Mayhew, the itinerant street folk of London are "a form of waste. They are the tailings of the commodified economy".[26] They have, as these authors put it, very little "range" not only in terms of the local spaces they inhabit but also in terms of their imagination: each character lives "mentally in a labyrinth that resembles the geography of his neighbourhood".[27] In Baker's *Heads of the People*, however, the pieman's pedestrianism massively *increases* his range and expands his economic capacity. He functions not at the tail end of the economy, but in its midst: everyone gets to taste his pies, sometimes more than once in the same day. It is only much later on, in fact, that his career unravelled and came to an end. Charged with being "of unsound mind" in 1860, he was taken to court; but even here, he insisted on the centrality of his role in the colony, telling the judge about "his own especial fitness to heal all the wounds of the state"[28] – as if he really *were* one of the "heads of the people". Sadly, he spent his final years as an inmate in Sydney's Liverpool asylum.

The kinds of micro-ethnographic, quasi-literary studies we find in the English and colonial Australian *Heads of the People* – and in Henry Mayhew's *London Labour and the London Poor* a few years later – can certainly confuse conventional distinctions between characters and actual people. John Frow teases out these distinctions in his book *Character and Person* (2014), a detailed account of the ways in which "social persons" are articulated (and articulate themselves) in literary narratives. What is the ontological relationship between (actual) social persons and literary characters? For Frow, they are in fact analogous and mutually constitutive:

> character is, in certain respects . . . the analogue of "real" persons, conforming more or less closely and more or less fully to the schemata that govern, in any particular society, what it means to be a person and to have a physical body, a moral character, a sense of self, and a capacity for action. I say "in certain respects" because fictional character happens in accordance with the modes of being specified by particular genres; it is of the order of representation rather than of the order of the real.[29]

---

25 Henry Mayhew, *London Labour and the London Poor*, vol.1 (New York: Dover Publications, 1968), 195.
26 Daniel Bivona and Roger B. Henkle, *The Imagination of Class: Masculinity and the Victorian Urban Poor* (Columbus: Ohio State University Press, 2006), 13.
27 Bivona and Henkle, *The Imagination of Class*, 20.
28 "Central Police Court", *Empire*, 14 June 1860, 3.
29 John Frow, *Character and Person* (Oxford: Oxford University Press, 2014), 24–5.

Genre is a key determinant here: it represents social persons *as* characters, but the "mode of being" is always specific to a particular genre's imperatives. In this book we shall look at a number of fictional genres – the squatter novel, colonial detective fiction, the bushranger romance, the hut shepherd's tale, and so on – each of which creates a distinctive set of character types and maps out their relationship to, and position within, a generically defined socio-economic framework. Baker's *Heads of the People* is interesting in this respect because it can indeed look as if it is not generic at all: just a series of arbitrarily strung-together character sketches. One of its editorials tries to defend itself against this charge:

> It has been objected that we have selected our HEADS rather indiscriminately. To this we reply... that we cannot undertake to please every one. We invariably make our selections, not only with a view to please our readers generally, but to bring into notice rising talent, and drag from obscurity real merit wherever we find it. Besides, our Head is only given as the type or representative of a class; we cannot, therefore, expect to please any number of persons, and at the same time exactly coincide with the opinions of some fastidious individual, who looks upon himself as a sort of index to the feelings and opinions of the great body of the people, which he estimates by his own.[30]

In this account, the critical, pedantic reader ("some fastidious individual") is created as a social type in order then to be refuted: there are now too many different types in colonial Sydney for any single point of view to dominate. *Heads of the People* therefore ran the opposite risk of being too "indiscriminate". But this is itself a generic determinant. By valuing "rising talent" and making "real merit" visible, the journal emphasised drive, energy and the capacity for even the most peripheral (or illicit) figure to be socially useful. In doing so, it self-consciously inverted prevailing assumptions about the role and nature of its chosen "social persons" – as we have seen with the night auctioneer, for example – and upset taken-for-granted social hierarchies to do with who was important to the Australian colonies, and who wasn't.

Minor and Eccentric Types

Alex Woloch has investigated the figure of the minor character in his book *The One vs the Many* (2003), which focuses mostly on the work of three nineteenth-century English and French novelists: Jane Austen, Charles Dickens and Honoré de Balzac. The weight of a reader's attention conventionally rests on the protagonist at the expense of the minor or "secondary" characters. But for Woloch, the realist novel during this time gave its minor characters increasing significance; when we get to Dickens, minor figures could even eclipse the protagonist through the sheer force of their dispositions or attributes. "Dickens's minor characters compel intense attention, in-and-of-themselves", Woloch writes, "through the configuration of their personalities and physiognomy, the texture of their speech, and their immediate and direct interaction with the protagonists".[31] Minor

---

30 Preface, *Heads of the People*, 17 April 1847, n.p.
31 Alex Woloch, *The One vs the Many: Minor Characters and the Space of the Protagonist in the Novel* (Princeton: Princeton University Press, 2003), 127.

characters go in two, contradictory directions: they perpetually run the risk of being "drowned out within the totality of the narrative"; and yet, as Woloch puts it, they have a "strange centrality to so many texts".[32] In other words, they are marginal and disproportionately significant at the same time. They are "engulfed" by an overall narrative that they nevertheless impact upon, often in unexpected, dramatic ways. We shall see exactly this predicament in – for example – our discussion in Chapter 3 of the colonial detective Wilmore in Hume Nisbet's *The Swampers* (1897): a minor character who radically alters the final course of events, even as his role in relation to a larger, critical narrative about the colonial Australian economy remains peripheral.

Minor characters are literally "eccentric": that is, situated outside the centre of the narrative. For Woloch, their eccentric situations are also a reflection of the increased specialisation of labour roles under industrialisation. A minor character is one kind of embodiment of the division of labour, a principle or phenomenon advocated at least as far back as Adam Smith in *An Inquiry into the Nature and Causes of the Wealth of Nations* (1776). Smith had seen the division of labour – where every worker is dedicated to a single task – as central to the creation of wealth and prosperity at home and abroad. Specialised labour is integral here not only to nation building but also to empire building, tied in Smith's book to colonial trade and the global exchange of goods. For Karl Marx in *Capital* (1867), on the other hand, the production of wealth through the division of labour works instead to alienate the worker from these larger frameworks: "all means for the development of production transform themselves into a means of domination over, and exploitation of, producers; they mutilate the labourer into a fragment of a man . . . "[33] Woloch's account of minor characters seems to draw on both of these accounts, leading him to identify the integrated character on the one hand, and the alienated character on the other. He writes: "Both . . . kinds of minor characters in the nineteenth-century novel – the functional worker and the deviant eccentric – can be structured by, or emerge as a consequence of, the division of labor".[34] Under the influence of Marx in particular, Woloch then reaches this fundamental insight: "*minor characters are the proletariat of the novel*", subordinated and significant at the same time.[35]

But the "deviant eccentric" suggests another identity here, that of the *lumpenproletariat*. This term was used to describe a loosely affiliated collection of types that have no obviously productive role to play in the larger economy (or, in the larger narrative). Perhaps the most famous account of the *lumpenproletariat* in the nineteenth century occurred just a few years after the publication of Baker's *Heads of the People*. Written not long after he moved to London, Karl Marx's account in the *Eighteenth Brumaire of Louis Napoleon* (1852) of the French *lumpenproletariat*'s participation in Bonaparte's suppression of the 1848 revolution strung together a spectacular litany of "deviant eccentric" minor character types:

---

32 Woloch, *The One vs the Many*, 38, 37.
33 Karl Marx, *Capital: A Critique of Political Economy*, vol. 1, book 1, trans. Samuel Moore and Edward Aveling, ed. Frederick Engels, 445: https://www.marxists.org/archive/marx/works/download/pdf/Capital-Volume-I.pdf.
34 Woloch, *The One vs the Many*, 161.
35 Woloch, *The One vs the Many*, 27.

> Alongside decayed *roués* with dubious means of subsistence and of dubious origin, alongside ruined and adventurous offshoots of the bourgeoisie, were vagabonds, discharged soldiers, discharged jailbirds, escaped galley slaves, swindlers, mountebanks, *lazzaroni*, pickpockets, tricksters, gamblers, *maquereaus*, brothel keepers, porters, *literati*, organ-grinders, ragpickers, knife grinders, tinkers, beggars – in short, the whole indefinite, disintegrated mass, thrown hither and thither, which the French term *la bohème* . . .[36]

Socially and economically, these figures are at once peripheral and central (not least, to Bonaparte's success in quelling the revolution). We find more detailed versions of some of them later on in Mayhew's account of metropolitan street folk and "nomads" in *London Labour and the London Poor* (knife grinders, tinkers, etc.), and in a whole raft of colonial Australian sketches and portraits, including some of those already featured in Baker's *Heads of the People*.

Thomas McCombie's second series of *Australian Sketches* was published in 1861: the same year as Mayhew's work. McCombie was a Scottish emigrant who arrived in Melbourne in 1841, working as a journalist and politician and, for a brief period, a squatter. He wrote an early history of the Victorian colony, as well as two novels. *Australian Sketches* looks in detail at four distinct colonial character types, "The Squatters", "The Gold Diggers", "The Convicts" and "The Aborigines". All of these are integrated into what the opening "Advertisement" (or preface) for the book calls "a very interesting episode in the great epic of Australian Colonisation". Although he could see that "Christian society" brutalised and "degraded" Aboriginal people in the name of "civilisation", McCombie nevertheless bought into a prevailing settler assumption that they would eventually die out. Henry Mayhew's moralising depiction of London's street "nomads" – which notes their "passion . . . for intoxicating fermented liquors", their "delight in warfare and all perilous sports", their "desire for vengeance", the "absence of chastity" among the women, etc.[37] – is precisely echoed in McCombie's account of Aboriginal people who, he tells us, have "no high estimation of female chastity", a "drunken, indolent" nature, a love of "war and the chase", and an obsession with the "duty of avenging" inter-tribal murders.[38] These are certainly familiar racist descriptions. But as we can see, they are also descriptions that draw on an ethnographic vernacular equally applied to character types identified as *lumpenproletarian*. This means that they could be applied to certain settler types, too. It turns out that Mayhew's account of London's street folk's "want of providence in laying up a store for the future", "vague sense of religion" and "utter absence of all appreciation of the mercy of the Divine Spirit" also finds an exact echo in McCombie's description of colonial convicts:

> The men who have been convicts are termed "old hands;" they are mostly rude, rough men, with no moral principle or religious feeling, who have little sympathy for humanity. They do not exhibit much desire to marry and settle, as is usually the case with free

---

36 Cited in Robert C. Tucker, ed., *The Marx-Engels Reader* (New York: W.W. Norton, 1972), 479.
37 Henry Mayhew, *London Labour and the London Poor*, 2.
38 Thomas McCombie, *Australian Sketches: The Gold Discovery, Bush Graves, &c., &c.* (London: Sampson Low, Son & Co., 1861), 156, 155, 157, 158. All subsequent references are to this edition and appear in parentheses in the text.

emigrants; they spend their wages as soon as they are earned, and seem to have little wish to accumulate money... Hardly one of them could be trusted in the vicinity of a public-house; whatever situation of trust he was in he could not resist the temptation to get drunk. (141)

Here, convicts are a type of "social person" represented as the *lumpenproletariat*: a dissolute underclass that doesn't even aspire to the most basic requirements of colonial settlement (accumulation of capital, marriage, settlement, etc.). Gertrude Himmelfarb has perceptively used the term *lumpenproletariat* to talk about Mayhew's study, which (as shown in the subtitle to *London Labour and the London Poor*) had divided London's street folk into those who "*will* work", those who "*cannot* work" and those who "*will* not work": "In fact", she writes, "as Mayhew presented them", London street folk "seem to have been less a class in the Marxist sense than a species in the Darwinian sense".[39] The interplay between *class* and *species* is important to register here, and it is something we shall return to as we continue to discuss colonial Australian character types in this book. In particular, this interplay brings together the economic and the ethnographic in ways that reveal precisely the social aspects of the division of labour that Woloch so strongly identifies with the "minor character".

Labour – in terms of the way it contributed to building the nation – was especially important to McCombie, but there is a paradox here: namely, that in order to *develop* the nation, specialised forms of labour needed to remain fixed or static. In some cases, it can be hard to distinguish the "deviant eccentric" from the "functional worker", as if the *lumpenproletariat* and the *proletariat* can somehow inhabit the same space. McCombie's convicts do indeed work. In spite of everything, they contribute to the "great epic of Australian Colonisation". But the specialisation of their labour holds them in place, both economically and socially: "From their expertise in splitting timber, building, fencing, and, indeed, all pursuits of bush life, and by their remaining single and evincing no disposition to emerge from their social position as menial servants, they are much liked by many squatters and farmers..." (141). The convict's *lumpenproletarian* disposition (choosing not to settle or marry, having no social aspirations) is precisely what, in this account, transforms this type into a labouring class or *proletariat*.

When McCombie looks at the gold digger, however, these configurations radically change. *Australian Sketches* was published about ten years after the beginning of the gold rush in Victoria, which had a profound effect on colonial development, releasing capital across the colonies and dramatically increasing the population. Because the gold rush gave so many people the chance to make their fortune quickly – and because the goldfields themselves were thriving, bustling, competitive places – it created unprecedented possibilities for social mobility and transformation.[40] One type could turn into another type almost overnight. Successful gold diggers transcended their *lumpenproletarian* condition through their capacity to generate what Graeme Davison has called "instant

---

39 Gertrude Himmelfarb, "The Culture of Poverty", in *The Victorian City*, vol. 2, ed. Jim Dyos and Michael Wolff (London: Routledge, 2002), 712.
40 In his account of this turbulent period in Australian history, David Goodman writes, "If there was one thing that contemporaries agreed upon about the gold rushes, it was that they were a disturbance to the normal order of things": *Gold Seeking: Victoria and California in the 1850s* (Stanford: Stanford University Press, 1994), xiv.

cities"[41] – something that McCombie also finds striking, as he describes what happens when gold diggers come to occupy a fresh site:

> A spot may be uninhabited, wild, and dreary but in a few days after it may be transformed into a large city ... The stranger who reaches a plain in the far bush, which only a short time before was destitute of any sign of civilisation, will find himself in a comfortable city, surrounded by stores, hotels, and theatres. That great civiliser, the newspaper press, is not long behind, and often makes its appearance in a week or two after the great rush has set in for a new digging. It thus happens, that in an incredibly short space of time all the appliances of civilised life are gathered together. (137)

Here, the digger literally paves the way for what Robert Dixon has called "colonial modernity", "a series of developments in the late nineteenth and early twentieth centuries that linked apparently provincial cultures like those of the Australian colonies into a busy traffic in personnel [and] cultural practices ... around the English-speaking world".[42] Diggers here are seen as nation builders; but because they could get so rich so quickly, they could also threaten the colonies' stability. McCombie writes, "the gold diggers form a gregarious order, containing so many intelligent and spirited members that no Government can trifle with their interests" (129). (We shall see something similar with squatters in Chapter 1.) The successful gold digger also ran the risk of being cast as improvident, just as careless about saving money as McCombie's convicts. The gold digger's rapid accumulation of wealth could lead to widespread investment and development, but it also opened the way to the growth of other *lumpenproletarian* classes. As Davison notes: "Instant cities catered to the demand of young, spendthrift men for instant pleasures ... Melbourne's thousands of immigrant bachelors, far from home and without the immediate prospect of matrimony, were a ready market for prostitution".[43] The unsuccessful gold digger, on the other hand, remains permanently *lumpenproletarian*, a parasitical and potentially dangerous figure that continually undercuts the "civilised" aspirations of the ever-expanding goldfields' economy. "There are numbers of reckless vagabonds", McCombie remarks, "who infest the purlieus of these busy scenes, and live by plunder" (137).

Colourful sketches of life on the Victorian goldfields were commonplace in the 1850s and 1860s, often focusing on the convergence of different social types and classes and the kinds of tensions and struggles that resulted. The English writer William Howitt spent a couple of years in Australia in the early 1850s, writing about the Victorian goldfields and city life, describing Australian flora and fauna, and offering critiques of broader colonial issues such as land policy and taxes. Howitt's two-volume *Land, Labour, and Gold* (1855) is full of distinctive character types: shepherds, squatters, bushrangers, horse stealers, speculators, "lady storekeepers", new chums, "cockatoo settlers", and many others, including gold diggers. The first volume opens with the excitement of arrival in Melbourne amidst news of the gold rush. An acute observer of street spectacles, Howitt's attention is

---

41 Graeme Davison, "Gold-Rush Melbourne", in *Gold: Forgotten Histories and Lost Objects of Australia*, ed. Iain McCalman et al. (Cambridge: Cambridge University Press, 2001), 59.
42 Robert Dixon, *Photography, Early Cinema, and Colonial Modernity: Frank Hurley's Synchronised Lecture Entertainments* (London: Anthem Press, 2011), xxix.
43 Davison, "Gold-Rush Melbourne", 58.

immediately captured by the vast numbers of convicts disembarking in Melbourne to head out to the diggings:

> The old lags, another name for convicts, are flocking over from Sydney and Van Diemen's Land by thousands, – there is no exaggeration in the word. And what subjects they would afford the sketcher! Yesterday as we went down to the ship, the steamers were coming in from those colonies. They were densely packed in the deck of the steamer, as you have seen Irish emigrants on the decks of vessels setting sail from Liverpool for America. What men! and what costumes! Huge burley fellows with broad, battered straw or cabbage-tree hats, huge beards, loose blue shirts, and trowsers yellow with clay and earth, many of them showing that they had already been digging in Sydney, where there is much gold, but according to fame, not so abundant or so pure as in this colony; almost every man had a gun, or pistols in his belt, and a huge dog, half hound half mastiff, led by a chain. Each had his bundle, containing his sacking to sleep upon, his blanket and such slight change of linen as these diggers carry. They had, besides, their spades and picks tied together; and thus they marched up the country, bearing with them all they want, and lying out under the trees.
>
> Every day this scene is repeated; thousands follow upon thousands in the same style, and take the road at once towards the Diggings.[44]

Here, the convict-as-digger is a spectacular but threatening figure who – far from being an agent for some sort of colonial modernity – is instead a kind of throwback to the earliest stages of colonial settlement. Every "old lag" looks exactly the same; as "thousands upon thousands" of them "flock" together, the character type not only multiplies but also literally grows in stature ("Huge burley fellows ... huge beards ... a huge dog ... "). Howitt's sketch lends the convict-as-digger a visceral force, casting this figure as powerful, self-sufficient and driven.

Clara Morison, Settlers and Diggers

In colonial Australian crime and adventure fiction, *lumpenproletarian* inhabitants of the goldfields invested these spaces with a villainous energy, and the convict-as-digger was a stock example. The detective stories in James Skipp Borlase's *The Night Fossickers* (1867) are full of ex-convicts and other "ruffians" and "scoundrels" on the goldfields, all of whom disrupt any attempt to regulate and police this vibrant economic and social realm. The first story in this collection, "The Shepherd's Hut", turns the threatening potential of Howitt's convict-as-digger into something sensational and explicitly criminal: "throughout the country round prowling ruffians – escaped convicts from Sydney or Van Diemen's Land – were ever ready to waylay and murder the wandering digger for the sake of the gold they expected to find on his person".[45] In the title story, the larger-than-life villain Spider-legged Ned, who works on the goldfields, turns out to be an escaped convict, the

---

44 William Howitt, *Land, Labour, and Gold: Two Years in Victoria: with Visits to Sydney and Van Diemen's Land* (Cambridge: Cambridge University Press, 2010), 21.
45 James Skipp Borlase, *The Night Fossickers, and Other Australian Tales of Peril and Adventure* (London: Frederick Warne & Co., 1867), 3.

revelation of which helps to justify his trial and execution. Benjamin Farjeon arrived at the Victorian goldfields in 1854; he migrated to New Zealand in 1861 to join the Otago gold rush, and returned to England in 1867, a successful journalist and author. His story "In Australian Wilds", published in Melbourne's weekly *Leader* in October 1870, introduces an ex-convict, Lilly Trott, who gives a vibrant account of criminal activity on the goldfields. To become a digger is a radically transformative process, where one character type evolves or emerges out of another, quite different one. The disposition of ex-convicts might very well be organically suited to life as a digger; but in the following passage we find that even antithetical types can metamorphose in the goldfields setting to become (from the perspective of what they once were) unrecognisable:

> You see, it was so easy for a man to lose himself. Take a clerk out of a city office, sprucely dressed, and with a nicely trimmed moustache; send him on to the gold-fields, and let him grow his beard and dress himself in moleskin trousers and Scotch twill shirt; let him work for a few weeks at the bottom of a twenty-foot shaft, or stand at the windlass all the day with his sleeves tucked up to his shoulders, with a black cutty pipe in his mouth and an old billycock on his head, and the sun blazing down upon him and browning every bit of flesh it could get at – why, in six months his own wife wouldn't know him![46]

Around the time of Farjeon's story, the journalist and (failed) prospector William Withers was creating a sense of the goldfields as an "exclusively masculine domain"; but as Claire Wright has noted, "women were there too, and . . . their stories are just as . . . vibrant as the stories of the men".[47] Ellen Clacy sailed from London to the Victorian goldfields with her brother in 1852, the same year as William Howitt. Her account of her experiences there, *A Lady's Visit to the Gold Diggings of Australia*, was published in 1853 and presents among other things a detailed understanding of the goldfields' micro-economics. In fact, for Clacy it is small business owners – and this is where the division of labour is most visible – who prosper most of all: "It is not only the diggers", she writes, "who make money at the Gold Fields. Carters, carpenters, storemen, wheelwrights, butchers, shoemakers, &c., usually in the long run make a fortune quicker than the diggers themselves, and certainly with less hard work or risk of life".[48] This distinction between specialised forms of respectable labour and the riskier practice of prospecting is one we often see in colonial accounts of the goldfields. It connects to a prevailing perspective on the question of colonial prosperity that is caught up with the problem of wanting wealth accumulation to happen but not so quickly that it distorts or destabilises social norms. In Clacy's account – as we saw with McCombie – there is also always a *lumpenproletarian* component that threatens social and economic security:

> Many – perhaps, nine-tenths – of the diggers are honest industrious men, desirous of getting a little there as a stepping-stone to independence elsewhere; but the other tenth is composed of outcasts and transports – the refuse of Van Diemen's Land – men of the

---

46 B.J. Farjeon, "In Australian Wilds", in *The Anthology of Colonial Australian Crime Fiction*, ed. Ken Gelder and Rachael Weaver (Melbourne: Melbourne University Press, 2008), 88.
47 Claire Wright, *The Forgotten Rebels of Eureka* (Melbourne: Text Publishing, 2013), i, iii.
48 Ellen Clacy, *A Lady's Visit to the Gold Diggings in Australia in 1852–53* (1853; Auckland: The Floating Press, 2010), 69.

most depraved and abandoned characters, who have sought and gained the lowest abyss of crime, and who would a short time ago have expiated their crimes on a scaffold. They generally work or rob for a space, and when well stocked with gold, retire to Melbourne for a month or so, living in drunkenness and debauchery... There is more drinking and rioting at the diggings than elsewhere, the privacy and risk gives the obtaining it an excitement which the diggers enjoy as much as the spirit itself.[49]

The association of rapid wealth accumulation, "drinking and rioting" and "risk" made the colonial goldfields an especially unstable place. Government policies prohibiting diggers from purchasing land and insisting on licence fee payments – along with heavy-handed policing – fostered a prolonged period of civil disobedience that culminated in the Eureka rebellion at Ballarat in 1854. Catherine Helen Spence's novel *Clara Morison: A Tale of South Australia During the Gold Fever*, was published in the same year. Spence's family had emigrated from Scotland to South Australia in 1839, when she was fourteen. A much-admired social and political reformer later on, Spence invested heavily in the utopian potential of South Australia, as a colony without a history of convictism and where land purchase was highly regulated. In her autobiography, Spence writes about her hope for "a new community where land, labour and capital work harmoniously together":[50] an aspiration that puts her at odds with the turbulence of life on the goldfields in colonial Victoria and New South Wales.

The emigrant journalist Frederick Sinnett, one of the founders of Melbourne *Punch*, thought that *Clara Morison* was "decidedly the best Australian novel that we have met with".[51] In an essay titled "The Fiction Fields of Australia" (1856) – the earliest example of an extended work of colonial literary criticism – Sinnett especially valued the novel's tendency to downplay "local colouring". Local fiction, he argued, should not be overburdened with ethnographic description:

> If Australian characteristics are too abundant – if blackfellows, kangaroos, emus, stringy barks, gums, and wattles, and any quantity of other things illustrative of the ethnology, zoology, and botany, of the country are crowded together, a greater amount of detailed information may be conveyed upon a given number of square inches of canvas than would otherwise be possible, but the picture loses character proportionately as a work of art.[52]

Sinnett wants to say that *Clara Morison* comes close to achieving the aspirations of a national literature precisely (and paradoxically) because it limits its use of local "characteristics": "The story is thoroughly Australian, but at the same time is not a deliberate attempt to describe the peculiar 'manners and customs' of the Australians".[53] But is Spence's novel really so free from ethnographic imperatives? In fact, *Clara Morison* is not "thoroughly Australian" at all; its frame of reference is adamantly *South* Australian, and it is from this particular colonial perspective that different character types are registered and

---

49 Clacy, *A Lady's Visit to the Gold Diggings*, 72.
50 Cited in Susan Magarey, *Unbridling the Tongues of Women: A Biography of Catherine Helen Spence*, rev. ed. (Adelaide: University of Adelaide Press, 2010), 28.
51 Frederick Sinnett, "The Fiction Fields of Australia", *Illustrated Journal of Australasia*, November 1856, 199.
52 Sinnett, "The Fiction Fields of Australia", 199.
53 Sinnett, "The Fiction Fields of Australia", 200.

organised. The central binary in this novel is a stark distinction between the colonies of South Australia and Victoria, which is then chiefly understood as a distinction between two colonial character types: settlers and diggers. The preface to the novel makes it clear which type it prefers:

> The South Australian settlers were remarkable for their good fortune – it may be added for their sobriety, and for the good example they set to the rest of the diggers. A few months, in many cases a few weeks, sufficed to gratify their desires. None of them took kindly to Victoria, or thought of making a permanent abode there. They remembered, too, that warm hearts were beating for them in their own loved and beautiful province ... many a green valley, and vine-clad cottage, bore witness to the welcoming back ... of wanderers laden with their golden spoil.[54]

In Spence's novel, "South Australian settlers" never settle in Victoria. But as the South Australian economy stagnates, many of that colony's young men do indeed set off to the Victorian goldfields to earn money. The goldfields themselves are distanced from the novel, spatially, socially and morally. Even as local opportunities for work become scarce, Mrs Handy advises her husband not to go prospecting: "You know that most of the diggers are old convicts", she warns him (vol. 1, 152). More and more settlers leave South Australia for the goldfields, however, and as they depart, Adelaide seems to regress, as if it is returning to the earliest stages of colonisation: "The chief streets are still full of a most unsettled-looking population", Anne Elliot complains, "but the outskirts of Adelaide are greatly thinned ... " (vol. 1, 222). Her sister Margaret worries that the gold rush will destabilise the local economy by artificially inflating it, with the virtues of respectable labour overturned by the short-sighted priorities of fortune-hunting: "I am grieved that gold has been found in these colonies ... We were avaricious enough before the discovery, and I fear it will only feed the restless desire of our population to make money as easily as possible – we meet with so many men who think it quite a virtue to be worldly-minded" (vol. 2, 207-08). Life on the Victorian goldfields is reported at a distance through a series of letters written by, among others, Margaret's brother Gilbert. "We cannot make a home in this sort of vagabond life at the gold diggings", he complains, before going on to represent the social world of the goldfields ethnographically, as a "nomadic system" (vol. 2, 47, 48).

Clara Morison is an early South Australian novel that values social respectability and responsibility, and keeps its characters' aspirations tastefully modest. It ideologically invests in settlement, with all its bourgeois connotations of achievement, stability and comfort. When Gilbert and the other prospectors finally return to South Australia, a chapter heading announces with some relief: "The Diggers Settle Down". In *Clara Morison*, domesticity and homeliness literally triumph: the "nomadic system" of the goldfields is refuted, and the diggers who had left their families return to South Australia to become settlers all over again.

---

54 Catherine Helen Spence, *Clara Morison: A Tale of South Australia During the Gold Fever*, vol. 1 (London: John W. Parker & Son, 1854), v. All subsequent references are to this edition and appear in parentheses in the text.

Introduction

New Chums and the Colonial-Born

By the 1840s, it was already a matter of routine for commentators to subdivide colonial populations ethnographically in terms of their capacity to work and contribute effectively to the development of an often-unforgiving local economy. New arrivals or "new chums" were by this time distinguished from native-born colonials; not yet assimilated, they remained conspicuous and even spectacular, a source of mirth but also a means by which colonial priorities can be scrutinised and arranged. This character type was one of the subjects of the anonymous writer "Crayon's" "Sketches in Sydney" series, published in the *Australasian Chronicle* in the early months of 1840. "The New Chum (for that is his title) comes ashore in the evening", he writes; "poor devil, he little knows the pleasures that await him . . . '.[55] The romance of arrival is soon dismantled by the hard realities of Sydney life: "All the golden dreams of happiness which have lured him from his home vanish the very moment he seeks for a situation". Unable to find a job, it dawns on the new chum that he is already redundant. Perhaps recalling the figure of the city clerk who becomes a digger in Farjeon's story, the realisation utterly transforms him: "The first face he sees in the morning (his own in the glass) very much astonishes him – he has indeed forgotten 'what manner of man he was', and is endeavouring to find out what kind of being he is".[56] The writer and journalist Horace Earle was another English visitor to the Victorian goldfields in the 1850s. In his story "The Hurricane; or, False Friends", from *Ups and Downs; or, Incidents of Australian Life* (1861), a new chum is cast as typically naïve and optimistic in order to play out a narrative of economic disillusionment at the diggings: "'New chums' are ever sanguine, and invariably feel almost heart-broken at the first goldless hole; being filled with the idea that out of every one something more valuable than earth is sure to be extracted. They are soon, however, undeceived . . ."[57]

The new chum can also be found in the writings of Frank Fowler, an English journalist who arrived in Sydney in 1855. During his short time in the colonies, Fowler edited a literary journal, the *Month*, joined the Stenhouse circle (a literary group that included Charles Harpur, Henry Kendall and John Sheridan Moore), and gave public lectures on writers such as Douglas Jerrold and topics that included literary portraiture. Ann-Mari Jordens wryly describes Fowler as "a loveable young enthusiast with a sometimes unfortunate talent for self-publicity".[58] His lively impressions of Australia, *Southern Lights and Shadows* (1859), gave a "new chum's" perspective on the highs and lows of colonial life, greatly offending local sensibilities. Fowler was well aware of colonial disdain for the new chum, which he saw as more exaggerated in Sydney than in Melbourne: "the battle of 'old-handism' against 'new-chumism'", he writes, "is not everlastingly waging in Victoria as it is in New South Wales, where the natives are more intolerant and intolerable than the Bowery boys of America".[59] Even so, Fowler subscribed to the prevailing sense that new chums (many of whom – as he did – stayed only briefly in Australia) were the complete

---

55 "Crayon", "Sketches in Sydney, No.VI: The New Chum", *Australasian Chronicle*, 11 February 1840, 2.
56 "Crayon", "The New Chum", 2.
57 Horace Earle, "The Hurricane; or, False Friends", in *Ups and Downs; or, Incidents of Australian Life* (London: A.W. Bennett, 1861), 342.
58 Ann-Mari Jordens, *The Stenhouse Circle: Literary Life in Mid-Nineteenth Century Sydney* (Carlton, Vic.: Melbourne University Press, 1979), 54.
59 Frank Fowler, *Southern Lights and Shadows* (1859; Sydney: Sydney University Press, 1975), 15.

opposite of what became known as the colonial "native-born". Here is Fowler on the "colonial young-stock", that is, on native-born colonials as an emergent character type:

> The Australian boy is a slim, dark-eyed, olive-complexioned young rascal ... and systematically insolent to all servant girls, policemen, and new-chums. His hair is shiny with grease, as are the knees of his breeches and the elbows of his jacket. He wears a cabbage-tree hat, with a dissipated wisp of black ribbon dangling behind, and loves to walk meditatively with his hands in his pockets, and, if cigarless, to chew a bit of straw in the extreme corner of his mouth. His face is soft, bloomless, and pasty, and you fancy if you touched his cheek you would leave the stamp of your finger behind ... He is christened ... a gumsucker and a cornstalk. He can fight like an Irishman or a Bashi-Bazouk; otherwise he is orientally indolent, and will swear with a quiet gusto if you push against him in the street, or request him politely to move on. Lazy as he is though, he is out in the world at ten years of age, earning good wages, and is a perfect little man, learned in all the ways and by-ways of life at twelve or thirteen. Dickens and Albert Smith have given high celebrity to the genuine cockney youth, though for shrewdness, effrontery, and mannish affectation, your London gamin pales into utter respectability before the young Australian.[60]

In this fascinating passage, new chums are one target among several others for the young colonial, who is already typologically divided: a "gumsucker" in Victoria, and a "cornstalk" in New South Wales. The character type is given a specific incarnation, not just a style of dress but also a set of mannerisms and an attitude. He has such a distinctive "complexion" that Fowler imagines for a moment touching his face and leaving an imprint. It seems as if this emergent type is still not quite fully formed, or is still literally impressionable. The Australian boy is at once "lazy" and industrious, volatile but capable of "earning good wages" even at such an early age. In this sense, he recalls our reading of Thomas McCombie's account of ex-convicts above: *lumpenproletarian* and *proletarian* at the same time. Fowler in fact claims a special rogue status for this emerging colonial type, who is both more calculating and more spectacular than his London counterparts.

We find the figure of the colonial-born distinguished from emigrant settler types early on. Peter Cunningham was a ship's surgeon who became a squatter in New South Wales in the late 1820s. In *Two Years in New South Wales* (1827), a series of sketches of early colonial life, he is already defining these types against each other: "Our colonial-born brethren are best known here by the name of *Currency*, in contradistinction to *Sterling*, or those born in the mother-country" – the former "bearing also the name of *corn stalks* (Indian corn), from the way in which they shoot up. This is the first grand division".[61] By the second half of the nineteenth century the colonies saw an increased ideological investment in the colonial-born Australian, whose vigour and motivation seemed to promise a prosperous future for the nation-to-come. The word *native* was soon appropriated as a substitute for *colonial-born*: the most visible manifestation of this, the Australian Natives' Association, was established in Melbourne in 1871. Restricting its membership to those born in the colonies,

---

60 Fowler, *Southern Lights and Shadows*, 22–3.
61 Peter Cunningham, *Two Years in New South Wales; A Series of Letters, Comprising Sketches of the Actual State of Society in that Colony; of Its Peculiar Advantages to Emigrants; of Its Topography, Natural History, &c., &c.*, vol.1 (London: Henry Colburn, 1827), 53, 116.

Introduction

it became "a vociferous advocate for federation of the Australian colonies, a strong federal government, economic protectionism, and the White Australia immigration policy".[62] In her account of the Australian Natives' Association, the historian Helen Irving writes: "To be native was a matter of pride, above all in the years leading to Australian Federation. To be native was to be young and free, with new ideas and lots of energy... All of this meant white. The Natives were White".[63] The shift in designation from colonial-born to native-born was, of course, an attempt to further legitimise non-Aboriginal settlement. It also routinely privileged this type over emigrant settlers, as an ideal embodiment of proletarian virtues, a model worker devoted to colonial development. The English novelist Anthony Trollope arrived in Australia in the same year that the Australian Natives' Association was established, giving his impressions of these colonial types in *Australia and New Zealand* (1873). "I have no doubt whatever", he remarked, "that the born colonist is superior to the emigrant colonist, – any more than I have that the emigrant is superior to his weaker brother whom he leaves behind him [sic]. The best of our workmen go from us, and produce a race superior to themselves".[64] In terms of his capacity to labour, the "colonial-born" outstrips his British counterpart – although in doing so (and consistent with the appropriation of the term *native*), his identity shifts to one determined by "race" rather than class.

The colonial- or native-born may, of course, seem like a major character type, not a minor one. But even this figure could unravel into subordinate components. Godfrey Mundy took up a military post in Sydney in 1846 and stayed there for five years. His chronicle of colonial life, *Our Antipodes* (1853), gives the colonial-born a much bleaker future, as if this character type begins to degenerate almost as soon as it emerges: "Many of the Cornstalks, or Colonial-born men, are tall and large-boned, but the majority of those attaining a standard above the middle height are spare, hollow chested, and have a certain weather-worn and time-worn look beyond their years".[65] This characterisation of the native-born young man as at once an embodiment of colonial vitality and a sign of deterioration-to-come persisted through the second half of the nineteenth century. Richard Twopeny was a journalist, entrepreneur and "colonial showman",[66] who helped to organise some important international exhibitions in Melbourne, Sydney, Christchurch, Calcutta and Paris. Peter H. Hoffenberg has noted the important role these exhibitions played in the promotion of colonial achievement in terms of cultural development as well as trade: "remaking the popular image of Australia created by novelists and journalists, among others", they were designed "to illustrate the 'progress' of the colonies and thus their suitability for new capital, emigrants, and self-government".[67] Twopeny's *Town Life in Australia* (1883) was a lively series of sketches of colonial cultural practices that worked according to the same logic; that is, it presents aspects of colonial life as "exhibits" around which it then builds a commentary outlining future prospects and opportunities. In a

---

62 Angela Woollacott, *To Try Her Fortune in London: Australian Women, Colonialism, and Modernity* (Oxford: Oxford University Press, 2001), 98.
63 Helen Irving, *To Constitute a Nation: A Cultural History of Australia's Constitution* (Cambridge: Cambridge University Press, 1999), 124.
64 Anthony Trollope, *Australia and New Zealand* (Leipzig: Bernhard Tauchnitz, 1873), 129.
65 Godfrey Charles Mundy, *Our Antipodes: or, Residence and Rambles in the Australasian Colonies*, vol. 1 (London: Richard Bentley, 1852), 50.
66 Peter H. Hoffenberg, *An Empire on Display: English, Indian, and Australian Exhibitions from the Crystal Palace to the Great War* (Berkeley and Los Angeles: University of California Press, 2001), 137.
67 Hoffenberg, *An Empire on Display*, 139.

section on "Young Australia", Twopeny divides young working men into three types: "old chums, new chums, and colonials".[68] Old chums, he writes, "are, on the whole, the best":

> For the most part they began life with a superabundance of animal spirits, and a love of adventure, which have been toned down by a practical experience of the hardships they dreamed of. They certainly drink most and swear most of the three sections, but with all their failings there are few men who can do a harder day's work than they. Barring pure misfortune, there is always some good reason for their still remaining in the class they sprang from.[69]

The "old chum" here is *proletarian* – still locked into a class that defines him – but he also displays *lumpenproletarian* characteristics: drinking, swearing, and "a superabundance of animal spirits". By the time we get to the colonial-born, however, these traits have become much less stable. The "thoroughbred colonial", as Twopeny puts it, is "the best workman when he chooses". But he can also be "as brutal as Coupeau" – the reference here is to a roof builder in Émile Zola's naturalistic novel *L'Assommoir* (1877), who degenerates into alcoholism and domestic violence – "and, except from a muscular point of view, he is often by no means a promising specimen of colonisation". Twopeny goes on to suggest that "thoroughbred colonial[s]" are unstable enough to mutate into a different type altogether, larrikins: "roughs of the worst description, insulting and often robbing people in Melbourne itself, and moving about in gangs with whose united force the police is powerless to cope".[70] The larrikin was the complete opposite of what one might have expected the "thoroughbred colonial" to become, a *lumpenproletarian* colonial criminal type that by the 1880s "was caught up in a moral panic about out-of-control adolescents who gathered in loosely composed street gangs known as 'pushes'".[71] Once again, it seems as if – to recall Woloch's distinction – the "functional worker" and the "deviant eccentric" are never far away from each other.

There is certainly a stark Hogarthian irony in showing (or anticipating) the degeneration of a character type that is supposed to stand for colonial "progress". A readily available narrative along these lines takes hold in the colonies and is soon reproduced, rapidly proliferating. Edward Oxford arrived in Melbourne in 1868 with a notorious history: twenty-eight years earlier, he had attempted to assassinate Queen Victoria. Finally released from a criminal asylum, Oxford was expelled to the colonies. Changing his name (significantly enough) to John Freeman, he began to chronicle life in Melbourne's slums for the *Argus* newspaper, collecting his various sketches in *Lights and Shadows of Melbourne Life* (1888). The title of this book clearly recalls Fowler's earlier *Southern Lights and Shadows*. As Jenny Sinclair notes, it also echoes James Payn's *Lights and Shadows of London Life* (1867) and James Dabney McCabe's *Lights and Shadows of New York Life* (1872) – as if "seeing darkness and light as part of the same thing" was a familiar ethnographic way of representing large cities across the Western world.[72] Perhaps more than any other example

---

68   R.E.N. Twopeny, *Town Life in Australia* (Harmondsworth: Penguin, 1973), 97.
69   Twopeny, *Town Life in Australia*, 97.
70   Twopeny, *Town Life in Australia*, 98.
71   Melissa Bellanta, *Larrikins: A History* (St Lucia: University of Queensland Press, 2012), xiv.
72   Jenny Sinclair, *A Walking Shadow: The Remarkable Double Life of Edward Oxford* (Melbourne: Arcade Publications, 2012), 129.

of colonial Australian "social zoology", Freeman's book – with its chapters on "costermongers", "match-sellers", "fish-hawkers", "watercress men" and so on – was conspicuously influenced by Mayhew's *London Labour and the London Poor*. But it also took the opportunity to think about a colonial future, turning to the figure of the colonial young man. "Like that of all young countries", he writes, "our native youth display a considerable amount of animal spirits"[73] – precisely echoing (or perhaps plagiarising) Twopeny's "superabundance of animal spirits". Just like Twopeny, Freeman saw the exuberance of colonial youth as both an advantage – since they become independent etc. – and a liability:

> The liveliness of a certain section of our boys takes the form of what is called "larrikinism" . . . Cowardly and treacherous as wolves [they] . . . require the confidence inspired by numbers before they can muster up sufficient courage to commence operations. Then, twenty or thirty, armed with road metal, will attack a solitary policeman; or three or four assault a decrepit old man or defenceless woman.[74]

Freeman and Towpeny's accounts of larrikins come relatively late in the day; E.E. Morris' *Austral English* (1898) in fact traces the earliest use of the term in print culture to local newspaper reports in February 1870.[75] In a column published in the *Australasian* just one month later, the colonial author, editor and satirist Marcus Clarke was already imagining the sensibility of this social type: "[t]he larrikin lives, he has an entity of his own, and he doesn't care a fig for you or anybody else. Why should he?"[76] Perhaps more than most colonial writers, Clarke was influenced by Balzac – "The life of Paris", he wrote in 1872, "is embalmed in the works of Balzac"[77] – and also Charles Dickens. In a long essay on Dickens that appeared in the *Argus* in July 1870, Clarke admired the novelist's ability to "sketch modern manners" and relished the exuberance of his minor characters. Clarke wrote novels, stories, plays and so on; but he also chronicled colonial metropolitan life – its lights and shadows – and imaginatively represented a remarkable variety of colonial character types. His weekly columns for the *Australasian* were collected and published in 1869 under the title *The Peripatetic Philosopher*, in which he self-consciously cast himself as an urban itinerant in Melbourne, a *flâneur*.[78] Mary L. Shannon has noted that Clarke's metropolitan character sketches were influenced by Dickens, Douglas Jerrold and Henry Mayhew; but she also suggests that Clarke developed a mocking, humorous relationship to those ethnographic literary traditions as a way of expressing both his geographical and generational distance from them.[79]

---

73 John Freeman, *Lights and Shadows of Melbourne Life* (London: Sampson Low, Marston, Searle, & Rivington, 1888), 12.
74 Freeman, *Lights and Shadows of Melbourne Life*, 12–13.
75 Morris quotes an article in the *Age*, 17 February 1870, that describes a "youngster of the rowdy class, commonly termed 'larrikins', who have been amusing themselves, in company with some twenty others of similar tastes, by insulting every person who passed them": see E.E. Morris, *Austral English: An Australasian Dictionary of Words, Phrases and Usages* (1898; Cambridge: Cambridge University Press, 2011), 260.
76 Marcus Clarke, "The Peripatetic Philosopher", *Australasian*, 19 March 1870, 17.
77 Marcus Clarke, "Of French Novels", in *A Colonial City: High and Low Life: Selected Journalism of Marcus Clarke*, ed. L.T. Hergenhan (St Lucia: University of Queensland Press, 1972), 292.
78 For a critical discussion of Clarke's role as colonial *flâneur* in relation to metropolitan "low life", see Andrew McCann, *Marcus Clarke's Bohemia: Literature and Modernity in Colonial Melbourne* (Melbourne: Melbourne University Press, 2004), 68–9.

Clarke's sketches of social types were also distinctively literary. He dramatised types in order to illuminate their key characteristics; he created scenes in which they participate; he described their "customs and manners", their costumes, their attitudes and aspirations; and significantly, he often gave them a name. L.T. Hergenhan has commented on Clarke's "vivid thumb-nail sketches of typical figures or groups of the time, in which he is able to isolate colonial characteristics – the parochial committee-man, share brokers, carmen (cabmen), colonial youth, politicians, squatters old and new . . . the working man, Victorian ladies, 'willing boys'", and so on.[80] In "The Working Man from His Own Point of View" (1870), Clarke ventriloquises the voice of a Melbourne worker he calls John Strong ("I ain't a swell. I don't pretend to be"). Strong's complaint is that Australian working men are routinely patronised by colonial intelligentsia: "We are sick of it", he tells us.[81] Clarke sympathetically inhabits the personas of some colonial character types, but distances himself from others: In "New Chums" (1868-69), he removes himself from a social type with which he had once identified, having emigrated to Australia just a few years earlier, in 1863. "I have been pent up in the society of new chums", he writes; "Not that I object to new chums as a body, because every man . . . must come here as a new chum some time or other".[82] Through the fictional character of Guy de Vere (the name is taken from Edgar Allan Poe's 1830 poem, "Lenore"), Clarke then creates a comical, exaggerated stereotype of an indolent, privileged and over-educated new chum who finds the colonies distasteful and cannot wait to return home: "On leaving for England, he remarked that Melbourne was not the place for an idle man, and that he should never again come farther south than the Mediterranean".[83] But what about the new chum who – like Clarke – never leaves? The paradox for Clarke is that the new chum who remains in the colonies also "disappears mysteriously": "As soon as one comes to know them by sight, they vanish from view altogether".[84] Clarke's account of the new chum precisely recalls Jules Janin's description, cited above, of Parisian social types as "brilliant meteors" that "appear and disappear, like the cloud or the smoke". The new chum is given a spectacular rise-and-fall narrative trajectory, visible at one moment, fading away in the next:

> Sometimes the gorgeous butterfly of Collins-street comes to unutterable grief. His cheap finery wears out. Messers. Moses' garments wax rusty, and the gilt wears off his Brummagem jewellery. He falls, and his fall is great. One fine day he disappears, and men shake their heads for a day or two . . . The haunters of the Café and Varieties miss a familiar face, and one asks, "What has become of young New Chum; I haven't seen him lately?" But the question is never satisfactorily answered, and I ask in vain – What becomes of all these young men?[85]

---

79 Mary L. Shannon, *Dickens, Reynolds, and Mayhew on Wellington Street: The Print Culture of a Victorian Street* (Farnham, UK: Ashgate Publishing, 2015), 200–2. For a general discussion of Clarke's European literary influences and their relationship to the "modernity of colonialism", see McCann, *Marcus Clarke's Bohemia*, 1–20.
80 L.T. Hergenhan, introduction to *A Colonial City*, xxviii.
81 Marcus Clarke, "The Working Man from His Own Point of View", *A Colonial City*, 79, 85.
82 Marcus Clarke, "New Chums", *A Colonial City*, 40.
83 Clarke, "New Chums", 41.
84 Clarke, "New Chums", 42.
85 Clarke, "New Chums", 44.

Much of the investment in colonial character types was precisely to do with what kind of future they had, and what kind of role they might have played in the colonies' development: productive, parasitical, and so on. The reporting of a character type's disappearance meant thinking about what would take its place, what would come next. The "Coming Man" emerged as an available "imperial myth" towards the end of the nineteenth century, an embodiment of the view that "the development of an active, competent colonial type" would "reinvigorate" the empire.[86] We have seen this already with Trollope's view of the colonial-born working man's ability to produce a "race superior" to the English. But the kind of emergence-and-decline narrative Clarke attributed to the new chum persisted alongside this view, and continually unravelled it. The novelist Rolf Boldrewood" gave us exactly this narrative in an article titled "Lapsed Gentlefolk", published in the *Australasian* in 1889. Lapsed gentlefolk are a social type, a version of the new chum; but instead of "disappearing mysteriously", they find themselves dispersed into an assortment of *proletarian* and *lumpenproletarian* colonial occupations:

> Ah, me! Who has not known and pitied them in this land of ours? The workman's paradise! Yet all too well adapted for converting the gently-nurtured waif into the resigned labourer, the homeless vagrant. The gradations through which, slowly, invisibly, but none the less surely, drifts to lower levels the luckless gentleman adventurer are fraught with a melancholy interest. How strange it seems to realise that of the hundreds of well-dressed, well-educated, high-hearted youngsters, fresh from pleasant homes, who every season land on our shores a certain proportion will in a few years of colonial experience (save the mark!) be transformed into misanthropic shepherds, shabby tramps, or reckless rouseabouts.[87]

This passage is different to Clarke's account above of the "working man" John Strong; rather than inhabiting the type and making it "speak", Boldrewood instead observes from a distance. Chronicling the slow decline (by "gradations") of educated emigrant gentlemen makes the novelist-ethnographer feel a kind of "melancholy" for what-might-have-been. On the other hand, the "transformation" of this kind of new chum into a range of debased, minor character types (shepherds, tramps, rouseabouts) also works to populate the colonial Australian fictional landscape.

In 1877, Clarke published a short booklet titled *The Future Australian Race*. "There has been much vaguely talked and written about the Coming Man", it begins – after which, it spirals off into an eccentric meditation on the physiognomic characteristics of different races in classical history. Clarke soon turns to English portraits of aristocratic and courtly figures across the centuries in order to trace developments in facial features. The eighteenth century is of particular importance here because it explicitly connected portraiture – and caricature – with physiognomy as an emerging field of scientific research: "[Thomas] Gainsborough, [Joshua] Reynolds, and [Thomas] Lawrence have reproduced

---

86 Ailise Bulfin, "Guy Boothby's 'Bid for Fortune': Constructing an Anglo-Australian Colonial Identity for the *Fin-de-Siècle* London Literary Marketplace", in *Changing the Victorian Subject*, ed. Maggie Tonkin et al. (Adelaide: University of Adelaide Press, 2014), 168. See also Robert Dixon, *Writing the Colonial Adventure: Race, Gender and Nation in Anglo-Australian Popular Fiction, 1875–1914* (Cambridge: Cambridge University Press, 1995), 147.
87 Rolf Boldrewood, "Lapsed Gentlefolk", *Australasian*, 13 July 1889, 37.

our ancestors in their habits as they lived; Hogarth, [Thomas] Rowlandson, and [James] Gillray have taught us how to recognise them, Lavatar how to talk with them".[88] The face itself becomes an important indicator of type for Clarke, and he touches promiscuously on a number of them: national ("an English face"), regional ("an Oriental face"), historical ("an Elizabethan face"), religious ("a Puritan face"), and fashionable ("a face for hair powder"). All this leads Clarke finally to talk about "an Australian face, and what that face might be like" (10).

It looks for a moment as if Clarke is reproducing the prevailing positive image of the "Coming Man": "Already there existed in the Australians much sturdy Anglo-Saxon stuff... It is only reasonable to expect that the children of such parents, transplanted to another atmosphere, dieted upon new foods, and restrained in their prime of life from sensual excess, should be at least *remarkable*" (15). Here, even convicts shed their *lumpenproletarian* characteristics to become "men of great courage, great strength, great powers of brain ... [with] astonishing talents for mechanics and the fine arts" (15). But as Clarke's satire becomes increasingly overt, the figure of the coming Australian begins to unravel. A clichéd, throwaway remark about the young male colonial-born – "The boys will be tall and slender – like cornstalks" – gives way to a list of degenerative features and qualities that lead to a series of idiosyncratic generalisations about the national type: "It will be rare to find girls with white and sound teeth ... Bad teeth mean bad digestion, and bad digestion means melancholy. The Australians will be a fretful, clever, perverse, irritable race" (20). Clarke assembles the characteristics of the "Coming Man" in order to expose the sheer impossibility of such a figure. It is as if a national type is unable to sustain itself: to glimpse its future is inevitably to predict its bitter end:

> The [Australian] will be a square-headed, masterful man, with full temples, plenty of beard, a keen eye, a stern and yet sensual mouth. His teeth will be bad, and his lungs good. He will suffer from liver disease, and become prematurely bald; average duration of life in the unmarried, fifty-nine; in the married, sixty-five and a decimal. (22)

In our book, we shall see many examples of character types assembling and disassembling; in the light of this, we shall also see just how difficult it is to maintain any coherent sense of a definitive or representative *national* type. Colonial Australian fiction is always about the interplay between major and minor character types. When this interplay happens, minor characters can radically extend their influence and the expected trajectories of major characters can be disturbed in interesting, ideologically loaded ways. In Chapter 1, for example, we will find squatters at loggerheads with shepherds and free selectors, and under siege from bushrangers and disgruntled bush workers; as all this unfolds, the squatter novel struggles to maintain this particular character type's socially (and financially) elevated position. In Chapter 2, the bushranger seems to occupy the centre and the periphery simultaneously, a character type that can seem at times to dominate the colonies even as he continually confronts the possibility of his own extinction. In Chapter 3, we chart the influence of colonial detectives on crime and social regulation as they encounter a wide range of antagonistic character types – including, in some cases, the police. In Chapter 4, we look into the fortunes and misfortunes of the hut shepherd and the

---

88 Marcus Clarke, *The Future Australian Race* (Melbourne: A.H. Massina & Co., 1877), 10. All subsequent references are to this edition and appear in parentheses in the text.

swagman; and we examine devious figures like the larrikin and the metropolitan dandy, both of whom are able to turn the colonial economy to their advantage. Finally, in Chapter 5, we see that the Australian girl is caught between a variety of suitors and opportunities, with a future that is precariously positioned between success and failure. What Thomas McCombie had called the "great epic of Australian Colonisation" turns out at the same time to be a whirl of micro-narratives, each of which prioritises certain character types over others – giving us narrative trajectories that can either underwrite or challenge the ongoing project of colonial nation-building.

1
The Reign of the Squatter

The squatter emerged as a recognisable type early on in colonial Australian writing and almost immediately generated controversy and debate. The term itself already suggested the illegal or opportunistic occupation of land;[1] even so, squatters were soon able to exert considerable political and ideological influence, in order to give their land tenure greater security and to lay legitimate claim to new leases and more extensive pastures elsewhere. It wasn't long before squatters acquired a kind of pseudo-aristocratic status, not only opening up the frontier for grazing cattle and sheep but also refashioning it in the image of the English estate, building stately homesteads, planting gardens and orchards, and establishing dynasties.[2] Philip McMichael has talked about a "pastoral ideology" in colonial Australia that was strongly shaped by the immense significance squatters gave to their economic value and social standing:

> Pastoral ideology in colonial Australia altered with the impact of squatting. The pioneering gentry (landowning graziers) saw themselves as the patriarchs of a stable social hierarchy, with the possibility of creating a colonial aristocracy sustained by the British state. Once squatting took hold, however, a more materialist ideology displaced the traditional conception. Squatters . . . emphasised their economic value to colony and empire alike.[3]

This "patriarchal" role was something squatters fought hard to maintain: through the successful management of a station and its labour force, by marrying well and establishing a family, by entering politics or becoming a magistrate in order to protect their interests, and – not least – by emphasising the importance of particular kinds of cultural knowledge and

---

1   E.E. Morris' *Austral English* traces the earliest use of the term "squatter" to 1835. An entry for 1843 describes squatters as "persons originally of depraved and lawless habits" who "have made their residence at the very outskirts of civilization a means of carrying on all manner of mischief": see *Austral English: An Australasian Dictionary of Words, Phrases and Usages* (1898; Cambridge: Cambridge University Press, 2011), 432.
2   See, for example, Paul de Serville, "The Gentleman Squatter", *Port Phillip Gentlemen, and Good Society in Melbourne before the Gold Rushes* (Melbourne: Oxford University Press, 1980), 82–105.
3   Philip McMichael, *Settlers and the Agrarian Question* (Cambridge: Cambridge University Press, 1984), 145.

literary tastes. In so many squatter novels, the squatter makes time for reading and looks forward to receiving the latest periodicals from England. For example, in Rolf Boldrewood's novella *The Fencing of Wanderowna: A Tale of Australian Squatting Life* (1873), the squatter Gilbert Elliot proudly declares, as he flicks through a copy of the *Cornhill* magazine, "Surely, few people can enjoy reading so thoroughly as we squatters do".[4] The squatter here is both the subject of the squatter novel and its ideal audience. Elliot and his brother read Sir Walter Scott, Shelley, Tennyson and a host of other canonical nineteenth-century English writers, whose work they casually cite at any opportunity. The squatter novel's emphasis on a squatter's love of reading adds to the refinement of this character type, but it also supplements McMichael's notion of a "pastoral ideology": as if, through the figure of the squatter, good economic management and literary cultivation can seamlessly merge together. In a later novel, *The Squatter's Dream* (1875), Boldrewood makes this point explicit:

> It is given to few active professions to afford and to justify as great a degree of leisure for realising an abstract thought, as to that of the Australian squatter. He may manage his property shrewdly and successfully, and still utilize a portion, at either end of the day, for history and chronicle of old; for poetry and politics; for rhyme and reason. He can vary intellectual exercise with hard bodily labour. He may possess, at small additional cost, the latest literary products of the old and new world.[5]

This passage takes the "pastoral ideology" of the squatter and frames it with literature (to be read "at either end of the day"). In doing so it helps to underwrite the sense that squatters – opportunistic as they may be – could call on a weight of literary tradition to legitimise their ownership of property.

The question of who could own property – and how much they could own – was a foundational one in colonial Australia. But one of the most influential early treatises on land ownership here came from an unlikely source. In 1827, Edward Gibbon Wakefield was serving a three-year sentence in Newgate Prison for the abduction of Ellen Turner, a fifteen-year-old heiress whom he had forced into a fraudulent marriage. Wakefield had never been to Australia, but he soon found himself becoming interested in matters to do with colonial reform. While in prison he wrote a series of papers in which he masqueraded as a young emigrant and settler, titled *A Letter from Sydney, the Principal Town of Australasia* (1829). Wakefield's account of early Sydney life was remarkably detailed, but his focus was primarily on the price of land and the management of labour resources. Buying a large property, his narrator is dismayed to discover that his servant – who had emigrated with him – has now left to purchase land for himself, quickly becoming so rich that he "feeds upon greasy dainties, drinks oceans of bottled porter and port wine, damns the Governor and swears by all his gods, Jupiter, Jingo, and Old Harry, that this Colony must soon be independent".[6] For Wakefield, the problem was that land in the

---

4 Rolf Boldrewood, *The Fencing of Wanderowna: A Tale of Australian Squatting Life*, *Australian Town and Country Journal*, 7 June 1873, 18. This serialised novella was later reprinted as *The Fencing of Wandaroona: A Riverina Reminiscence* in *A Romance of Canvas Town* (London: Macmillan & Co., 1898).
5 Rolf Boldrewood, *The Squatter's Dream*, *Australian Town and Country Journal*, 27 November 1875, 23. This serialised novel was published under the more prosaic title *Ups and Downs* by George Robertson in 1878, and later reprinted as *The Squatter's Dream: A Story of Australian Life* (London: Macmillan & Co., 1891).

colonies was so cheap that even servants and farm workers could buy it, which meant that the colonies ran a significant risk of losing their labouring classes. His solution – which he called "systematic colonisation" – went on to become integral to processes of colonial reform across the dominions.

In a later book, *A View of the Art of Colonisation* (1849), Wakefield advocated what he called a "sufficient price" for colonial land that would, as he put it, "prevent labourers from turning landlords too soon" – while nevertheless allowing smaller-scale farming enterprises to flourish.[7] His proposals for colonial land pricing, and the need to preserve a labouring class by raising the cost to such an extent that they were unable to afford property, had their exponents and detractors. Karl Marx famously commented on Wakefield in a chapter titled "The Modern Theory of Colonisation" at the end of volume one of *Capital* (1867), which began by noting the colonies' enthusiasm for turning everyone, even labourers, into landowning capitalists. "Think of the horror!" Marx scoffed. "The excellent capitalist has imported bodily from Europe, with his own good money, his own competitors! The end of the world has come!"[8] Marx took issue with Wakefield's notion of a "sufficient price" because it meant that labourers would be too dependent on a landowning class. But he agreed with Wakefield that colonisation in Australia had also brought with it the "shameless lavishing of uncultivated colonial land on aristocrats and capitalists", that is, on squatters. It is therefore not surprising that the squatter novel itself was unsympathetic to Wakefield's reforms.

The first squatter novel was in fact Thomas McCombie's *Adventures of a Colonist; or, Godfrey Arabin, the Settler* (1845), which we briefly discussed in the introduction to this book. McCombie's hero, the English-born Godfrey Arabin, is a "young man of enthusiastic temperament" who is obsessed with Sir Walter Scott and the Romantic poets. His literary background helps him to conceive emigration as a romance and adventure, but it also encourages him to take financial risks: "he would rush heedlessly", the novel tells us, "into the most absurd speculations".[9] The novel follows Arabin's experiences in Australia and provides him with a range of different models for settler life: some of his acquaintances do well, while others go under. In the meantime, Arabin realises that hard work and industriousness are essential in order to thrive in a fledgling colonial economy; so he buys a squatter's station and devotes himself to its success. The squatter novel was generally picaresque and episodic, full of stories-within-stories driven by character types like the boundary rider or the bushranger. But it also addressed the economic realities of a squatter's predicament in a direct (but still partisan) way. The price of land, the question of how much land can yield, and the impact of government legislation, were all explicitly laid out for consideration and debate. In McCombie's novel, the chronicle of an emigrant's first-hand experiences of becoming a squatter is sufficient in itself to condemn Wakefield's policies (which were in any case devised in a London prison) as remote from actual colonial needs and practices. In fact, Wakefield becomes representative here of a

---

6   E.G. Wakefield, *A Letter from Sydney, the Principal Town of Australasia* (London: Joseph Cross, 1829), 12.
7   E.G. Wakefield, *A View of the Art of Colonisation* (London: J.W. Parker, 1849), xii.
8   Karl Marx, *Capital: A Critique of Political Economy*, vol. 1, book 1, trans. Samuel Moore and Edward Aveling, ed. Frederick Engels, 539: https://www.marxists.org/archive/marx/works/download/pdf/Capital-Volume-I.pdf.
9   Thomas McCombie, *Adventures of a Colonist; or, Godfrey Arabin, the Settler* (London: John & Daniel A. Darling, 1845), 6, 12.

particular colonial administrative type, someone who influences local legislation from a great distance and who thereby dooms it to failure: "Edward Gibbon Wakefield ranks at the head of these fireside economists . . . and since that time everything has gone wrong with our Colonies in the East" (17). What the novel calls "the Utopian systems of Wakefield" (55) put rules and regulations into place for land sale and land management in the colonies that end up pitting squatters' interests against the state. Since those interests are so often cast as crucial to colonial prosperity, Wakefield's land reforms are seen to work against not only the squatters' "pastoral ideology" but also, more broadly, the "independent spirit" of all colonists (21).

Wakefield's idea of a "sufficient price" for colonial land (although he never actually said what that price might be) also attracted the attention of Samuel Sidney, an English journalist and hunting enthusiast. Like Wakefield, Sidney had never actually been to Australia. But he became interested in colonial affairs, drawing on his brother's experiences as a squatter; and in fact, he went on to write a lively squatter novel, *Gallops and Gossips in the Bush of Australia; or, Passages in the Life of Alfred Barnard* (1854), parts of which were first published in his friend Charles Dickens' *Household Words*. Sidney thought that the rising cost of land in the colonies would slow the rates of emigration; his popular *Australian Handbook* (1848) was one of a spate of publications around this time designed to increase the volume of new arrivals. In a later publication, *The Three Colonies of Australia* (1853), Sidney outlined his objections to Wakefield's "systematic colonisation" – which he dismissed as "land monopoly" – and worked carefully through the subsequent conflicts between landowners and colonial politicians. "At that period", he writes – meaning the 1830s and early 1840s – "opposition to the Wakefield system was considered wild and democratic".[10] Sidney is often taken as a progressive champion of the working or labouring classes because he thought Wakefield's system of colonisation unfairly prevented these people from becoming freeholders. But in fact, he thought that the kind of legislation that derived from Wakefield's theories disadvantaged everyone, including squatters. A great deal of the criticism in *The Three Colonies of Australia* was directed at the Whig politician Sir George Gipps, Governor of New South Wales during much of this time. Gipps had raised the price of land significantly and limited its availability: "I was sent here to carry out the Wakefield system of land sales", Sidney quotes him as saying, "and whether it suits the colony or not, it must be done".[11] As a result, Sidney writes, "the small settlers were deeply discontented" and the "great pastoral proprietors, or squatters . . . were worried".[12]

Given that he never actually came to Australia, Sidney's *Gallops and Gossips in the Bush of Australia* is an audacious attempt to convey the experiences of a young emigrant in the colonies. A "propagandist of emigration", as Andrew Hassan describes him, Sidney puts a positive spin on his protagonist's hardships and allows him to succeed quite early on.[13] Having arrived in Australia, Alfred Barnard begins his colonial career by becoming a partner in a cattle station and later buys a station of his own. The accumulation of wealth

---

10 Samuel Sidney, *The Three Colonies of Australia: New South Wales, Victoria, South Australia; Their Pastures, Copper Mines, and Gold Fields*, second edition (London: Ingram, Cooke & Co., 1853), iii.
11 Sidney, *The Three Colonies of Australia*, 122.
12 Sidney, *The Three Colonies of Australia*, 123.
13 Andrew Hassan, *Sailing to Australia: Shipboard Diaries by Nineteenth-Century British Emigrants* (Manchester: Manchester University Press, 1994), 185.

comes quite easily to him; but the novel wants to say that, because he is still a bachelor, his good fortune has not yet been secured. "A bachelor's station in the Bush", Barnard remarks, "or even a bachelor's farm, is generally a wretched place. Founded to make money and nothing else, decency and comfort are little cultivated".[14] He provides a touching image of the solitary squatter: "a young man, who may often be found dirty, barefooted, in his shirt sleeves, sitting alone, in melancholy state, on an old tea-chest..."[15] The squatter novel generally presents marriage as a necessary destination, a proper endpoint to the narrative – although the path a squatter novel takes in relation to heterosexual romance can vary widely.[16] Barnard's marriage is presented in a fairly matter-of-fact way, but it works ideologically to further legitimate his occupation of the land. Marriage transforms the squatter's station from a rudimentary, barren place into one that is now fully "cultivated" in terms of both successful land management and aesthetic tastes – literary tastes in particular. It allows the squatter novel to switch genres, replacing frontier adventure and the Gothic – built around the "melancholy" bachelor/pioneer – with the post-frontier pastoral. In this way, it can offer an idealised image of country settlement that brings the novel to a close. Everything has now calmed down, and even the local Aboriginal people are seen to be subdued under the influence of squatter domestication:

> I was no longer a discontented turbulent boy; I was a successful man. My heart had changed... The pen, once so hateful, had become my favourite resource in hours of leisure; and I filled long letters with my thoughts, my feelings, my regrets. Books once neglected were learnt by heart... The rich district in which I was one of the earliest pioneers had become settled and pacified, as far as the river ran; the wild Myals [sic] had grown into the tame, blanket-clothed dependents [sic] of the settlers. Thousands of fine-woolled flocks upon the hills, and cattle upon the rich flats, were mine; the bark hut had changed into a verandahed cottage, where books and pictures formed no insignificant part of the furniture; neighbours were within a ride; the voices of children often floated sweetly along the waters of the river.[17]

Songs of the Squatters

Early on, Sidney's novel approvingly quotes a poem, titled "The Bushman to His Bride", taken from "a satirical Sydney paper". In fact, this poem is one of several "Songs of the Squatters" that the lawyer and politician Robert Lowe had published in the *Atlas* in

---

14 Samuel Sidney, *Gallops and Gossips in the Bush of Australia; or, Passages in the Life of Alfred Barnard* (London: Longman, Brown, Green & Longmans, 1854), 95.
15 Sidney, *Gallops and Gossips in the Bush of Australia*, 95.
16 An interesting variation on the squatter romance is the writer and publisher Donald Cameron's "The Adventures of a Squatter", serialised in the *Australian Journal* between October and December 1866. Two mutually admiring young men, Edward and Harry, emigrate to Australia and purchase neighbouring properties in western New South Wales. But neither man marries; instead, when Edward finally makes Harry a partner in his own property, they become romantically joined in what Toni Johnson-Woods calls "a pseudo-marriage". Johnson-Woods stops short of calling this narrative "a homosexual story", but only just. See Toni Johnson-Woods, "'Adventures of a Squatter': A Colonial Male Romance", *Southerly* 70:2 (2010), 138–9.
17 Sidney, *Gallops and Gossips in the Bush of Australia*, 222.

early 1845. Lowe lived and worked in Australia from 1842 to 1850, returning to England to become a key figure in Gladstone's Liberal government and, eventually, Viscount Sherbrooke. A close friend and confidant of Sir George Gipps, he was initially hostile to the squattocracy. But in 1844, Lowe fell out with Gipps over new legislation that increased the price of land, limited the leasehold and made squatters bid for their properties at public auctions.[18] The newly established Pastoral Association – founded, as Sidney puts it, "to resist unjust confiscation and taxation" – was horrified by these developments.[19] As Peter Cochrane writes, "This was not the security they wanted".[20] Demonstrating his opposition to government interference, Lowe joined the Pastoral Association. Around this time, he became involved with the *Atlas*, a magazine that spoke up for squatter independence and was fiercely critical of what it saw as Gipps' excessive regulations. "The Bushman to His Bride" is the third of Lowe's squatter songs, with a squatter carefully yet optimistically laying out all the hardships that his new wife will have to face as she accompanies him to his bush station. The first of his squatter songs is a tribute to the squatter's pioneer spirit, ending with a plea for "men of the city" not to force them off the land. But it is the second squatter song that most vehemently criticises government interference, offering a squatter's first-hand perspective on colonial bureaucracy as petty, corrupt and relentlessly self-interested:

> The Commissioner bet me a pony – I won,
> So he cut off exactly two thirds of my run,
> For he said I was making a fortune too fast;
> And profit gained slower the longer would last.[21]

The *Atlas*' most vocal opponent at this time was the *Weekly Register*, edited by William Duncan. The *Weekly Register* opposed the "monstrous disproportions" of land distribution in the colonies, attacked the influence of the squatters, and supported Gipps' emphasis on the need to limit squatter leaseholds and inhibit reckless land speculation by insisting on improved levels of productivity.[22] It was also very critical of Lowe. A few weeks after Lowe's poems appeared in the *Atlas*, the *Weekly Register* answered with its own series of "squatter songs" by a colonial poet Duncan greatly admired, Charles Harpur. Harpur's "Squatter Songs. No. I" begins by satirising the familiar image of the squatter as a romantic embodiment of male beauty:

> Where the wandering Barwin [sic] delighteth the eye,
> Befringed with the myal [sic] and golden bloom'd gorse,
> Oh, a beautiful Squatter came galloping by,

---

18   See R.L. Knight, "Robert Lowe (1811–1892)", in *Australian Dictionary of Biography*: http://adb.anu.edu.au/biography/lowe-robert-2376.
19   Sidney, *The Three Colonies of Australia*, 135.
20   Peter Cochrane, *Colonial Ambition: Foundations of Australian Democracy* (Melbourne: Melbourne University Press, 2006), 88.
21   Robert Lowe, "Songs of the Squatters No. 2", *Atlas*, 22 February 1845, 149.
22   "Squatters and Landholders: Fixity of Tenure and District Corporations", *Weekly Register*, 22 March 1845, 133.

> With a beard on his chin like the tail of a horse;
> And his locks trained all round to so equal a pitch,
> That his mother herself, it may truly be said,
> Had been puzzled in no small degree to find which
> Was the front, or the back, or the sides of his head.[23]

This coiffured young man goes on to bribe, seduce and "ruin" an Aboriginal woman. When he abandons her soon afterwards, the men in her tribe immediately take revenge:

> And that beautiful squatter, one beautiful day,
> Was waddied to death in the bloom of his charms![24]

Harpur's squatter songs offer a number of different trajectories for a squatter's career, each of which highlights this figure's greed, his casual abuse of power, his overblown sense of entitlement, and so on. In "Squatter Songs. No. II", a squatter is overwhelmed by the idea that a small landholder, Tom Brown, could settle beside his "noble" estate. It is as if the self-assumed aristocratic status of his position is now under attack, or (as the poem says) "curst". The squatter tries to bribe a land commissioner to evict Brown, but to no avail; as a consequence, the squatter spirals down into drink and destitution. "Squatter Songs. No. III" also captures these aristocratic pretensions when a squatter blames Gipps, rather than a natural disaster, for his inability to make his "Earldom" last "For me and mine for ever".[25]

Old and New Squatters

Ken Stewart suggests that Harpur's squatter songs give us a number of different "paradigms of the squatter figure": "the wise, genteel Englishman; the quasi-aristocratic self-made man; the rapacious, ill-dressed scrooge; the struggling young son; the ruthless explorer-land-taker; [and] the acquisitive Anglo-Australian revenant". But he adds that these are all contained by an overriding sense of the squatter as a "model of acquisitive selfishness who cruelly or meanly exploits his workers . . . "[26] In the squatter novel, this kind of model also prevails; but levels of sympathy for the squatter type can vary, and they also generate other kinds of critiques and comparisons. McCombie's *Adventures of a Colonist* was published in the same year as Harpur's squatter songs, but even though it is critical of Wakefield it is only briefly explicit about its investment in the land debates that so absorbed the *Atlas* and the *Weekly Register*. Taking a pro-squatter stance, McCombie's novel insists that "the Government must grant the squatter's right to the soil upon moderate terms" (108). Its protagonist, Godfrey Arabin, is a belated squatter, purchasing his station late in the novel. In the meantime, other squatter types flow through the narrative: for example, the fake merchant, Captain Thomson, who sells his station to Arabin to pursue a failed business

---

23 Charles Harpur, "Squatter Songs. No. I", *Weekly Register*, 15 March 1845, 124.
24 Harpur, "Squatter Songs. No. I", 124.
25 Charles Harpur, "Squatter Songs. No. III", *Weekly Register*, 26 April 1845, 198.
26 Ken Stewart, "Transcendentalism, Emerson and Nineteenth-Century Australian Literary Culture", in *Reading Across the Pacific: Australia–United States Intellectual Histories*, ed. Robert Dixon and Nicholas Birns (Sydney: Sydney University Press, 2010), 44.

venture back in England; or the unstable, profligate Mr Willis, a dandy squatter whose "dress was finer in quality than squatters commonly" and whose reckless, desperate greed brings about madness and ruin (93). As we noted in the previous chapter, the novel also introduces a gathering of men described as "excellent specimens of the squatting interest": "There was the outlandish settler, a rough, half-civilised (in manner) kind of fellow. There was a more dandified settler, whose station was just across the river; and a stock-owner and jobber, who had stations in different parts of the country" (240). By this time, the "squatter" and the "settler" are sometimes used interchangeably; but they still break down into distinct subcategories that are sufficiently defined to drive narratives of their own. The "outlandish settler", for example, tells a gruesome story about bushrangers raiding a station and violating a pregnant woman.

The squatter novel also charts the history of the squatter type, often contrasting older colonial figures with newly evolving ones. Like Samuel Sidney, William Howitt was an acquaintance of Charles Dickens who published articles and sketches in *Household Words*. Unlike Sidney, however, Howitt came to Australia in the early 1850s to work on the goldfields. A devout Quaker, he had written the influential *Christianity and Colonisation* (1838), a passionate condemnation of the treatment of indigenous people around the world. After his time in the colonies, Howitt produced, among other things, a squatter novel, *Tallangetta, the Squatter's Home: A Story of Australian Life* (1856). Some of the chapters in *Tallangetta* were first published in *Household Words*, including "The Old and New Squatters", serialised in December 1855. In "The New Squatter", Howitt describes a young Glaswegian, David Macleod, who emigrates to Australia and makes a fortune as a merchant. When the economic depression of the early 1840s hits the colonies, many squatters go broke – and Macleod happily takes possession of their properties. One day, he visits one of the largest of these properties and is transported by its size and splendour: "Readers", the narrator says (speaking, of course, to the English readers of *Household Words*),

> lift up your imaginations; spread them out on their broadest pinions, and conceive the Squatter occupying the county of Kent, or Surrey for his run, at a rate, including licence-fee, and head-money, of some fifty pounds a-year, and you form a tolerable idea of the Squatter's domain; a domain which this country has so bountifully consigned to him, and perceive why he should so fervently desire to hold it forever.[27]

Standing alone in the homestead, Macleod suddenly sees "a strange and startling figure standing before him". "The man, if man it were", the narrative says,

> stood tall, gaunt, and clad in a rude, coarse, green jacket, ragged and soiled. A belt round his waist showed a brace of large pistols, his left hand held upright as a support a long gun. On his head was a slouching brown wide-awake, and an enormous beard buried the lower half of his face. It was a face that seemed shaped to inspire horror; long, bony, and withered; tanned by sun and breeze into a mahogany hue, and from the deep sunken sockets, his eyes gleamed fiery, yet still and fixed with a spectral expression on the squatter.[28]

---

27 William Howitt, "The New Squatter", *Household Words*, 15 December 1855, 475.
28 Howitt, "The New Squatter", 476.

This is a Gothic encounter that takes place on a squatter's property in the middle of a sun-lit day in December. It introduces the ghost of a bitter old squatter called Tom Scott, who cries for "justice" and tells Macleod that he put his life's work into establishing the station that Macleod has now bought for a pittance. Howitt's sketch invokes Dickens' "A Christmas Carol", published twelve years earlier in 1843; but as a morality tale, it contradicts everything Dickens' story had stood for. Macleod is not a scrooge but a successful property speculator, and the spectral squatter's visitation has no effect at all on his attitude or his wealth, which continues to increase in the wake of the gold rush. The squatter-from-the-past's harsh experiences are in fact soon forgotten as a new wave of wealthy squatters emerges from the turbulent 1840s, richer than ever: "Each party held their estates on equally cheap tenure, that is, just about for nothing; but the balance of profit was infinitely in favour of the patriarchs of the antipodes".[29]

This kind of radical distinction between old and new squatters might recall Raymond Williams' influential cultural categories of the "residual" and the "emergent". For Williams, the "residual . . . has been effectively formed in the past, but it is still active in the cultural process"; the "emergent", on the other hand, is a term that gives expression to "the new meanings and values, new practices, new relationships and kinds of relationship [that] are continually being created".[30] The ghostly visitation in Howitt's sketch on the new squatter brings these two categories into direct contact. But perhaps it also consigns the ghostly old squatter to the more distant category of the "archaic", which divests him of any influence in the present.[31] Even so, there remains the sense that the new or emergent squatter is a pale imitation of an earlier, hardier squatter type. In Marcus Clarke's "Squatters – Old Style and New", first published in the *Brisbane Courier* in March 1870, all the affection and sentiment is given to an old squatter named Robin Ruff, who had arrived in Australia in 1836 and survived the depression to live a prosperous, undistinguished but charitable life: "he is not aristocratic, nor even deistical; but he is a fine, honest, kind-hearted old man, and has not been without his use in this brand-new-go-ahead colony of ours".[32] This hard-working old squatter contrasts with the brash, faux-aristocratic character of young Dudley Smooth, "a very different stamp":

> He had but lately come down from the station, but was arrayed in the most fashionable of fashionable garments. His trousers were so tight, that his legs looked as if they had been patented by some mono-maniac player on the flute, as cleaning machines for that instrument of music. His waistcoat yawned like a whited sepulchre. He wore half-a-yard of black satin tied round his neck, or rather his shirt collar. His feet were encased in shoes of that high-heeled class affected by step-dancers, and the suddenly expanded trouser ends flapped around his ankles – entwined, like two barber's poles, by the red stripes of his silk stockings.[33]

---

29 Howitt, "The New Squatter", 477.
30 Raymond Williams, *Marxism and Literature* (Oxford: Oxford University Press, 1977), 123.
31 Williams describes the "archaic" as "that which is wholly recognized as an element of the past, to be observed, to be examined, or even on occasion to be consciously 'revived', in a deliberately specializing way": *Marxism and Literature*, 122.
32 Marcus Clarke, "Squatters – Old Style and New", *Brisbane Courier*, 10 March 1870, 3.
33 Clarke, "Squatters – Old Style and New", 3.

This new squatter dandy is the object of much scorn in Clarke's character sketch, a sort of by-product of the "brand-new-go-ahead colony", effortlessly successful and strikingly stylish, but lacking in content. He has no moral framework, no work ethic, and no particular dedication to the maintenance of his own station. Significantly, he is uncultivated, with no interest in literature or art: "Books, music, pictures, &c., are 'rot'".[34]

We shall come to other examples of the squatter dandy shortly; it is one of a large number of "paradigms of the squatter figure" that inhabit and shape the squatter novel. In Howitt's *Tallangetta*, the Fitzpatrick family arrive from England and take possession of a splendid bush property; soon, they meet their neighbours, who offer them an array of squatter paradigms or "specimens" (a word the novel repeats many times). Captain Ponceford has served in India and is now happily married and immersed in colonial life; he presents "the life of a squatter in so pleasant a point of view" but thinks that a squatter's entitlements should be "limited by the public rights".[35] Mr Metcalfe is an older squatter type, someone who has worked hard to build his property; a cultivated man, he has "a great knowledge of books, and managed to keep up an acquaintance with what was going on in Europe, and in literature in a remarkable degree" (76). Mr Quarrier is a successful dynastic squatter who agitates for squatters' rights against "the radicals in Melbourne" (66); his wife is "a most favourable specimen of the native-born white population" (68), their daughters are "splendid specimens of Australian beauty" (92) and their son is "one of the most affluent of [the] squatter lords" (93). The novel's map of colonial Australia – its literary geography – is in fact charted primarily in terms of squatters' properties. There is also Peter Martin's station, Bongubine, furnished with literary magazines such as *Punch* and the *Illustrated London News*. And there is Mr Farbrother's station, which is full of collections of native birds and insects: an amateur naturalist, he proudly shows his visitors a copy of John Gould's *The Birds of Australia* (1840–48).

All of these squatter types are presented as relatively benign, their properties now fully established. But at Farbrother's station, the novel suddenly lurches into a long description that plunges the orderly, pastoral world of these squatters back into the Gothic. Farbrother tells a story called "The Land-Shark": another chapter from the novel that was first published in Dickens' *Household Words*. The story introduces a doctor who has been attending Peter Stonecrop, a dying land speculator. Stonecrop has accumulated massive tracts of land and is a perfect example of Ken Stewart's notion of the squatter as a "model of acquisitive selfishness who cruelly or meanly exploits his workers . . ." The 1850s gold rushes had given him new energy, along with many other speculators: enough, in fact, to form what the doctor calls a "tribe of voracious, yet indigesting land-sharks". Stonecrop is a bit like David Macleod, in that he makes his fortune out of buying up already-established squatters' properties: "the in-rushing torrents of gold-seekers have found the squatter and the land-shark in a coalition terrible as an Antarctic frost. What the one was reluctantly compelled to let go, the other seized".[36] In South Australia, Wakefield's influence had enabled settlers to keep the land-shark at bay, restricting land purchases

---

34 Paul Eggert, "Textual Criticism and Folklore: The Ned Kelly Story and *Robbery Under Arms*", *Script and Print* 31:2 (2007), 72.
35 William Howitt, *Tallangetta, the Squatter's Home: A Story of Australian Life*, vol. 1 (London: Longman, Brown, Green, Longmans & Roberts, 1857), 69. All subsequent references are to this edition and appear in parentheses in the text.
36 William Howitt, "The Land-Shark", *Household Words*, 12 January 1856, 568.

to the "small capitalist" and the "small farm". As we have seen in Spence's *Clara Morison* (1854), for example, the South Australian smallholder's relationship to the land is regarded as much stronger than the squatter's.[37] But in Victoria "the squatter and the land-shark reign", locked together in a struggle over land supremacy. The impassioned doctor casts the land-shark in a strikingly Gothic way, as a "devourer of his kind", a colonial monstrosity that "swallows up earth by acres and leagues":

> Australia has produced no lion, tiger, grizzly bear, or such ferocious monsters, but it has produced the land-shark, and that is a *monstrum horrendum* worse than all of them put together. It is worse, because it wears the shape of a man; and, with a face as innocent, as meek, and placid as a manticora or a siren, takes shelter under human laws. In a word, a land-shark is a thing which combines all the attributes of the incubus, the cannibal, the vampyre, and the choke-damp. Where it lives nobody else can live. It is the upas-tree become animated and, walking over the southern world like a new Frankenstein, producing stagnation, distortion, death-in-life, and desolation wherever it arrives.[38]

In this remarkable passage, the land-shark emerges in the wake of the squattocracy, feeding off its past success while shutting down the values and traditions that had underpinned and driven its "pastoral ideology": not least, the squatters' sense that they were essential to the project of national development and prosperity.

Henry Kingsley's Squatters

Henry Kingsley wrote the two best-known Australian squatter novels of the mid-nineteenth century: *The Recollections of Geoffry Hamlyn* (1859) and *The Hillyars and the Burtons* (1865).[39] Like William Howitt, Kingsley visited Australia in the early 1850s, staying for about five years. He became "well acquainted" with the Western District of Victoria and visited a number of stations there, including William Mitchell's property Langi Willi near Skipton[40] – which no doubt helped to inform Kingsley about the details of squatter life. There are three prevailing views of Kingsley's squatter novels that we can identify here. The first sees them as a kind of positive antidote to the bleaker, more Gothic atmosphere of so much colonial Australian writing – offering instead a benign chronicle of a "golden age" of Australian life that pays tribute to the squattocracy as an exemplary class of established (or establishment) settlers. The successful squatter Sam Buckley in *Geoffry Hamlyn* is a good example, "the very Brummel of bush-dandies ... altogether as

---

37 See the South Australian Gilbert Elliot's letter from the Victorian goldfields: "Our working farmers, struggling for and obtaining comfort and even opulence, buying section after section, and making the value of their land tend times greater by their labour, have a much stronger attachment to the soil than the squatters here": Catherine Helen Spence, *Clara Morison: A Tale of South Australia During the Gold Fever*, vol. 2 (London: John W. Parker & Son, 1854), 48.
38 Howitt, "The Land-Shark", 567.
39 *The Hillyars and the Burtons* was first serialised in *Macmillan's Magazine* from November 1863 to April 1865.
40 Stanton Mellick, Patrick Morgan and Paul Eggert, introduction to Henry Kingsley's *The Recollections of Geoffry Hamlyn* (St Lucia: University of Queensland Press, 1996), xxviii, xxx.

fine a looking young fellow, as well dressed, and as well mounted too, as you will find on the country side"; he goes on to become "one of the richest of her Majesty's subjects in the Southern hemisphere".[41] For Marcus Clarke, *Geoffry Hamlyn* was in fact the definitive squatter novel: "The best Australian novel that has been, and probably will be written, is 'Geoffrey [sic] Hamlyn', and any attempt to paint the ordinary squatting life of the colonies, could not fail to challenge unfavourable comparison with that admirable story".[42] The following newspaper article from 1930, honouring Kingsley's centenary, gave eloquent expression to this novel's idealised view of Australian pastoral prosperity:

> To re-read *Geoffry Hamlyn*... is to be reminded that Australia of the early colonial days was not altogether made up of double-dyed convicts, drought-stricken settlers, and the ructions of New South Wales Governors, but had, away from the Sydney-siders, whole pastoral communities where the old English culture and courtesy blended with the unconventional frankness and open-handed hospitality of Australia Felix.[43]

The second view is the complete opposite of this, however, offering a much more critical account of Kingsley's unadulterated apology for this powerful ruling class. The best expression of this is probably Tom Collins' spirited denunciation of Kingsley in Joseph Furphy's novel *Such Is Life* (1903):

> Those whose knowledge of the pastoral regions is drawn from a course of novels of the Geoffrey [sic] Hamlyn class, cannot fail to hold a most erroneous notion of the squatter. Of course, we use the term "squatter" indifferently to denote a station-owner, a managing partner, or a salaried manager. Lacking generations of development, there is no typical squatter. Or, if you like, there are a thousand types. Hungry M'Intyre is one type; Smythe – petty, genteel, and parsimonious – is another; patriarchal Royce is another; Montgomery – kind, yet haughty and imperious – is another; Stewart is another. My diary might, just as likely as not, have compelled me to introduce, instead of these, a few of the remaining nine-hundred and ninety-five types – any type conceivable, in fact, except the slender-witted, virgin-souled, overgrown schoolboys who fill Henry Kingsley's exceedingly trashy and misleading novel with their insufferable twaddle.[44]

The third prevailing view – presented in some more recent critical accounts – sees Kingsley in the framework of a taken-for-granted colonial racism that (in this case) routinely casts Aboriginal people as debased or enslaved or both. Catherine Hall notes that Kingsley's mother "came from a long line of Barbadian plantation owners", giving Kingsley a historical background that enabled him to take for granted the oppression of Aboriginal people: conceding the ultimate failure of colonialism's "civilising" project, in order then to casually reproduce the various "extinction discourses" in currency at this time.[45] To "civilise" Aboriginal people is, from a settler perspective, to "save" them. To admit that the

---

41 Henry Kingsley, *The Recollections of Geoffry Hamlyn*, ed. Stanton Mellick, Patrick Morgan and Paul Eggert (1859; St Lucia: University of Queensland Press, 1996), 303–4. All subsequent references are to this edition and appear in parentheses in the text.
42 Marcus Clarke, preface to *Long Odds: A Novel* (Melbourne: Clarson, Massina, 1869), n.p.
43 "Henry Kingsley Centenary", *Brisbane Courier*, 4 January 1930, 14.
44 Joseph Furphy, *Such Is Life* (1903; Text Publishing: Melbourne, 2013), 239. Here, Collins interestingly both typecasts the squatter and preserves his individuality ("there are a thousand types").

civilising mission of colonialism doesn't work then licenses a sense that Aboriginal people are a "dying race", inherently unable to survive the pressures of contemporary life. Paul Giles sees Kingsley in a similar way, arguing that he was "completely untroubled by the kind of continuities between colonialism and racism that were then widely regarded, even by liberals, as inevitable".[46]

Our readings of Kingsley's novels certainly bear out each of these views. But we also want to say that the squatter novel as a genre can draw together distinct, even contradictory representations and dispositions. In fact, it is possible to say that Kingsley's two squatter novels take their readers in quite different ideological directions. *The Recollections of Geoffry Hamlyn* is indeed a celebration of squatter prosperity – and supremacy – bringing a group of English immigrants over to Australia and charting their rapid accumulation of money and property. "We had had but little trouble with the blacks", Hamlyn tells us, "and, having taken possession of a fine piece of country, were flourishing and well to do" (192). Even so, the novel ties its squatters to a militant colonialism that leads to a couple of ultra-violent struggles over land occupation. After a servant is speared by Aboriginal people, a young squatter, James Stockbridge, regrets that "any of our party has had this collision with them. I cannot bear shooting the poor brutes" (267). This combination of stark racism and humanitarian compassion is a familiar expression of the kinds of "extinction discourses" that Hall mentions above. Soon afterwards, Stockbridge himself is speared, and killed, as the squatters violently clash with a large group of Aboriginal people: as if even the slightest expression of settler sympathy has to be erased from the novel's framework. Frontier violence impinges on squatter prosperity only occasionally, however; bushrangers are the main threat in this novel, described by one character as "more detestably ferocious than savages, when they once get loose" (339). Aboriginal people are generally cast here as either "wild" and ferocious or debased and enslaved – like Jerry, "a tame black belonging to us", who is used as a tracker by the squatters during a kangaroo hunt (331).

There is one scene in *The Recollections of Geoffry Hamlyn*, however, that complicates this racist binary, and it stands out as one of the more unusual representations of settler–Aboriginal encounters in colonial Australian fiction. A group of squatters swim in a river where some Aboriginal people are camped, gleefully stripping off their clothes to frolic with them in the water. The scene presents a visual problem for Hamlyn, the narrator: "Had Etty been on the spot", he writes, referring to William Etty, the controversial English painter of relatively realistic female nudes, "he would have got a hint for one of his finest pictures; though I can give but little idea of it in writing, however, let me try" (213). But it also presents an ideological problem, namely, how to represent this settler–Aboriginal encounter without turning it into either an example of frontier conflict or a manifestation of the comic grotesque so often applied in colonial writing to Aboriginal people identified as "harmless". When the squatters emerge from the water, they sit on the riverbank and watch an elderly Aboriginal woman guiding a canoe along the river. "She was entirely without clothes", the novel tells us, before invoking Botticelli's famous painting, "The Birth of Venus": "and in spite of her decrepitude stood upright in the

---

45 Catherine Hall, "The Slave Owner and the Settler", in *Indigenous Networks: Mobility, Connections and Exchange*, ed. Jane Carey and Jane Lydon (London and New York: Routledge, 2014), 41, 46.
46 Paul Giles, *Antipodean Australia: Australasia and the Constitution of US Literature* (Oxford: Oxford University Press, 2013), 223.

cockleshell, handling it with great dexterity" (214). Some Aboriginal children in the river play a trick on her, tipping her out of the canoe. "It was amazing to see how boldly and well the old woman struck out for the shore", Hamlyn comments, "keeping her white head well out of the water; and, having reached dry land once more, sat down on her haunches, and began scolding with a volubility and power which would soon have silenced the loudest tongue in old Billingsgate" (214). There is admiration for this figure, but it collapses back into caricature at the end by likening the old woman to a fishwife in a London market. The scene momentarily absorbs Aboriginal people into the squatters' version of the pastoral ideal, but this soon unravels and the woman becomes a source for the squatters' high-handed amusement.

In *The Hillyars and the Burtons*, published six years later, frontier violence seems more remote and there is now a sense that the squattocracy has completely succeeded in dominating, and domesticating, Aboriginal populations. As she makes her way to a squatter's property, Gerty Hillyar – a squatter's daughter and the sister-in-law of another squatter, the Colonial Secretary, James Oxton – is not in the least "alarmed" by the prospect of encountering local Aboriginal people: "There were none but *tame* blacks on that line of country", the novel says; "there was not a wild black within a hundred miles".[47] *The Hillyars and the Burtons* is in fact full of squatters, many of whom, like Oxton, are very successful. Like all squatter novels, it gives expression to the triumphs of a "pastoral ideology". But unlike *The Recollections of Geoffry Hamlyn*, it doesn't really celebrate every achievement and the fortunes of different characters spill out quite unevenly. The narrator, Jim Burton, begins the novel in England, with his blacksmith father and his family. A number of connections are established between the Burtons and a much wealthier family, the Hillyars; among other things, Sir George Hillyar's son from a second marriage, Erne, is attracted to Jim's sister, Emma. In the meantime, Sir George's first son – also called George – is an effective Inspector of Police in Australia; and Samuel Burton, one of Jim's relatives, is an escaped convict. When he emigrates to Australia with his family, Jim meets two squatters on board the ship: Abiram Pollifex, a colonial Governor who "did the dirty work [of being a squatter] as cleanly as he could" (236); and Charles Morton, an Eton-educated squatter, "expensive and useless", a "thriftless horse-riding dandy" who has been sent out to Australia to improve himself (237, 239). These squatter models provide a cynical edge to the otherwise triumphalist account of squatter success. But they also give Jim a sense of just how possible it is to start over again in Australia and do well. One of the first people Jim meets in Australia is Mr Dawson, a politician and the owner of "many stations", with "pockets full of money" (276, 309). Dawson is an embodiment of the excesses of "pastoral ideology", owning (from one perspective) far too much; in the wake of Gipps' failed attempts to regulate the squatter economy, he makes the connections between money, property and political influence all too visible. As he gets to know Dawson – and this also distinguishes this novel from *The Recollections of Geoffry Hamlyn* – Jim realises that his "humble story" is now becoming "mixed up with the course of colonial politics" (265).

The Hillyars and the Burtons in fact returns us to a set of political questions concerning colonial land and labour management – that is, colonial reform. Oxton, the Colonial Secretary, wants an assisted emigration program in order to secure a large labour force in the colonies, to be funded out of land sales. But his program runs the risk of flooding

---

47   Henry Kingsley, *The Hillyars and the Burtons: A Story of Two Families* (Boston: Ticknor & Fields, 1865), 339. All subsequent references are to this edition and appear in parentheses in the text.

the workforce with labourers, "creating a lower class, and depressing the price of labour by denying them land" (325). This puts Oxton in conflict with the "Radicals", who want to legislate for smaller selections of land; it also puts him in conflict with Dawson, who opposes assisted emigration and wants a native-born labouring class. The novel thus sketches out a set of post-Wakefieldian predicaments. But Oxton is a squatter, and – as well as working against the interests of colonial labourers – he transparently supports the squattocracy: "James Oxton, a 'squatter', a wool-grower among wool-growers ... had unworthily blinded himself so far as to legislate for his own class" (325). Defeated in parliament, Oxton resigns. Whereas *The Recollections of Geoffry Hamlyn* had (more or less) presented an unwavering portrait of squatter prosperity, this novel troubles the seamlessness of that taken-for-granted connection between squatters, political power and financial success. Oxton is also disturbed at a personal level, feeling responsible for his wife's sister Gerty's failed marriage; Gerty herself becomes a solitary sort of Gothic figure by the end of the novel, "the only dark thing in a blazing landscape" (419). Jim Burton's father buys an apparently unappealing block of land and goes on to become "the proprietor of the richest copper mine in the world" (312) – making his fortune outside the prevailing logics of pastoral land use. In *The Recollections of Geoffry Hamlyn*, marriage, happiness and prosperity combine as the squatter romance concludes. But in *The Hillyars and the Burtons*, the long, fraught romance between Emma and Erne never reaches fruition. In a bleak, apocalyptic ending, Emma is killed in a cyclone and Erne, distraught, "turned his back on a country which had become hateful to him" (419). Unusually for the squatter novel, *The Hillyars and the Burtons* does not end with an image of pastoral domesticity, and there is no concluding celebration of squatter success.

Squatters vs Selectors

How troubled can a triumphant expression of "pastoral ideology" be? The acclaimed English novelist Anthony Trollope wrote a squatter novel, *Harry Heathcote of Gangoil: A Tale of Australian Bush Life*, serialised in Melbourne's *Age* newspaper from the end of 1872 to January 1874, which introduced a new squatter type: the paranoid squatter. Like Howitt and Kingsley, Trollope visited Australia on two occasions, first in 1871 and again in 1875. His son Frederick had already emigrated to Australia, becoming a squatter at Mortray, an inland property around 400 kilometres west of Sydney. But Frederick's station quickly fell into debt, despite his father's financial assistance; later on, ironically enough, he took a job as an Inspector of Conditional Purchases, presiding over land claims by small selectors.[48] By the 1860s, the interests of squatters and small selectors were in open conflict. In 1861, the New South Wales premier John Robertson had introduced the Robertson Land Acts, which made Crown lands open to free selection and installed "a new system in response to the mass immigration of people of small means who had experienced difficulty establishing themselves under the old regulations".[49] Rodney Harrison notes

---

48 See R.B. Joyce, "Anthony Trollope (1815–1882)", in *Australian Dictionary of Biography*: http://adb.anu.edu.au/biography/trollope-anthony-4750. See also, for example, "Death of Mr Fred Trollope", *Riverine Grazier*, 7 June 1910, 2.
49 Rodney Harrison, *Shared Landscapes: Archaeologies of Attachment and the Pastoral Industry in New South Wales* (Sydney: UNSW Press, 2004), 36.

that until this time "vast areas of grazing lands were under the control of the squatters". The Robertson Land Acts, however, challenged this supremacy by reducing "the tenure of pastoral leases" and enabling "selectors, whether *bona fide* settlers or speculators" to purchase land much more easily.[50] The claims of the "Radicals" in Kingsley's *The Hillyars and the Burtons* have now become a reality – although, as we have seen, squatters and small holders were defined in opposition to one another as early as Wakefield. Not least because of his son's predicament, Trollope was all too aware of this opposition. He wrote about it in his chronicle of his travels across the colonies, *Australia and New Zealand*, allowing his admiration for the hospitable squatter to be challenged by his liberal politics. Surprisingly, perhaps, Trollope urges "travellers" like himself to take the side of the free selector:

> In this great question between the squatter and free-selecter [sic] of land, – for with its different ramifications in regard to immigration, agricultural produce, and pastoral success, it is the greatest of all questions in Australian life, – it is almost impossible for the normal traveller not to sympathise with the squatter. The normal traveller comes out with introductions to the gentlemen of the colony, and the gentlemen of the colony are squatters. The squatters' houses are open to him. They introduce the traveller to their clubs. They lend their horses and buggies. Their wives and daughters are pretty and agreeable. They exercise all the duties of hospitality with a free hand. They get up kangaroo hunts and make picnics. It is always pleasant to sympathize with an aristocracy when an aristocracy will open its arms to you . . . But the traveller ought to sympathize with the free-selecter [sic], – always premising that the man keep his hands from picking and stealing his neighbour's cattle. He, we may say, is the man for whom colonial life and colonial prosperity is [sic] especially intended, and without whom no colony can rise to national importance. The pastoral squatter occupying tens of thousands of acres, and producing wool that has made Australia what she now is, has done great things for the infancy of the country. But in all discussions on this question it must be remembered that he has no right to the permanent occupation of the land on which his flocks wander.[51]

In *Harry Heathcote of Gangoil*, Trollope turned the open conflict between squatter and free selector into a Christmas story in the Australian bush. Heathcote is a young squatter and magistrate, with a large sheep station near the Mary River in southeast Queensland.[52] An orphan in England, Heathcote inherits some money and emigrates to Australia. Marrying the daughter of a bankrupt squatter, he settles at Gangoil with his wife and her sister Kate, and soon develops an overblown sense of his power and capacity to control others. He is, the novel tells us, "not only his own master, but the master also of all with whom he was brought into contact from day to day. In his life he conversed but seldom with any except those who were dependent on him . . . " (2). His wife idolises him, and his sister-

---

50   Harrison, *Shared Landscapes*, 36.
51   Anthony Trollope, *Australia and New Zealand* (Leipzig: Bernhard Tauchnitz, 1873), 41.
52   P.D. Edwards notes that "the scenes of bush life in *Harry Heathcote of Gangoil* are based almost exclusively on Trollope's observations while staying with his son. He saw little of the Mary River district in Queensland, where Gangoil is supposed to be located, and did not visit any sheep stations there": Introduction to *Harry Heathcote of Gangoil: A Tale of Australian Bush Life*, ed. P.D. Edwards (1874; London: The Trollope Society, 1998), vii. All subsequent references are to this edition and appear in parentheses in the text.

in-law "feared him also somewhat" (3). But the more Heathcote insists on his authority, the more fragile he becomes. In the heat of mid-summer he obsesses over the threat of bushfires, worrying about swagmen smoking their pipes and discarding their matches, and disgruntled employees setting fire to shearing sheds. The spectre of financial ruin plagues him; his greatest fear is of one day becoming "the servant instead of the master of men" (27). When he sacks a boundary rider, Nokes, he is immediately anxious about retaliation. What makes things worse is that Nokes then goes to work for a neighbouring free selector, Giles Medlicot, who grows sugar cane. Heathcote gruffly tells Kate, "I can't understand why free-selectors and mosquitoes should have been introduced into the arrangements of the world" (4). Reluctantly, he visits Medlicot and urges him to have Nokes "watched", but Medlicot refuses: "I'll encourage no such espionage as that" (32). Later, Nokes tells Medlicot that Heathcote has made a lot of enemies.

When his wife Mary and her sister Kate invite Medlicot to dinner, Heathcote thinks they are "against him". Distancing himself even from his family, he comes to embody the dark side of the settler's independent spirit, alienated and alone: "He had chosen to manage everything himself, without contradiction and almost without counsel; but, like other such imperious masters, he now found that when trouble came the privilege of dictatorship brought with it an almost insupportable burden" (35). We have already noted Philip McMichael's view that the "pastoral ideology" of squatters enabled them to represent themselves as "patriarchs of a stable social hierarchy". But Trollope's patriarchal squatter has only a partial grip on power, and the social hierarchy beneath him turns out to be both radically unstable and potentially menacing. A very different family of squatters also lives nearby, at a station called Boolabong. The Brownbies run cattle, not sheep; the father, Old Brownbie, is an emancipated convict who lives with several of his sons, "uneducated, ill-conditioned, drunken fellows"; and they are all "hated by the respectable squatters", not least because they drive their cattle across other properties, picking up stolen stock along the way (42). Their noisy, run-down property is the exact opposite of Heathcote's tidy homestead. Among other things, there are very few women (and no prospect of squatter romance) there, which means Boolabong remains both undomesticated and uncultivated. Even so, the novel speaks up for the Brownbies' hospitality, especially in relation to a lower class of itinerant bush worker. There is a patriarch, Old Brownbie, but he is "obsolete" and his sons don't respect him. As a consequence, there is very little sense of "social hierarchy" at this station:

> Boolabong was certainly a miserable place; and yet, such as it was, it was frequented by many guests. The vagabondism of the colonies is proverbial. Vagabonds are taken in almost everywhere throughout the bush; but the welcome given to them varies ... Boolabong was a very paradise for vagabonds. (45)

A squatter's station is usually an expression of settler domination, where social hierarchies are clearly held in place. But the Brownbies' station is linked to "vagabonds", to bush travellers, people without credentials and without property, who come and go indiscriminately. The metropolitan vagabond had, of course, entered popular currency through Henry Mayhew's *London Labour and the London Poor* in the late 1850s and early 1860s. Drawing on the earlier "taxonomic ethnography" of James Prichard,[53] Mayhew began his work with a famous distinction between "wanderers and settlers – the vagabond and the citizen": "not only are all races divisible into wanderers and settlers", he wrote, "but ... each civilised or settled tribe has generally some wandering horde intermingled with, and in a measure preying upon, it".[54] The squatter novel relies on exactly this distinction between settlers and vagabonds in the bush. The former own very large properties, while the latter have nothing much at all and are therefore routinely seen as threatening or parasitical – recalling our discussion of the colonial *lumpenproletariat* in the Introduction. But in Trollope's novel, the Brownbies' cattle station is a place where this distinction between squatter and vagabond is confused. There is no family dynasty on this property, with the various sons becoming drifters or criminals: one does indeed become "a vagabond in the country", while another languishes in jail. As both a respectable squatter and a magistrate, Heathcote despises the Brownbies: "The Brownbies were rascals", he thinks, "and should therefore be exterminated" (43).

One of the jokes in this novel is that Heathcote trespasses on the Brownbies' property (rather than vice versa) when a bushfire breaks out. The resulting fight between them brings Heathcote and Medlicot, the respectable squatter and the free selector, closer together. Soon afterwards, Medlicot asks Kate to marry him and she accepts. *Harry Heathcote of Gangoil* is a squatter romance that literally accommodates the free selector, which might suggest a more flexible vision of settler land ownership. But Medlicot is already cast as an atypical free selector, gentlemanly and well dressed: "he was not of their class". In fact, he is really a kind of squatter by default, Heathcote's "equal in education, intelligence, and fortune, if not in birth" (20). Trollope's novel is a Christmas story that reconciles two otherwise opposed settler character types, bringing the free selector into the squatter's family circle. But it is able to do so only because Medlicot and Heathcote share similar social aspirations and character traits.

Rolf Boldrewood's Squatters

In January 1881, Trollope's son Frederick wrote to him about meeting "a man named Browne" in Dubbo, New South Wales, a magistrate who "scribbles a bit and has written several passable stories".[55] In fact, Thomas Alexander Browne – the colonial writer best known as "Rolf Boldrewood" – probably met Anthony Trollope ten years earlier, in 1871, when he spoke at a public banquet at Gulgong in Trollope's honour. Boldrewood was a Police Magistrate by this time, but he was also an experienced squatter. In 1845 he had taken up a station in the Port Phillip District that he named Squattlesea Mere, after a fictional property owned by a character named Wildrake in Sir Walter Scott's historical novel *Woodstock* (1826). In his biography of Boldrewood, Paul de Serville notes that Squattlesea Mere "was one of the few Port Phillip runs with a literary derivation. [Boldrewood] obviously knew his Scott well".[56] Boldrewood wrote about his time at Squattlesea Mere in *Old Melbourne Memories* (1884): building and furnishing a small house on the station, he remarks, "I had a few books which I had brought up with

---

53   Gillian Beer, *Open Fields: Science in Cultural Encounter* (Cambridge: Cambridge University Press, 1996), 87.
54   Henry Mayhew, *London Labour and the London Poor*, vol. 1 (New York: Dover Publications, 1968), 1.
55   N. John Hall, ed. *The Letters of Anthony Trollope, Volume 2, 1871–1882* (Stanford, Calif.: Stanford University Press, 1983), 894.
56   Paul de Serville, *Rolf Boldrewood: A Life* (Melbourne: Miegunyah Press, 2000), 60.

me in the dray – Byron, Scott, Shakespeare . . . with half a score of other authors, in whom there was *pabulum mentis* for a year or two".[57] De Serville writes that the mid- to late-1840s was a "golden age for pastoralism in Port Phillip".[58] In one sense this is true, and Boldrewood looked back very fondly on these early squatting days. But this was also the time of the long-running Eumeralla War, where squatters fought against the local Gunditjmara people for land occupation. Tom Griffiths notes that Boldrewood's writing in fact made this conflict "famous", not least by bringing to it "the theatrical glamour of overseas frontiers" – comparing it to battles with first nations Americans or, in hindsight, to the 1857 Indian Mutiny.[59] In this context, the neighbourliness of squatters can come to mean something quite different. Boldrewood wrote about squatters in the district with great admiration. But as Jan Critchett has observed in relation to regional conflicts around this time, squatters often "closed ranks to protect each other" from legal scrutiny when they took it upon themselves to aggressively defend their stock and properties.[60] In Boldrewood's writing, the military overtones to squatter life – some of his neighbours and acquaintances were retired officers – are seamlessly merged with cultivated literary tastes and moral integrity. As de Serville writes, "he had little to do with squatters who were not gentlemen":[61] what Boldrewood went on to call "men of high principle, great energy, early culture, and refined habits".[62]

Perhaps it is not surprising to find that Boldrewood was an admirer of Kingsley's *The Recollections of Geoffry Hamlyn*, "that immortal work, the best Australian novel, and for long the only one".[63] The squatter became a major character type for Boldrewood, the focal point for many of his colonial adventure novels and stories. *The Squatter's Dream* first appeared a year or so after Trollope's *Harry Heathcote of Gangoil*, serialised in the *Australian Town and Country Journal* in 1875. A semi-autobiographical novel, it chronicles the life and fortunes of Jack Redgrave, "a jolly, well-to-do young squatter". Redgrave owns a small but successful and picturesque cattle station, Marshmead; but, ambitious to expand, he soon sells it to purchase a much larger but less cultivated property in the Riverina called Gondaree. The "squatter's dream" is precisely this persistent desire for growth and accumulation. One of the first characters he encounters at Gondaree, however, is an Aboriginal woman, an accomplished stockrider called Wildduck (her name perhaps an echo of Scott's landowner Wildrake). A station employee, Wildduck's stories remind Redgrave of the Aboriginal history of Gondaree. In fact, she even makes an explicit land claim: "Everybody say Gondaree people live like black fellows. What for you not give it us back again?"[64] She also reminds Redgrave of his station's history of violent conflict, talking openly about the massacres of Aboriginal people and the shooting of her own father. Later on, Redgrave and a neighbouring squatter's sister, Maud Stangrove, go picnicking at a

---

57 Rolf Boldrewood, *Old Melbourne Memories* (London: Macmillan & Co., Ltd.: 1896), 47.
58 de Serville, *Rolf Boldrewood*, 82.
59 Tom Griffiths, *Hunters and Collectors: The Antiquarian Imagination in Australia* (Cambridge: Cambridge University Press, 1996), 109.
60 Jan Critchett, *Untold Stories: Memories and Lives of Victorian Kooris* (Carlton: Melbourne University Press, 1998), 230.
61 de Serville, *Rolf Boldrewood*, 61.
62 Boldrewood, *Old Melbourne Memories*, 39.
63 Boldrewood, *Old Melbourne Memories*, 172.
64 Rolf Boldrewood, *The Squatter's Dream: A Story of Australian Life* (London: Macmillan & Co., 1891), 32. All subsequent references are to this edition and appear in parentheses in the text.

massacre site called Murdering Lake. Wildduck arrives with her husband, Old Jack, and tells the story of the massacre – noting that her husband had once killed a bushman who had shot an Aboriginal child. Even though they are acknowledged, the conflicts themselves are distanced in time here. Redgrave's comment to Maud – "You see there is more good, solid tragedy in Australian life than you fancied" (116) – also works to neutralise these earlier hostilities, casting them in a clichéd, generalised way as an unproblematic aspect of colonial Australian history (rather than a specific form of injustice).

The Squatter's Dream is about the life cycle of a squatter, seen almost exclusively in terms of economic drives and imperatives that are both national and global. Redgrave is advised early on to buy sheep – "for wool, you had the world for a market" – whereas cattle are only for a "limited and surely decreasing local demand" (40). A huge capital outlay is required, carefully calculated in numbers of sheep and levels of accumulating debt. Redgrave soon finds himself talking to bankers, like Mr Shrood and the younger Mr Smith: the latter

> had many a time and oft envied the bronzed squatter lounging in on a bright morning, throwing down a cheque and stuffing the five-pound notes carelessly into his waistcoat-pocket. But young as he was, he had more than once seen a careworn, grizzled man waiting outside the bank parlour, with ill-concealed anxiety for the interview which was to tell him whether or not he went forth a ruined and hopelessly broken man. (86-7)

Mr Smith's recollections put the successful and the failed squatter side by side, the one seeming to foreshadow the other. Different squatter models appear in the novel, each reflecting a different perspective on good practice and sound investment. Redgrave's neighbour, Mark Stangrove, is a "very staunch conservative", cultivated but cautious about spending money on improvements such as fencing. Other squatters, like Mr Blockham, are frugal to the point of mean-spiritedness, "mole-blind to the pleasures of the intellect, the claims of sympathy, the duties of society" (245). Redgrave, on the other hand, is much more ambitious, and speculative. With the help of an excellent station manager, Sandy M'Nab, he purchases thousands of sheep, builds a solid stone house – with a library that receives "the excellent weekly papers of the colonies" (68) – and finds himself in "magnificent surplus" (174). But the market is soon glutted, levels of debt increase, and the banks carry a motion "to close *all pastoral accounts under a certain amount*" (198). Redgrave is forced to sell Gondaree and – since a squatter's financial security is invariably tied to marriage and domesticity – he postpones his romance with Maud. In Samuel Sidney's squatter novel, *Gallops and Gossips in the Bush of Australia*, we saw a "pastoral ideology" that connects a squatter's success to the subduing, or repression, of local Aboriginal people. Boldrewood's novel takes this a step further. As if embodying Redgrave's failure – and the increasing desolation of the property because of drought, over-stocking, and so on – Wildduck falls ill and dies. The novel therefore binds the fate of this Aboriginal woman to the fate of Gondaree itself. Wildduck dies at exactly the point at which Gondaree is sold; when Redgrave leaves the station, her people have already gone. As he walks away, Redgrave explicitly connects the post-settlement history of her short life to the early promise and subsequent declining fortunes of his property. He recalls

> the day of their first muster of the cattle – the glorious day, the abundant herbage, the free gallop after the half-wild herd, in which poor Wildduck had distinguished herself;

and, fairer than all, the glowing hope which had invested the unaccustomed scene with brightest colours. How different was the aspect of the spot now! The bare pastures, the prosaic fence-line – the Great Enterprise carried through to the point of conspicuous failure; the reckless, joyous child of these lone wastes lying in her grave, under the whispering streamers of the great coubah tree yonder. And is every hope as cold and dead as she? (232)

We would generally expect squatting itself – the settlement and cultivation of large tracts of land in colonial Australia – to invest heavily in the reproduction of racist "extinction discourses": and, as Sidney's novel shows, it certainly did. In Boldrewood's novel, however, "extinction discourses" are linked instead to the failure of squatting. When the "Great Enterprise" comes undone, an Aboriginal woman dies, her people disappear, and the squatter leaves his property in a bizarre mimicry of an Aboriginal predicament – where Redgrave becomes a "landless and dispossessed proprietor", a "wanderer, a beggar": a sort of vagabond (232).

In the event, Redgrave "recovers his spirits" almost immediately and becomes speculative once more. He befriends an Oxford-educated Englishman, Guy Waldron, and – along with an Aboriginal station hand, Doorival – they travel north to search for new lands to purchase. Far from being chastened by failure, Redgrave is now more ambitious than ever, spurred on by Waldron's yearning for "a colossal fortune". They push further inland, continually hungry for better pasture: "with the insatiable greed of their kind", the novel tells us in an explicit typecasting gesture, "they were not disposed to content themselves with anything short of the magnificent and exalted standard which they had set up for themselves" (245-6). The squatter novel shifts genre slightly at this point as the characters head to the edge of the frontier and play out the role of "successful explorer[s]".[65] Here, Aboriginal people are "wild", not domesticated; Waldron is speared and dies, and Doorival and Redgrave become delirious with thirst. Finding water at last, Redgrave returns to the Pioneer's Royal Hotel where he meets Frank Forestall and tells him about the properties he plans to claim. Soon afterwards, Redgrave is surprised to find that Forestall has already tendered for the properties, winning the leasehold. It is now the early 1860s and the Robertson Land Acts have bureaucratised land claims processes, with little regard for individual nuance or moral obligation. As an official tells Redgrave, "the department can only deal with tenders or applications for pastoral leases of unoccupied Crown lands as brought before it, without reference to the characters or motives of applicants" (284).

Redgrave's bitter disappointment at being defrauded by Forestall is sufficient to transform him into the complete opposite of a squatter: not a vagabond, in fact, but a shepherd. Boldrewood gives a stark example of the squatter's view of shepherds in "The Fencing of Wanderowna", when Hobbie grumbles, "'I wish every shepherd between here and Carpentaria was boiled down'".[66] When a Chinese gardener mistakes a squatter for a shepherd in *The Squatter's Dream*, the squatter is grossly insulted: "Do I look like a

---

65   Colonial explorers were often seen as promoting frontier land for potential use by squatters. See, for example, the remarks about Major Thomas Mitchell in Alan Lester and Fae Dussart, *Colonisation and the Origins of Humanitarian Governance: Protecting Aborigines across the Nineteenth-Century British Empire* (Cambridge: Cambridge University Press, 2014) whose explorations across eastern Australia "had advertised the richness of the land available for squatters to occupy", 106.
66   Boldrewood, "The Fencing of Wanderowna", 18.

slouching, 'possum-eating, billy-carrying crawler of a shepherd?" (67). Broke and with no property, Redgrave falls into a kind of Gothic delirium, collapsing in the bush: "The form of the wanderer lay beneath the forest tree, which swayed and rocked beneath the rising blast. With the moaning of the melancholy shrill-voiced wind, wailing all night, as if in half-remembered dirges, mingled the cries of a fever-stricken man" (288). Close to death, he is saved by Old Jock, an experienced shepherd who takes him to Jimburah Station. Old Jock is from Ettrickshire, in Scotland: he is meant to recall the Scottish author James Hogg, who wrote under the pseudonym "Ettrick Shepherd", a vernacular figure "full of naïve folk-wisdom".[67] Initially thinking that shepherding in colonial Australia would be "like slavery", Old Jock has turned it into a dignified vocation, tied to the pastoral genre and a love of nature: where "the vara sheep, puir dumb beasties, seem to acknowledge the influence of the scene, and there's a calm sense o' joy and peace unknown to the dwellers in town" (291). Old Jock's advice, along with his "Arcadian" identity, influences Redgrave, who changes his name, becomes a shepherd and regains his health. It is certainly unusual in the squatter novel – which is generally so dismissive of shepherds – to see a shepherd become a squatter's "humble mentor" and help him revive his fortunes. Redgrave then hears that Forestall has been speared by Aboriginal people; afterwards, he returns to the Land Office to resubmit his claim, gaining the lease and turning his outback station into a financial success. Three years later, he sells it and buys back his original station, Marshmead; he is also now in a position to propose marriage to Maud. *The Squatter's Dream* ends conventionally enough for a squatter novel. But it also reflects critically on the squatter's predicament, and the forces that continue to disturb or trouble his equilibrium. "What he thinks right to do", the novel concludes, "he will perform if he can, maugre land-sharks, agitators, or even his very respectable and slightly democratic farmer neighbours" (311). The squatter's "pastoral ideology" is affirmed here, but the novel also reminds us of its fragility – which it links both to external factors (the global economy, drought, "land-sharks", neighbours, etc.) and the characteristics of the squatter himself. In the framework of the novel, Redgrave is *too* speculative: too easily "enthralled", as the novel beautifully puts it, "by the Circe of the new world" (311). Greedy squatters like Redgrave have "abandoned the substance for the shadow" (312); they cross a threshold, where the rapid accumulation of property and stock plunges them into a world of debt and solitude, and the solid, pastoral promise of the genre risks lapsing into delirium and despair.

We saw something like this at the end of Kingsley's *The Hillyars and the Burtons*, where that investment in a vision of pastoral ascendency and settler triumph is routinely destabilised by its opposite, the Gothic. The squatter novel is as much preoccupied with failure as it is with success, and this can mean that the Gothic and the squatter's pastoral romance are much closer to each other than we might first have thought. McCombie's insane settler Willis; Howitt's spectre of the bitter, old squatter; Boldrewood's delirious failed speculator: these are all dark visions of what the successful squatter might become. In Trollope's novel, squatters can also be vagabonds; and in *The Squatter's Dream*, a squatter becomes a shepherd. Although its "pastoral ideology" can be pervasive – and single-mindedly upheld and fought for – the squatter novel is therefore also a surprisingly accommodating genre. It plays host to all sort of yarns and stories-within-stories, to do with bushrangers, ex-convicts, shepherds, "land-sharks", and so on. It embraces the

---

67 See John Barrell, "Putting Down the Rising", in *Scotland and the Borders of Romanticism*, ed. Leith Davis, Ian Duncan and Janet Sorensen (Cambridge: Cambridge University Press, 2004), 130.

romance as the primary way of domesticating a squatter's sometimes rudimentary relationship to property. It unleashes moments of brutal frontier violence, although it can also push this into the recent past or revise it by (for example) sentimentalising a squatter's interactions with particular Aboriginal characters, like Wildduck or Doorival. And it touches the pastoral itself, not as a return-to-Nature narrative but as an expression of a squatter's cultivated, aristocratic tastes and status. The squatter novel is literally hospitable, assembling a range of genres and a variety of character types which it then tirelessly arranges into hierarchies of value and significance: with the squatter and his "pastoral ideology" always, or ultimately, on the highest rung.

2
Bushrangers

The colonial bushranger was a ubiquitous character who appeared in many Australian novels right across the nineteenth century. He was in fact there from the beginning: James Boyce writes that "the first book of general literature published in Australia" is Thomas Wells' *Michael Howe: The Last and Worst of the Bushrangers of Van Diemen's Land*, "printed in Hobart Town in 1818".[1] We can note that this first book about Australia's first bushranger is already confidently announcing the end of this character type ("the *last* bushranger"). In fact, colonial fiction and commentary made a habit of declaring the bushranger's demise, as if it could hardly wait to close this particular chapter of Australia's history: to make this figure *residual*. Even so, the bushranger persisted, and colonial romance increasingly turned to him as a powerful and charismatic figure, compelling enough to become a protagonist. By the time we get to Captain Starlight in Rolf Boldrewood's *Robbery Under Arms* (1882-83), the bushranger is likeable, cultivated and heroic. In the earliest accounts, however, the bushranger was generally cast in the opposite way, as feral and primitive, and wantonly cruel: as in Thomas McCombie's *Adventures of a Colonist* (1845), where the "outlandish settler" tells his story about bushrangers "of the old days" who "were of a more ferocious character".[2] Thomas Wells' 1818 account of Michael Howe works steadily towards this particular bushranger's "extinction", as the murderous Howe flees his pursuers to live in solitude in the remote forests of Van Diemen's Land. Losing his grip on civilisation, he soon becomes a wild figure immersed in the natural world: a kind of *homo ferus*, the hybrid species identified by Carl Linnaeus at the end of the eighteenth century that posed a challenge to conventional distinctions between human and animal. Wells writes that "Howe was of athletic make: he wore at the time of his death a dress made of kangaroo skins; had an extraordinary long beard, and presented altogether a terrific appearance".[3] Alone in the forest, he keeps "a sort of journal of dreams" written in "kangaroo blood" which "shew[ed] strongly the distressed state of his mind, and some

---

1 James Boyce, *Van Diemen's Land: A History* (Melbourne: Black Inc., 2008), 79.
2 Thomas McCombie, *Adventures of a Colonist; or, Godfrey Arabin, the Settler* (London: John & Daniel A. Darling, 1845), 241: "They had no pity . . . they violated maid and matron before the eyes of their husbands and relatives. They were refined at torture. Many a cruel story I know of them . . ."
3 Thomas Wells, *Michael Howe: The Last and Worst of the Bushrangers of Van Diemen's Land* (Hobart: Andrew Bent, 1818), 33.

tincture of superstition". In this deranged, primal state, Howe nevertheless still clings to the promise of a domesticated, cultivated future, even in the bush: "he had always an idea of settling in the woods; for [the journal] contains long lists of such seeds as he wished to have, of vegetables, fruits, and even flowers!"[4]

Hayden White has captured the imaginative force of the wild man in literature in the following passage:

> He is just out of sight, over the horizon, in the nearby forest, desert, mountains, or hills. He sleeps in crevices, under great trees, or in the caves of wild animals, to which he carries off helpless children, or women, there to do unspeakable things to them. And he is also sly: he steals the sheep from the fold, the chicken from the coop, tricks the shepherd, and befuddles the gamekeeper.[5]

Paul Keal notes that this account "equally well describes the image of North American Indians and Australian Aboriginals held by many Europeans during the nineteenth century".[6] Bushrangers and Aboriginal people are indeed sometimes affiliated in colonial fiction, as we shall note below; Wells relates that Michael Howe travelled with a "native girl" named "Black Mary", but had treated her so badly that she later helped the colony's soldiers to track him down. Wells' account of Howe is resolutely unromantic, and unforgiving. But a few decades later, Howe's story was revisited and opened out in terms of scale and affective capacity. James Bonwick's *The Bushrangers* was published by George Robertson in 1856: the same year that the name Van Diemen's Land (with all its ties to those "early days") was cast aside, the island now officially renamed Tasmania. Bonwick's description of Howe's last days in the wilderness begins with an allusion to the wild man in a popular fifteenth-century French romance, *Valentine and Orson*:

> Clad in raw kangaroo skins, and with a long, shaggy, black beard, he had a very Orson-like aspect. Badgered on all sides, he chose a retreat among the mountain fastness of the Upper Shannon, a dreary solitude of cloud-land, the rocky home of hermit eagles. On this elevated plateau, – contiguous to the almost bottomless lakes, from whose crater-formed recesses in ancient days torrents of liquid fire poured forth upon the plains of Tasmania, or rose uplifted in balsatic masses like frowning Wellington; – within sight of lofty hills of snow, having the Peak of Teneriffe to the south, Frenchman's Cap and Byron to the west, Miller's Bluff to the east, and the serrated crest of the Western Tier to the north; entrenched in dense woods, with surrounding forests of dead poles, through whose leafless passages the wind harshly whistled in a storm; – thus situated amidst some of the sublimest scenes of nature, away from suffering and degraded humanity, the lonely Bushranger was confronted with his God and his own conscience.[7]

---

4 Wells, *Michael Howe*, 31.
5 Hayden White, "The Forms of Wildness", in *The Wild Man Within: An Image in Western Thought from the Renaissance to Romanticism*, ed. Edward Dudley and Maximillian E. Novak (Pittsburgh, Penn.: University of Pittsburgh Press, 1972), 20–1.
6 Paul Keal, *European Conquest and the Rights of Indigenous Peoples: The Moral Backwardness of International Society* (Cambridge: Cambridge University Press, 2003), 68.
7 James Bonwick, *The Bushrangers; Illustrating the Early Days of Van Diemen's Land* (Melbourne: George Robertson, 1856), 53.

In this passage, the bushranger is "elevated" in an expansive, Romantic landscape, described with geographical – and geological – precision. Everything that is contemporary and social is dispensed with here, leaving Howe to stand alone as *the* representative of his type: the "Bushranger", with a capital B. The endpoint of Bonwick's mid-nineteenth century chronicle is in sharp contrast to Boyce's contemporary account of Michael Howe, as someone who posed "a genuine alternative to the colonial government's political authority" by controlling the flow of resources and supplies and doing economic deals with powerful families.[8] Even so, the image of Howe as a wild and solitary figure surrounded by mountains and forests was a powerful one. One of the earliest bushranger novels is Charles Rowcroft's *The Bushranger of Van Diemen's Land*, first serialised in the London-based *Hood's Magazine and Comic Miscellany* in 1845-46 (Rowcroft was its editor at the time) and published in England in 1846 by Smith, Elder & Co. Rowcroft had lived in Van Diemen's Land in the early 1820s, returning to England around the beginning of what Boyce calls the "bushranger emergency years of 1825-26".[9] The introduction to *The Bushranger of Van Diemen's Land* makes the ironic observation that transportation to the colonies turns out, for some, to be more about reward than punishment: not least "for the sake of licentious liberty of action which the wild wilderness holds forth the promise of, and which, to restless minds, presents so fascinating an attraction".[10] The novel introduces Mark Brandon and a group of convicts who are watching the arrival of a family of emigrants by ship: Major Horton and his two daughters. Brandon, already a notorious bushranger, kidnaps the eldest daughter, Helen, and the novel offers the possibility of a romance between the two. But her father and an English suitor – along with constables and soldiers – soon go in pursuit; not long afterwards, Aboriginal people attack Brandon's camp and take Helen captive. Searching for the young woman, Brandon realises that he loves her: "she was a girl after his own heart – bold, brave, ready-witted in difficulty and in danger, and resolute in her determination . . . If his lot, he thought, had been cast in happier circumstances, the companionship of such a woman might have spurred him on to noble enterprises . . ." (vol. 2, 264). But the novel doesn't allow Brandon to be redeemed by romance. Instead, he evades his pursuers and flees into the wilderness, alone and abandoned. In the closing scenes of the novel, Rowcroft draws directly on Wells' earlier account of Michael Howe. Brandon is now "The Bushranger", an increasingly deranged, hallucinatory figure, shot at by police and attacked by Aboriginal people. At one point he eats a raw kangaroo rat. Howe had written his journal in kangaroo blood; but Brandon "takes grim pleasure in writing with his own blood", using an eagle feather as a quill (vol. 3, 215). Wells had placed Michael Howe in "a dreary solitude of cloud-land, the rocky home of hermit eagles". In Rowcroft's novel, what seems to be "a passing cloud" suddenly casts a shadow over Brandon's journal: it turns out to be "one of the largest of the great eagles of Australia", descending towards him (vol. 3, 215). When Helen and a search party discover Brandon, the bushranger is already dead, with the eagle devouring his corpse. (We might say here that the bushranger is literally swallowed up by Nature.)

Rowcroft's earlier novel, *Tales of the Colonies* (1843), works in quite a different way by placing the bushranger in the midst of a populated, dynamic settler economy – and

---

8 Boyce, *Van Diemen's Land*, 77.
9 Boyce, *Van Diemen's Land*, 147.
10 Charles Rowcroft, *The Bushranger of Van Diemen's Land* (London: Smith, Elder & Co., 1846), vol. 1, 1. All subsequent references are to this edition and appear in parentheses in the text.

linking him more explicitly to Aboriginal people. Mr Crab is a bad-tempered settler with a cynical view of the colony's future: "Now, gentleman and lady", he declares, "don't you be guiled into sinking your money in this country: it's all bad, and every thing's bad. My friend here was only just saved the other day from being shot by the bushrangers and burnt by the natives".[11] The novel repeatedly connects bushrangers and Aboriginal people as the two primary (and most proximate) threats to settler prosperity. The narrator, Mr Thornley, encounters a desperate bushranger, Gypsey, who is being pursued by constables. Gypsey is carrying his baby daughter; entrusting her to Mr Thornley's care, he rides to his death over a precipice as the constables arrive. The novel then introduces Musqueeto, a notorious Aboriginal bushranger who regards himself as Gypsey's "brother"; thinking that Thornley had killed Gypsey, Musqueeto kidnaps the girl and offers her protection. This character is based on an actual Aboriginal man from Sydney known colloquially as "Mosquito", who was arrested for acts of resistance against settlers and transported first to Norfolk Island and then to Van Diemen's Land. Engaged as a black tracker by the authorities, Mosquito helped to find the bushranger Michael Howe in October 1818. He was also a servant to one of the wealthiest men in the colony, Edward Lord. It is possible that Rowcroft – who was prosecuted by Lord for having an affair with his wife – had known Mosquito first hand. In the early 1820s, Mosquito joined forces with local Aboriginal people to conduct a series of raids against settlers, thus becoming the colony's first "Aboriginal bushranger".[12] Rowcroft's novel gives a relatively sympathetic view of this figure, allowing him to express his anti-settler perspective but also to demonstrate his moral framework. When Thornley and a magistrate and constables visit Musqueeto's camp to retrieve the girl, the settlers give full expression to their colonial racism: Aboriginal people are "savages", "treacherous" etc. The girl, however, provides a point of mediation for them, forcing the settlers to revise their assumptions as they recognise Musqueeto's loyalty to Gypsey and his child. At the same time, their racism remains untroubled because Musqueeto is presented as an exception, someone who literally stands apart from the Aboriginal community around him: "Almost the whole party was naked; – but one man, whom by his stature and bearing we recognised as Musqueeto, was distinguished by a black hat, with waistcoat and trowsers . . . "[13]

Ned Kelly's Jerilderie Letter

Cassandra Pybus has suggested that the colonies were concerned about the idea of alliances between escaped convicts, Aboriginal people and "disaffected settlers" – which created what she calls "a parallel community beyond the boundaries of the settlement".[14] The term "bushranger" becomes fluid and inclusive here, giving expression to a range of different (anti-)settler predicaments. The explorer Thomas Mitchell's *Three Expeditions into the Interior of Eastern Australia* (1839) opens, perhaps surprisingly, with "A Bushranger's Story". George Clarke, a runaway convict who escapes "the vigilance of the police,

---

11 Charles Rowcroft, *Tales of the Colonies; or, the Adventures of an Emigrant*, vol. 2 (London: Saunders & Otley, 1843), 208.
12 Angela Woollacott, *Settler Society in the Australian Colonies: Self-Government and Imperial Culture* (Oxford: Oxford University Press, 2015), 155–6.
13 Rowcroft, *Tales of the Colonies*, 155.
14 Cassandra Pybus, *Epic Journeys of Freedom: Runaway Slaves of the American Revolution and Their Global Quest for Liberty* (Boston, Mass.: Beacon Press, 2006), 203.

by disguising himself as an aboriginal native", then "assembles" Aboriginal people together "with a view to drive off the cattle of the colonists".[15] He is even initiated into the local Gamilaraay community. Eventually, however, this bushranger is captured by mounted police "with the help of Aboriginal trackers".[16] Philip A. Clarke has noted that bushrangers sometimes "had Aboriginal women travelling with them"[17] – as Michael Howe had done with "Black Mary". The notorious bushranger Frederick Ward (or "Thunderbolt") was "assisted" by his Aboriginal wife, Mary Ann (also sometimes known as "Black Mary"), described as "Australia's only recognised female bushranger".[18] Some recent commentators have wanted to emphasise the ethnic diversity of colonial bushrangers: Angela Woollacott, for example, notes that "the first person to be identified as a bushranger was 'Black Caesar', a convict of African descent who had arrived on the First Fleet in 1788 . . . "[19] Murray Johnson has similarly drawn attention to the "tragic" Sam Poo, a Chinese bushranger who was hanged in Bathurst in 1865 "for the murder of a police trooper".[20] As our discussion of Hume Nisbet's novels will suggest below, bushrangers in colonial fiction do indeed form interesting "alliances" with ethnically diverse characters. Invariably, however, these fictional bushrangers are Anglo-Australian men; women (mothers, daughters, sweethearts), Aboriginal people and characters outside the Anglo-Australian frame usually play secondary, although often significant, roles.

The most famous example of a bushranger narrative's investment in ethnic difference is, of course, Ned Kelly's Jerilderie Letter (1878-79). This is a first person account of an actual bushranger's life: the unmediated voice of a character type. The document was in fact Kelly's second attempt to chronicle his experiences, a revision of an earlier document transcribed by gang member Joe Byrne and sent on to a police superintendent and a local politician, but never published. Publicity turns out to be important here: the Jerilderie Letter is the opposite of Michael Howe's private journal composed in the wilderness because it was produced with the explicit intention of gaining widespread public recognition. Holding up the bank in this small New South Wales town, Kelly tried to give his revised document to the editor of the *Jerilderie and Urana Gazette*. Political interference was the thing that prevented colonial newspapers from rapidly disseminating this sensational first-hand account; in the event, the Jerilderie Letter was not published in its entirety until 1930. It is indeed a remarkable document – a history of Kelly's life, a petition to the authorities, a list of grievances, and an escalating promise of revenge and retribution. It has a kind of delirious poetics, filling itself up with striking images and metaphors, often to do with violent intent: for example, "we will blow him into pieces as small as paper".[21] The letter begins with an account of a bush hawker's wagon bogged in a

---

15 Thomas Livingstone Mitchell, *Three Expeditions into the Interior of Eastern Australia*, vol. 1 (London: T. & W. Boone, 1839), 22.
16 Philip A. Clarke, *Aboriginal Plant Collectors: Botanists and Australian Aboriginal People in the Nineteenth Century* (Kenthurst, NSW: Rosenberg Publishing, 2008), 33.
17 Clarke, *Aboriginal Plant Collectors*, 33.
18 Murray Johnson, "Australian Bushrangers: Law, Retribution and the Public Imagination", in *Crime Over Time: Temporal Perspectives on Crime and Punishment in Australia*, ed. Robyn Lincoln and Shirleene Robinson (Newcastle upon Tyne, UK: Cambridge Scholars Publishing, 2010), 11.
19 Woollacott, *Settler Society in the Australian Colonies*, 9.
20 Johnson, "Australian Bushrangers", 4.
21 Jerilderie Letter transcription, National Museum of Australia, 24: http://www.nma.gov.au/collections/collection_interactives/jerilderie_letter/page_1.

nearby creek. The bushrangers, by contrast, have a remarkable mobility, circulating freely through the region. Kelly also moves casually through a range of different jobs, shifting stock and other items of property from one place to another. Bushranging is understood here as a useful and profitable enterprise, making its own distinctive contributions to the colonial economy: "Therefore", Kelly writes, "I started wholesale and retail horse and cattle dealing".[22] As troopers harass his family and invade his home, however, he increasingly (and self-consciously) emphasises his Irish, working-class background. This is where Kelly identifies his revolutionary potential, if only rhetorically: by the end of the document he is invoking a mythical tradition of Irish rebellion fighting to free itself from the "tyrannism of the English yoke".[23] The ethnic distinction between English troopers and Irish bushrangers is also a class distinction, and in fact Kelly uses it, finally, as the basis for the declaration of class warfare. "I would advise all those who joined the Stock Protection", he writes, "to withdraw their money and give it to the poor of Greta . . . all those that have reason to fear me had better sell out and give £10 out of every hundred to the widow and orphan fund".[24] Here, the bushranger's project is nothing less than the redistribution of income in the colonies. Meanwhile, the colonies themselves invest an immense amount in tracking the bushrangers and bringing them to justice. In his memoir of the capture of the Kelly gang, titled (yet again) *The Last of the Bushrangers* (1892), the police superintendent Francis Augustus Hare reflects on whether the extent of that investment was worth it: "the cost would have been over £115,000 – a large price to pay for the capture of four desperadoes and the destruction of a gang of malefactors".[25]

Robbery Under Arms

Rolf Boldrewood's *Robbery Under Arms* was first serialised in the *Sydney Mail* less than two years after Ned Kelly was hanged in Melbourne. This was the first colonial novel to fully redeem the bushranger, saving him from public execution and rescuing him from a solitary, "uncivilised" ending in order, finally, to absorb him back into the developing colonies as a settled, productive figure. These changes in the fortunes of the bushranger also help to explain how *Robbery Under Arms* came to launch this colonial Australian character type into an internationally recognisable genre of adventure romance.[26] The influential London weekly, the *Graphic*, made exactly this point in its review of Remington & Co.'s 1888 three-volume publication of Boldrewood's novel:

> The bushranger would not strike most people as very promising material for a hero of romance. In the hands of Mr Rolf Boldrewood, however . . . he becomes at any rate a very efficient rival to such heroes as Claude Duval, or even as the old Border cattle thieves,

---

22 Jerilderie Letter transcription, 15.
23 Jerilderie Letter transcription, 32.
24 Jerilderie Letter transcription, 38–9.
25 Francis Augustus Hare, *The Last of the Bushrangers: An Account of the Capture of the Kelly Gang* (London: Hurst & Blackett, 1895), 325–6.
26 For a full discussion of colonial Australian adventure romances, see Robert Dixon, *Writing the Colonial Adventure: Race, Gender and Nation in Anglo-Australian Popular Fiction, 1875–1914)* (Cambridge: Cambridge University Press, 1995); see also Ken Gelder and Rachael Weaver, eds, *The Anthology of Colonial Australian Adventure Fiction* (Melbourne: Melbourne University Press, 2011).

or the Calabrian brigands... *Robbery Under Arms* is not to be classed with criminal fiction in general. The tone is thoroughly wholesome, and is assuredly not likely to throw a glamour over lawlessness and ruffianism in the mind of the most impressionable reader.[27]

The circulation of *Robbery Under Arms* increased both internationally and locally when Macmillan published it as an abridged single volume in 1889, as part of its Colonial Library series.[28] By 1890 the influential Melbourne columnist "Telemachus" (Francis Myers) was declaring in the *Argus* that *Robbery Under Arms* "ranks as an Australian classic" – not least because it chronicles "some phases of our early life which are rapidly passing away".[29] Boldrewood agreed, writing soon afterwards (in response to some criticisms that his novel contains factual and historical errors) that his novel gave "a vivid pictorial record of wild times long passed".[30] *Robbery Under Arms* is in fact a historical adventure novel, set mostly in the late 1840s and 1850s. The notion that the colonies have already moved on is taken for granted right from the beginning, with its bushranger protagonist, Dick Marston, in prison and the rest of the gang – Dick's brother Jim and father Ben, Captain Starlight, and Warrigal, an Aboriginal tracker who works for Starlight – all dead. As the novel unfolds, the bushrangers increasingly entertain a sense of themselves as residual characters, especially during the gold rush period in the mid-1850s when prospectors are literally opening up every bit of the landscape. Their hideout, a secret place called Terrible Hollow, is cast here as the last uncharted part of a landscape that is increasingly plundered, developed and *revealed* by a rapidly growing colonial economy:

> Sooner or later, we began to see, the secret of the Hollow would be found out. There was no great chance in the old times with only a few shepherds and stock riders wandering through the bush, once in a way straggling over the country. But now the whole colony swarmed with miners... They would try every creek, gully, and hillside, and river bed. If they found the colour of gold... they would at once settle down themselves. If it went rich the news would soon spread, and a thousand men might be gathered in one spot... within a fortnight, with ten thousand more sure to follow within a month.[31]

Robbery Under Arms takes up the now-familiar notion of "the last of the bushrangers" and puts it to work as a romantic anachronism. But it also reinvests in this notion, giving it a prolonged currency. One of the colonial newspaper articles in the novel – and these bushrangers compulsively read media reports on their exploits – carries the title "Bushranging Revived". "The good old days", it announces, "have apparently not passed away forever... We shall be agreeably surprised if this be the end and not the commencement..." (363-4). *Robbery Under Arms* in fact works by continually postponing

---

27 "New Novels", *Graphic*, 1 December 1888, 586.
28 For a detailed publication history, see Paul Eggert and Elizabeth Webby's introduction to the Australian Academy of the Humanities edition of Rolf Boldrewood's *Robbery Under Arms* (St Lucia: University of Queensland Press, 2006), xxxv–lxxiv.
29 "Telemachus", "A Good Australian Book", *Argus*, 18 January 1890, 4.
30 Rolf Boldrewood, *Robbery Under Arms*, *Argus*, 4 February 1890, 11.
31 Rolf Boldrewood, *Robbery Under Arms* (1888; St Lucia: University of Queensland Press, 2006), ed. Paul Eggert and Elizabeth Webby, 360. All subsequent references are to this edition and appear in parentheses in the text.

the "end" of the bushrangers, allowing these residual figures to inhabit a kind of extended aftermath: as Dick Marston writes optimistically at a late stage in the novel, "we might last a few years yet" (401).

Boldrewood was himself held up by bushrangers in 1867. In September 1864 he had written that "New South Wales is suffering an epidemic of bushrangers", highlighting the role of the "scoundrel" Daniel Morgan and concluding, sourly, that "the benign influences of liberty and a new country with unlimited wages, food etc. are not to be relied on".[32] Morgan became the model for the most vicious bushranger in *Robbery Under Arms*, the "black-hearted" Dan Moran; in contrast, the Marston brothers and Starlight are presented as noble and fundamentally decent, although equally opportunistic. At one point Moran's gang raids a squatter's station when only the womenfolk are at home – including the daughter of another squatter, Mr Falkland, who had spoken up for the Marstons at an earlier trial. Dick, Jim and Starlight intervene, rescuing the women, evicting the bushrangers and protecting the station. In an attack on another property, Moran and his gang are defeated by a well-armed squatter ("He'd been in India . . . and was a great hunting man") and his courageous wife. We noted in Chapter 1 that Boldrewood was himself an experienced squatter, connected to a network of elite pastoralists in the region. *Robbery Under Arms* predictably valorises the squatter type, using this figure as a way of measuring the bushranger's qualities and capacities. We can see this especially when Starlight and the Marstons join forces with Moran and his gang to raid a third squatter's property. The squatter here is Mr Knightley, a "tall, handsome man" who "walked like a lord"; his wife is the "handsomest woman in the whole country side" (509). When Knightley kills one of Moran's gang, Moran wants revenge. But Starlight and Dick Marston fall under the spell of the Knightleys' aristocratic influence and turn against Moran; in doing so, they effectively protect the squatter's interests (Starlight even gives him a revolver). The sympathetic alignment of squatters and bushrangers here makes *Robbery Under Arms* a distinctly conservative novel, especially when we compare it to the very different "anti-settler" alliances – ex-convicts, Aboriginal people, and so on – that Cassandra Pybus describes in relation to earlier bushranger narratives.

This squatter/bushranger affiliation is partly secured through Starlight's own qualities, a man (as Dick Marston describes him) "that's born and bred a gentleman" (56). A literate and cultivated figure, with a library of books at his disposal, Starlight is the complete opposite to the "wild" Michael Howe or the working-class Irishman Ned Kelly. But his history is mysterious. "He was an Englishman – that was certain", Marston tells us, "but he must have come young to the colony" (441). On the other hand, Starlight is also not local: "He'd been all over the world. In the Islands and New Zealand; in America and among Malays and other strange people that we'd hardly ever heard of" (105). He seems to have lived with islander tribes and witnessed the horror of slave trading in the Pacific; and yet he exercises a kind of brutal mastery over a young Aboriginal tracker, Warrigal, who responds with slave-like devotion. The gentleman bushranger, as a character type, is already a localised version of a cliché: the novel itself describes Starlight as "the Australian Claude Duval", citing this well-known seventeenth-century gentleman highwayman as a precedent (as the *Graphic* review had done, above) (499). But there is also a sense that this particular gentleman bushranger can never be fully absorbed into colonial Australian life.

---

32 Rolf Boldrewood quoted in Paul de Serville, *Rolf Boldrewood: A Life* (Melbourne: Miegunyah Press, 2000), 141–2.

Dick Marston's sister Aileen falls in love with Starlight, but (like Rowcroft's *Tales of the Colonies*) the novel refuses to let this romance develop. And Starlight is never redeemed: he dies spectacularly in a shoot-out with the police, reminding the astonished Police Inspector Sir Ferdinand Morringer in his dying breath that they once shot pigeons together at Hurlingham, an exclusive sports club in London. In his 1890 *Argus* review, "Telemachus" had found the character type of the gentleman bushranger in Australia far too incredible to believe. Calling him "the impossible 'Starlight'", he writes, "I do not think there was ever such a man on the roads in Australia". "Telemachus" tells his readers that Boldrewood "has been a gentleman amongst gentlemen all his days"; this view of the novelist makes the gentleman bushranger seem, by contrast, like "a perverted image of his own order".[33]

Robbery Under Arms is interested in how young Australian men can become bushrangers – and how, if at all, they can be drawn back into legitimate participation in the colonies through productive employment and (in this case) agricultural enterprise. It asks a question that is central to all bushranger narratives: how far outside the boundaries of "civilisation" can this character type go before he becomes irredeemable? Dick Marston is the narrator of *Robbery Under Arms*, although the young bushranger's "attractive, semi-literate"[34] voice is heavily mediated through a gentleman-novelist who represents the interests of the squatter class and (as a police magistrate and justice of the peace) the law. Marston is the colonial-born son of an ex-convict selector, restless and looking for excitement; his father is already a bushranger. Interestingly, the innate "wildness" of bushrangers – an expression of their naturally anti-authoritarian disposition – is also often denoted through their affinity with native animal species. In Rowcroft's *The Bushranger of Van Diemen's Land*, for example, Mark Brandon is "as quick as a bandicoot and as cunning as a platypus".[35] Dick Marston characterises himself in the same way right at the beginning of his narrative: "I can . . . swim like a musk-duck . . . [and I am] as active as a rock-wallaby" (9). When he escapes from prison, his sheer delight at being free inspires an imaginative bond to a host of native animals teeming around him: "Everything . . . I seemed to notice and to be pleased with somehow. Sometimes it was a rock wallaby . . . Then an old 'possum would sing out, or a black-furred flying squirrel – pongos the blacks call them – would come sailing down from the top of an ironbark tree . . . " (198). This structural link to native species and their sheer freedom of movement makes it difficult for Marston to commit to the ordinary life of a settler. When his friend and neighbour, George Storefield, offers him a contract to build fences, Marston refuses and walks away. Storefield is Marston's opposite, a smallholder who works hard and grows increasingly prosperous, finally owning a number of large stations. Like Boldrewood, he goes on to become a squatter and a magistrate: tying together land ownership, wealth and the authority of the law. Dick Marston's family farm, by contrast, is steadily impoverished and, finally, abandoned. His brother Jim is killed, his mother dies of grief, his sister Aileen (after Starlight is shot dead) goes off to a convent, and his father commits suicide. The novel is then left with the problem of what to do with its narrator, a problem it solves by drawing once again on the power and influence of the squattocracy. Mr Falkland and his daughter ("looking like a queen") visit Marston in jail and begin to plan his release. An influential group of squatters – "the Hon. Mr

---

33 "Telemachus", "A Good Australian Book", 4.
34 Paul Eggert, "Textual Criticism and Folklore: The Ned Kelly Story and *Robbery Under Arms*", *Script and Print* 31:2 (2007), 72.
35 Rowcroft, *The Bushranger of Van Diemen's Land*, vol. 1, 239.

Falkland, the Hon. Mr Storefield, and other gentlemen who have interested themselves in your case" (582) – finally succeed in having Marston's death sentence commuted to twelve years in prison. When he is released, Storefield offers him a job as station manager on one of his properties in Queensland, which Marston willingly accepts. It is as if the squattocracy has been waiting patiently simply in order to integrate this troubled character into its world. What is also interesting here is the role that women play in Marston's redemption. Storefield's sister Grace remains absurdly loyal to the ex-bushranger, sitting out his prison sentence and then throwing herself into his arms when he is released – and marrying him soon afterwards. Robert Dixon has noted that the women in *Robbery Under Arms* are "marginalised . . . by the code of adventure", which is true.[36] Women are certainly well and truly in the background in this bushranger novel. Even so, characters like Grace and Miss Falkland have important roles to play in the business of Dick Marston's redemption: they lend the squattocracy a feminine, sentimentalised quality, smoothing the way for his entry into the squatter's "pastoral ideology". Earlier bushrangers like Michael Howe, as we have seen, were finally consumed by nature. Here, the bushranger is finally absorbed into the most elite, powerful circles of the colonial economy.

Outlaw and Lawmaker

Robbery Under Arms gave expression to an influential set of conventions for bushranger characters in colonial Australian adventure fiction: the dark, doomed romantic figure of Starlight, the residual ex-convict figure of Ben Marston (also doomed), and the itinerant, excitement-seeking bush worker who defines himself against the solid, dependable settler-farmer. The relationship between bushrangers and squatters is especially interesting here. In Boldrewood's novel, squatters are masculine, aristocratic types who successfully defend their properties and work hard to reabsorb the reformed bushranger into their nation-building agenda and cultural milieu (where the bushranger marries Storefield's sister, etc.). Rosa Praed's novel *Outlaw and Lawmaker* (1893) is obviously indebted to *Robbery Under Arms*. Its charismatic bushranger Moonlight is, like Starlight, a well-travelled, cultivated man with a mysterious, aristocratic past. But it alters Boldrewood's squatter/bushranger paradigm in several important ways. Moonlight himself poses no physical threat to the local squatters: as Frank Hallett says, "the squatters don't seem so down on Moonlight as you'd suppose. He hasn't bailed up any of them yet".[37] Moonlight's public identity is Morres Blake of Barolin, an aspiring colonial politician who in fact stands in direct opposition to the squatter ascendancy. "I mean to go against your Squatters Land Bill", he tells the novel's heroine, Elsie Valliant (vol. 1, 141). It is generally agreed that Blake/Moonlight's character was loosely based on the figure of John Boyle O'Reilly,[38] an Irish writer and republican who was transported as a convict to Fremantle in 1868 – remaining there for a year or so before absconding and sailing to America. O'Reilly had written a novel

---

36   Dixon, *Writing the Colonial Adventure*, 38.
37   Rosa Praed, *Outlaw and Lawmaker*, vol. 1 (London: Chatto & Windus, 1893), 73. All subsequent references are to this edition and appear in parentheses in the text.
38   See, for example, Kay Ferres, "Shrouded Histories: *Outlaw and Lawmaker*, Republican Politics and Women's Interests", *Australian Literary Studies* 21:1 (2003), 32–42.

about convict transportation to Western Australia, *Moondyne* (1879), which took its title from a local ex-convict and bushranger, Joseph Bolitho Jones, also known as Moondyne Joe. *Moondyne* is not a bushranger novel, but it does present an escaped convict who leads a double life as, ironically enough, a colonial prison reformer: Mr Wyville, "the most influential man in the West Australian penal colony".[39] In Praed's novel, Blake/Moonlight brings some of O'Reilly's Fenianism and rhetorical skill to bear on his political career and social success, making influential speeches in the gallery and drawing popular admiration. Ned Kelly's earlier Irish complaints are transformed into a publicly recognised, self-empowering discourse here, as Blake goes on to defeat Frank Hallett and win the seat of Luya (in Praed's fictionalised Queensland setting, "Leichardt's Land"). Kay Ferres has also noted that the "correspondences" between Blake and the famous Irish republican politician Charles Stewart Parnell "are inescapable".[40] Blake in fact goes on to become Colonial Secretary, an official role that puts him (among other things) in charge of the police. This is the revelation of the title of Praed's novel, *Outlaw and Lawmaker*: that bushrangers who once (in Cassandra Pybus' words) existed "beyond the boundaries of the settlement" now find themselves at the centre of public and political life in the colonies. A minor character becomes, if only for a moment, a major one.

Another important point of contrast between *Outlaw and Lawmaker* and *Robbery Under Arms* is that women are central to Praed's novel. The heroine is Elsie Valliant, a beautiful and "flirtatious" young woman who draws the attention of pretty much every man in the district. "I am very selfish and very frivolous and very mercenary and very ambitious..." (vol. 1, 84), she says, defiantly – partly as a reaction against her own poverty (the novel harshly describes her as "the penniless daughter of a defunct scab inspector") but partly also as a gesture of decadent self-fashioning that brings her closer in kind to the character of the bushranger (vol. 2, 225). In *Robbery Under Arms*, women like Miss Falkland and Gracey Storefield helped to stabilise the squattocracy. But in *Outlaw and Lawmaker*, Elsie rejects Frank Hallett's advances. Local squatters like Hallett seem to Elsie to be "dull" and "prosaic": she "did not admire the typical bushman. She would have preferred the product of a more complex civilisation. In this she resembled what indeed she was, the typical Australian girl" (vol. 1, 13, 176). This is a passage about *types*; but the question of how typical Elsie is remains open. Craving excitement, she is instead drawn to Moonlight. "He's a picturesque figure", she says at one point; "We haven't much that is picturesque in the bush" (vol. 1, 74). The word *picturesque* is used repeatedly in this novel to denote a kind of cultivated romantic wildness – giving us something far removed from Hayden White's predatory "wild man". When Elsie fantasises about being abducted by Moonlight, she is both unleashing her desires and placing them in the reassuring conventions of chivalrous masculinity – with Moonlight, just like Starlight in *Robbery Under Arms*, likened to the gentleman highwayman Claude Duval.

Moonlight's political objections to the squattocracy are reflected in the region's geography: Hallett's station Tunimbah, "one of the most beautiful stations on the Luya", is contrasted to Barolin Gorge where Moonlight has his lair, a remote "misty cleft" that "seemed to Elsie's imagination the passage to a realm of mystery" (vol. 1, 197): rather like Starlight's Terrible Hollow. Blake/Moonlight reinforces his distance from the "prosaic"

---

39   John Boyle O'Reilly, *Moondyne: A Story of Life in Western Australia* (1880; Sydney: Sydney University Press, 2003), 85.
40   Ferres, "Shrouded Histories", 34.

world of the squatter when he calls himself "a Bohemian rebel" and tells Elsie (whom he imagines has a future as a squatter's wife): "You will never rise above the level of prosperous Australian Philistinism. You will never taste the finest aroma of romance" (vol. 1, 21, 117). The passion between Moonlight and Elsie overtakes them, perhaps surprisingly, when they go with a group of settlers to watch an Aboriginal corroboree – an event that seems primal and profane to them, full of "grotesque forms", "demoniac beings", dark shadows, and naked bodies (vol. 3, 58-60). Moonlight is "infected" by the "excitement" of the scene and draws Elsie into the bush, passionately kissing her. By this time, Elsie is engaged to Frank Hallett and it looks as if she may indeed have a future as a squatter's wife, but the romance with the bushranger persists. She is with Moonlight when his identity is exposed and she stays with him when Hallett and the police arrive, only to see the bushranger escape arrest (rather like Gypsey in Rowcroft's novel) by throwing himself over a precipice to his death, "swallowed up for ever in the depths of the Barolin waterhole" (vol. 3, 303). The novel then concludes by placing these events in the colony's distant past, as a "strange tragic episode". Perhaps this is consistent with the tendency of the bushranger novel to regard every bushranger as the last of his kind. But it means *Outlaw and Lawmaker* also finally distances itself from Blake's radical political agenda. The ending for Elsie, however, is less conventional. Kay Ferres notes that colonial marriage – especially for a "typical Australian girl" like Elsie – is always "a question bound up with a national ethos".[41] In Praed's novel, this is suggested as a possibility through Elsie's engagement to Hallett, who goes on to become "a prominent Australian politician" and presumably continues to represent the interests of the squattocracy. But Elsie is caught up in the scandal of her relationship to Blake. She leaves Frank (who later marries her more dependable sister, Ina) and travels with her mother to Italy, where she develops a taste for fine art. The bushranger therefore plays an interesting role here: helping to detach a "typical Australian girl" from the squattocracy and, eventually, from the nation itself. On the other hand, while Elsie's relationship with Moonlight allows her to reject the very idea of marriage as a woman's "natural" destination, his demise also effectively excludes her from a social economy of romance and desire. As Robert Dixon notes, "She may not be sent to a nunnery like Aileen Marston, but she is still effectively removed from the sexual world".[42]

Hume Nisbet's Bushrangers

In Boldrewood's *Robbery Under Arms*, squatters are powerful (and patient) enough to redeem a bushranger and absorb him into their world. The squatter is central to Praed's novel, too, but in this case more as a "prosaic" point of contrast to the bushranger's "picturesque", romantic character. Although *Outlaw and Lawmaker* challenges some of the conventions found in *Robbery Under Arms* – especially through the central role played by Elsie – it shares that novel's focus on the squatter/bushranger paradigm. Even their geographies reflect this, largely remaining within a circuit of pastoral properties and remote hideouts. However, if we look at Hume Nisbet's bushranger novels from the early 1890s – *Bail Up!* (1890), *The Bushranger's Sweetheart* (1892) and *The Bush Girl's Romance* (1894) – we can see how this paradigm begins to unravel.[43] Born in Scotland, Nisbet

---

41 Ferres, "Shrouded Histories", 39.
42 Dixon, *Writing the Colonial Adventure*, 44.

came to Australia as a teenager, travelling and working as an actor. He later trained as an artist in London and knew John Ruskin, whom he affectionately criticised in his book about painting and photography, *Where Art Begins* (1892). Returning to Australia in 1886, Nisbet again travelled extensively; his first novel, published in 1888, was a tropical adventure set in Papua New Guinea, which he had visited the previous year.[44] He went on to become a prolific author, writing across a range of popular genres – adventure, romance, historical sagas, pirate novels, horror – and beautifully illustrating many of his own works. *Bail Up!* begins in southern Queensland, where Raike Morris, "a young colonial stonemason", is hired to build a station for a wealthy squatter, Harley Graves. When the squatter and his manager, Jerry Owen, refuse to pay Morris for his labour, the young man violently confronts Owen and is knocked unconscious by the manager's wife. The actions (or transactions) of this disreputable squatter then trigger a complex series of events. Morris awakens to find himself in jail and hears the news that Owen has been robbed and murdered. A mysterious Chinese man, Wung-Ti, helps the young man to escape and directs him to a secret cave – a place sacred to Aboriginal people – where he goes into hiding. Later on, a coach rides past with Owen's niece, Judith Higgins, on board: she is to become a governess on Harley Grave's station. Morris bails up the coach and begins his career as a bushranger, taking the name "Captain Deadwood" and declaring that he will only rob the rich. He also falls in love with Judith.

Like William Howitt, Nisbet was often critical of colonialism, especially its brutal treatment of Aboriginal people. In the introduction to his New Guinea novel, *The Land of the Hibiscus Blossom*, he gives a scathing account of the civilising mission: "We who are the favoured ones of earth teach the naked races how to dress themselves before we bury them".[45] Nisbet's travel writing and adventure fiction inevitably resorted to the prevailing racial stereotypes of the period; but as Ouyang Yu suggests, he "showed more liberal mindedness than his contemporaries in that he realised the evils of Western civilisation and what disastrous effects it had on indigenous people".[46] Ouyang also sees Nisbet as an "exception" in terms of his representations of the Chinese, especially given prevailing anti-Chinese attitudes in the colonies. *Bail Up!* and *The Bushranger's Sweetheart* both feature Chinese characters who are intimately connected to the bushranger, a constituent part of what Cassandra Pybus had referred to as this type's "parallel community". In *The Bushranger's Sweetheart*, the bushranger Rainbow regards a Chinese boy, Dicky, as a son, and relies on the boy's ability to carry out surveillance and accompany him on various heists. "As long as that remarkable boy remains near to me", he says, "I don't think that I shall be caught ... What a detective that boy would make if he were not a born thief and the watchdog of an outlaw!"[47] Rainbow's remarks valorise the Chinese boy's intellect (he could be a "detective"), but they also insist on his subordinate position,

---

43 Nisbet's novel *The Savage Queen: A Romance of the Natives of Van Diemen's Land* (1891) is not a bushranger novel, but – set in 1813 – it does present extended character sketches of Michael Howe ("the Governor of the Ranges") and "Mosquito" ("the black tracker, bushranger, and murderer").
44 See Peter Cowan, "James Hume Nisbet (1849–1923)", in *Australian Dictionary of Biography*: http://adb.anu.edu.au/biography/nisbet-james-hume-7850.
45 Hume Nisbet, *The Land of the Hibiscus Blossom: A Yarn of the Papuan Gulf* (London: Ward & Downey, 1888), x.
46 Ouyang Yu, *The Chinese in Australian Fiction, 1888–1988* (Amherst, NY: Cambria Press, 2008), 101.
47 Hume Nisbet, *The Bushranger's Sweetheart: An Australian Romance* (London: F.V. White & Co., 1892), 165. All subsequent references are to this edition and appear in parentheses in the text.

constantly in the service of the bushranger. *Bail Up!*, on the other hand, gives us a much more empowered Chinese character in Wung-Ti, an all-seeing figure who appears and disappears at will throughout the narrative. Just like Dicky, Wung-Ti works tirelessly to protect the bushranger's interests. He is colonial-born, a " cornstalk Chinaman", described as strong, graceful and good-looking.[48] An "astute reader of character" (129), Wung-Ti is also able to anticipate the villainous plans of Harley Graves, watching the young squatter as he robs his father and, later on, as he robs and murders the station manager's widow, Mrs Owen. He functions in this sense as a kind of moral nemesis, violently calling criminals to account for their misdeeds: killing Harley Graves for the murder of Mrs Owen, exposing a corrupt church minister and, at the end of the novel, throwing a cannibalistic ex-convict to the sharks. He also supplies opium to Morris, who has several hallucinatory experiences. For Ouyang Yu, Wung-Ti is "a curious mixture of positive Orientalism and racism", in many respects an "admirable Other" – in stark contrast to the comic grotesquery of, say, Henry Lawson's Chinese characters.[49] Recalling our discussion in the Introduction, we can perhaps think of Wung-Ti as a "minor" character in Alex Woloch's terms: that is, as marginal in one sense and influential in another, possessing what Woloch had called "a strange centrality" to the text.[50]

Bail Up! owes an obvious debt to Boldrewood's *Robbery Under Arms*, re-staging some of its key scenes and events. Raike Morris is arrested and sent to jail about halfway through the novel, just as Dick Marston was; and just as Warrigal helps Marston to escape, so Wung-Ti – with the help of an Aboriginal boy called Dan Harris – helps Morris to break out.[51] After Marston escapes, he goes in disguise to the goldfields with Starlight and the other bushrangers. The same thing happens in *Bail Up!*: after escaping from jail, Morris, Judith, Wung-Ti and some other characters head to the goldfields where, posing as diggers, they work hard and finally discover a number of gold nuggets. But Nisbet's novel is much more cynical about the nature of colonial enterprise than *Robbery Under Arms*. *Bail Up!* breaks at this point to give us a brief account of failed colonial land speculation on a flood-prone swamp ironically called Paradise Plain (probably One Mile Swamp or what is now Woolloongabba, in Brisbane). Investors come and go; a hotel is built, called the Tree of Knowledge; Chinese traders are involved; and finally, under Wung-Ti's advice, the hotel is sold to Jerry Owen's widow (who is also Wung-Ti's lover). The profligate young squatter Harley Graves is drawn to the hotel's seedy attractions; desperate for money, he robs and murders Mrs Owen and is killed in retribution by Wung-Ti. The hotel then burns to the ground, wiping out all traces of its history, after which, the narrative returns to the goldfields and the fortunes of the escaped bushranger. Nisbet gives us an interesting colonial version of the Fall in this short digression, where investments produce

---

48 Hume Nisbet, *Bail Up! A Romance of Bushrangers and Blacks* (London: Chatto & Windus, 1890), 88. All subsequent references are to this edition and appear in parentheses in the text.
49 Ouyang Yu, *The Chinese in Australian Fiction*, 109.
50 Alex Woloch, *The One vs the Many: Minor Characters and the Space of the Protagonist in the Novel* (Princeton: Princeton University Press, 2003), 37.
51 Raike Morris is sent to jail in a chapter titled "For the Term of His Natural Life"; but *Bail Up!* wants to distance itself from Marcus Clarke's famous novel, insisting that Australian prisons are less brutal now and that Clarke's account of early prison life was "masterly" but "morbid" (186). In *The Bushranger's Sweetheart,* the apprentice bushranger Luck Mort spends some time in prison in a chapter titled "Melbourne Free Hydropathic Establishment"; a few pages earlier, Rainbow confesses, "In prison I began and finished my education as a bushranger" (109, 106).

an increasingly squalid business enterprise (gambling, opium dens, prostitution) that leads only to tragedy and death. In *Robbery Under Arms*, squatters are principled, aristocratic figures, committed to the future of the squattocracy – and the nation. But in Nisbet's *Bail Up!*, Harley Graves abandons the squattocracy all too readily for an illicit economy built around dishonesty and self-interest.

Nisbet's bushranger, Raike Morris, is by contrast much more trustworthy and fair-minded. Although he discovers gold, the novel doesn't let him keep it; pursued by troopers and Aboriginal trackers, Morris, Judith, Wung-Ti and the others make their way to the Pacific coast. After the ship they board catches fire, the group is rescued by some local islanders who have recently escaped enslavement by a "blackbirding" expedition that has been kidnapping workers for the Queensland sugar plantations. Morris and the others finally find themselves living on a South Sea island, in a closing scene that provides a kind of utopian counterpart to the earlier narrative about the Tree of Knowledge. The newspapers report that Morris and his party have been "massacred" by Aboriginal people, his gold abandoned. But the novel (in contrast to the ending of Praed's *Outlaw and Lawmaker*) projects an imaginary future for the colonial bushranger. Five years later, Morris and Judith have moved to their own island in the Pacific. They have, the final paragraphs tell us, "established another station and conquered another kingdom farther on – they are colonising it also, for Judith has already four lovely children" (318). This is not that far away from Dick Marston's final destination, as a married station manager in northern Queensland – except that in this case it can only happen *outside* Australia, as if the local economy were too debased and corrupt to accommodate such a benign colonial vision. We will see something similar at the end of Nisbet's *The Swampers* (1897) in the next chapter: showing us that a novelist who is otherwise critical of the civilising mission and capacity of the colonial economy to flourish in some kind of ethical way, is still willing to imagine a space where these things might yet happen.

In his preface to *The Bushranger's Sweetheart*, Nisbet begins by recalling the death of Ned Kelly: "Twelve years ago the last of the bushrangers was cut short in his public career, and the ground left entirely open for less ostentatious professors of his unholy craft . . . " (vii). Paradoxically, the death of Ned Kelly in this account, far from closing this character type down, paves the way for a range of new bushranger possibilities. Even so, *The Bushranger's Sweetheart* is a digressive, densely populated novel, full of other vibrant character types, each with their own narrative trajectory. Nisbet's preface also talks about the sundowner, for example, or the larrikin: we shall return to these figures in Chapter 4 of this book. Because Nisbet's novel is so fissured with sub-plots and intrigues, it can seem as if Boldrewood's squatter/bushranger paradigm is no longer dominant. But in fact, *The Bushranger's Sweetheart* has a squatter, Mr Condon, with an important role to play. The narrator is Lucknow Mortimer, his first name taken from "the Indian city where I was born during the mutiny" (2); he is known more colloquially as Luck Mort. Mort comes from an old, reputable British family that has lost its money, so his uncle's lawyer advises him to go to the colonies where he can "learn to be useful" and "return with a fortune" (10). On a ship bound for Melbourne, he is introduced to a number of characters who will shape his future – including the mysterious speculator Ovinius Hardwake, the "Melbourne larrikin" Stringy Bark, and the "sinister" Alexander "Sandy" Macintosh (25). Later, at a notorious Coffee Palace in Melbourne, Mort meets a squatter's beautiful fifteen-year-old daughter, Sabina Condon, who is lodging there with her alcoholic mother. He also meets

James Walker, a man "in a digging costume" who enjoys the theatre and studies "all the colonial papers" (70-1).

Walker turns out to be Captain Rainbow, a charismatic gentleman bushranger in the tradition of Boldrewood's Starlight and Praed's Moonlight. Mort is drawn to him, just as Dick Marston was drawn to Starlight: as if colonial young men are open-minded enough (that is, unconstrained by law, morality and social convention) to be seduced by this particular character type:

> I am afraid also that there must be rather a large assemblage of disreputable microbes in my composition, a hereditary inclination towards more broad boundaries than mere Bohemianism, for ... I did not feel the least repugnance to my friend James Walker because he happened to be Captain Rainbow, the notorious bushranger. (102)

We have noted the colonial bushranger's transition over time from "wildness" to civility, from social estrangement to social participation (if we think, for example, of Blake/Moonlight's political role as a Member of Parliament in *Outlaw and Lawmaker*). In *The Bushranger's Sweetheart*, James Walker in fact begins his career as a published author: "I wrote and published two or three books which at the first got fair notices, but met with very indifferent success in the market" (104). This is certainly a major departure from Michael Howe (who ends his career by writing his diary in blood) or Ned Kelly (whose autobiographical "letter" is only published many years after his death). Here, it is what comes *after* publication – the social networks, the various literary frustrations, etc. – that leads to the decision to become a bushranger. It turns out that Walker is being falsely flattered by a network of other, equally ambitious writers, a "colonial gang" under the influence of a leading critic, a "treacherous pirate". After he violently attacks the critic, Walker is sent to prison where he meets "new companions, which, I think, on the whole, were honester [sic] fellows than the literary clique whom I had left outside" (106). As a bushranger some years later, Walker begins to fetishise his literary publications, using the distribution of his books as the basis for deciding whether or not to raid a squatter's property: "Who ever had the gumption to buy a book of mine when they were for sale, and provident enough to keep and display it on their shelves, are sacred to me and my gang of thieves now; we pass them over" (104). In Chapter 1, we noted that the squatter's love of literature adds to the refinement of this character type. In Nisbet's novel, the bushranger amusingly exploits this quality by insisting not only that squatters own copies of his books but that they must also have *read* them. He tells Mort,

> as all my men know my peculiarity, the first thing they do when they break into a strange house is to go to the book-case and overhaul it. If a book of mine is there *uncut*, they punish the owner by making him cut it and read aloud from it for his former neglect of the author, while they carry off what provisions they may require. If the book has been cut and well used, they apologise for their intrusion. When it is absent, then they take whatever they can carry. (104)

It might seem odd (a "peculiarity") to transition from literary author to bushranger, but there are in fact significant correspondences between the socio-cultural identities of these two types. We have seen the bushranger in Praed's *Outlaw and Lawmaker* identify as "a Bohemian rebel"; while in *The Bushranger's Sweetheart*, Mort's attraction to the life of a bushranger takes "mere Bohemianism" as its point of departure. The squatter/bushranger paradigm here is thus also a version of the familiar cultural distinction between bourgeois aspirations and bohemian self-fashioning. On the other hand, we have also seen gentleman bushrangers like Starlight defined by their cultivated literary tastes – something that *connects* them to the squatters. We can begin to see why the gentleman bushranger and the squatter might enjoy each other's company, even as they remain essentially antagonistic. Judith R. Halasz writes: "While bohemians have expressed their disdain for the bourgeoisie openly, bohemian creative types have depended on the bourgeoisie to patronise the private art market, attend the theatre, and consume popular literature".[52] In Nisbet's bushranger novel – itself an example of popular literature – this predicament is given literal expression. Walker begins his career as a literary author who meets with only "very indifferent success in the market" (104). Like so many colonial writers – even when they publish in the popular genres – his commercial prospects are limited. Bohemianism is usually taken to be disdainful of the market and of commercial success. By the 1860s and early 1870s it becomes a recognisable literary disposition in Australia, strongly identified with Marcus Clarke and his metropolitan literary circles.[53] But Walker's bohemianism is compromised here, because he expects a return on his literary investments. He has little time for what Pierre Bourdieu had called the "economic world reversed", where a writer's symbolic capital (his prestige, his reputation) might far outstrip his income.[54] Even so, when he becomes a bushranger later on, his literary career continues to determine his actions. He searches for copies of his books at every property he raids, he makes the squatters open those books and read them aloud, and then he robs them. This is a literary author's belated revenge on an indifferent public: recouping the profits (and the recognition) that were denied to him by the failure of his work to gain popular success at the time of publication. Bushranging here is thus about symbolic *and* economic capital, which is why connecting the bushranger to the literary author is both a "peculiarity" and an understandable expression of a shared quasi-bohemian disposition.

Walker also hands out free copies of his books to a select few, including the squatter's daughter, Sabina: an act that guarantees the protection of her father's property from the bushranger's gang. By this time, Mort is in love with Sabina, and Walker's lover Jessie Carew is working on the station as a housekeeper. Jessie is the "bushranger's sweetheart" of Nisbet's title, a rough-riding, capable young woman who can beat a man in a fight – – although the novel also emphasises her feminine, domestic qualities. When "Sandy" Macintosh and a group of men attack Mr Condon's station, the bushrangers come to the squatter's aid – just as they did in Boldrewood's novel. Walker, the boy Dicky and Jessie are all killed in the shoot-outs that follow, which makes the novel generic in the sense that (like *The Bushranger of Van Diemen's Land*, *Robbery Under Arms* and *Outlaw and Lawmaker*) it concludes by bringing the bushranger's career to a melodramatic close. Mort and Sabina, however, survive and later marry, further uniting the worlds of the bushranger

---

52 Judith R. Halasz, *The Bohemian Ethos: Questioning Work and Making a Scene on the Lower East Side* (New York and London: Routledge, 2015), 22.
53 Andrew McCann notes that Clarke's arrival in Melbourne makes the local literary scene "seem more self-consciously Bohemian"; *Marcus Clarke's Bohemia: Literature and Modernity in Colonial Melbourne* (Melbourne: Melbourne University Press, 2004), 31. We briefly discussed Clarke's European literary influences and their effects on the representation of local character types in the Introduction to this book.
54 See Pierre Bourdieu, *The Field of Cultural Production*, trans. Randal Johnson (Oxford: Polity Press, 1993), 29–73.

and the squatter. Enriched with bushranger gold and recovering his family's lost wealth, Mort leaves Australia with Sabina, travelling around the world and spending freely for a couple of years before returning to his English property. The bushranger dies in this novel so that this young couple can live – and indulge themselves. They are not interested in investing in the future of the squattocracy like Dick Marston and Gracey Storefield in *Robbery Under Arms*; and unlike Raike Morris and Judith in *Bail Up!*, they have no critical role to play in relation to the social and economic life of the colonies, which the novel represents as debased and corrupt.

The "bohemian" character of the bushranger in late colonial Australian fiction gives a different complexion to Pybus' point that early bushrangers formed a "parallel community beyond the boundaries of the settlement". Pierre Bourdieu has talked about the nineteenth-century literary bohemian not so much as an outsider but as part of a "society *within* a society", devoted to the pursuit of a purer kind of aesthetic sensibility but dependent on broader "public recognition". Bohemianism, as Bourdieu puts it, "makes the art of living into one of the fine arts".[55] We see something of this in Walker/Rainbow's obsession with his literary reputation in *The Bushranger's Sweetheart*. But in Nisbet's third bushranger novel, *A Bush Girl's Romance*, the sense that this character type might be a practitioner of the fine arts is pushed to a kind of logical conclusion. With Derrick Wild, we are (despite his surname) a long way from those earlier, *homo ferus* bushrangers who wrote their diaries in blood and ate raw kangaroo rat. Wild is "a bushranger with aesthetic principles"; he educates and disciplines his gang so that they are as capable of the "enjoyment of life's richest pleasures, as he was himself".[56] The role of the gentleman bushranger here is in fact precisely to cultivate the *un*cultivated: his gang "had been beasts before, without discrimination; they had become philosophers" (174). When Wild and his gang raid Crocodile Station, he is appalled to see a group of debauched, intoxicated squatters covered in filth and surrounded by Aboriginal women, one of whom they have violently flogged. This scene inverts Boldrewood's squatter/bushranger paradigm in *Robbery Under Arms*, with squatters now far more debased than bushrangers. (Crocodile Station might also recall Boolabong Station in Trollope's *Harry Heathcote of Gangoil*.) What especially disgusts Wild about these squatters, however, is their food, a "mess of potatoes, onions and fat mutton" (142). Wild is an epicurean and an excellent chef, a "true artist"; he uses the proceeds of his robberies to go to Paris, taking "lessons from some celebrated chef" and "cultivating his gastronomic tastes" (178-9). We have noted that colonial bushrangers like Dick Marston are often sympathetically connected to native species. Derrick Wild's speciality as a chef is in fact native cuisine: he prepares and cooks things like "Cockatoos, parroquets, and bush-turkey served with mushrooms", "Snakes and lizards . . . with stewed muurang", and so on (186).[57] "He was", the novel tells us, "an epicure and monomaniac on cooking" (274).

The term *monomaniac* is worth briefly considering here. It was introduced by the French psychiatrist Jean-Étienne Esquirol in the early nineteenth century, initially to

---

55 Pierre Bourdieu, *The Rules of Art: Genesis and Structure of the Literary Field*, trans. Susan Emanuel (Stanford, Calif.: Stanford University Press, 1996), 56.
56 Hume Nisbet, *A Bush Girl's Romance* (London: F.V. White & Co., 1894), 174, 180. All subsequent references are to this edition and appear in parentheses in the text.
57 Even this aspect of the gentleman bushranger's character has its precedent in *Robbery Under Arms*: Starlight cooks black duck "with every care" (268).

denote "an *idée fixe*, a single pathological preoccupation in an otherwise sound mind".[58] Monomania soon "became a favourite term among the intelligentsia", finding its way into literature as a common explanation for a character's aberrant, obsessive and excitable behaviour: think, for example, of Heathcliff in *Wuthering Heights* (1847), or Melville's Captain Ahab. Stephen Kern notes that "Victorian writers routinely used monomania to explain murders".[59] In Nisbet's novel, monomania becomes a way of describing a bushranger's absolute commitment to his craft: "when he had fixed his mind upon the gaining of a pleasure, [he] counted no price too high, no obstacle too great to get it..." (274). Wild is a ruthless figure who single-mindedly pursues his goal of becoming rich at the colony's expense. In Perth, he robs the bank, impoverishes some of the local squatters, seduces several "rich, free and independent widows", and buys a schooner – intending to sail to South America and invest in "the South Sea trade" (227, 229). *A Bush Girl's Romance* is contemporaneous with the radical journalist William Lane's journey to Paraguay in July 1893 to establish a utopian community: a project that resonates with the Pacific island ending of *Bail Up!*. Wild's monomania, however, is driven not by communal ideals but by self-interest and the pursuit of "pleasure". At one point, disguised as a police officer – his assumed name, Captain Wildrake, indicates that his identity as a bushranger is never far away (and again recalls the character in Scott's *Woodstock*) – he is employed by squatters to "disperse" a group of local Aboriginal people. It seems here as if Wild is now instrumental to the wider project of settler expansion, but this is entirely a mercenary role that suits his own interests (because those Aboriginal people know his true identity and could betray him). In a gruesome manifestation of the squatter/bushranger paradigm, Wild and his gang carry out a large-scale massacre. The violence of the scene is skewed by the bushranger's monomaniacal obsession with gastronomy, which then distorts the way he rationalises his actions. Wild decides to prepare an extravagant meal for the Aboriginal people he is about to slaughter: "if I can only give them one real thrill of pure gastronomic pleasure before they leave this world", he says, "it must compensate for my share in the taking off of those innocents" (173). We have seen the critic "Telemachus" complain in the *Argus* that the gentleman bushranger seems like "a perverted image" of the gentlemanly type. In Nisbet's novel, this is now taken to an extreme position, where the gentleman bushranger is both a sociopath and self-justifying agent of the civilising mission. By preparing an extraordinary meal of native produce for Aboriginal people just before he massacres them, Wild gives literal expression to Nisbet's colonial critique: "We...teach the naked races how to dress themselves before we bury them". But Wild is also a bohemian figure who heavily invests in what Bourdieu had called "the fine arts". Killing Aboriginal people, for him, is filtered through precisely this kind of ultra-cultivated disposition; it becomes, as the novel puts it, "a question of expediency that only the tactics of the most refined civilisation can justify" (173).

A Bush Girl's Romance remains more or less within the squatter/bushranger paradigm, introducing the successful squatter, Richard Craven, and his daughter Helen, the "bush girl" of the novel's title. In contrast to Elsie Valliant in Praed's *Outlaw and Lawmaker*, Helen is "wholesome in her mind", carefully distanced from any decadent influences (10).

---

[58] Jan Goldstein, *Console and Classify: The French Psychiatric Profession in the Nineteenth Century* (Chicago and London: University of Chicago Press, 2001), 155–6.
[59] Stephen Kern, *A Cultural History of Causality: Science, Murder Novels, and Systems of Thought* (Princeton, NJ: Princeton University Press, 2004), 248.

Her reading tastes (remembering the squatter's investment in literary cultivation) precisely reflect her "healthy" temperament:

> Never having read any of the so-called realistic or morbidly psychical rubbish with which some of the young authors expend their mental energies and debauch their unsophisticated readers in this latter end of the nineteenth century, she had therefore no idea about the wickedness of the world or the depravity of the human soul in its natural state . . . (11)

Wild attempts to seduce Helen; but although she finds him "young, good-looking and gentlemanly, with large black eyes", she responds to his presence with "anger and abhorrence . . . mixed with a chill fear" (42). Her "instinctive" reaction to Wild's dark, predatory nature associates him with the debased literature she otherwise avoids, bringing a naive "bush girl" into reluctant proximity with *fin-de-siècle* decadent tastes. George du Maurier's immensely popular novel *Trilby* was serialised in America the same year Nisbet's *A Bush Girl's Romance* was published, and gives us another unsettling, predatory figure through the notorious mesmerist, Svengali. For David Glover, Svengali is a "true bohemian in only caring about his art"; what turns this character's bohemianism into an example of "monomania", however, is his "brazen disregard for human suffering".[60] We can say something similar about the bushranger Derrick Wild, a seducer of women, a mass murderer, and an absurdly obsessive "gastronomic artist" (304). Awaiting execution at the end of the novel, Wild completes a recipe book that he dedicates to Helen: it is, he says, "reparation for my less worthy actions; it is the best part of myself" (305). The book goes on to sell across the colonies "like a newspaper": reaching the kind of audiences Ned Kelly had in mind, perhaps, when he handed his autobiography over to the editor of the *Jerilderie and Urana Gazette*. We have come a long way from early, feral bushrangers like Michael Howe who wrote solitary journals in remote locations. At the end of the nineteenth century, the bushranger is now a *fin-de-siècle* bohemian ruthlessly dedicated to the "fine arts" – and paradoxically, in a work of popular literature, producing a bestseller.

---

60 David Glover, *Literature, Immigration and Diaspora in Fin-de-Siècle England: A Cultural History of the 1905 Aliens Act* (Cambridge: Cambridge University Press, 2012), 96.

3
Colonial Australian Detectives

John Lang's *The Forger's Wife* (1855) – first serialised in *Fraser's Magazine* in 1853 under the title *Emily Orford* – is, we think, the first detective novel in Australia and, most likely, the world. Lang was born in Parramatta in 1816 and, after studying law in England, practised as a Sydney barrister in the early 1840s. He later worked in India as a lawyer and a journalist, and then moved to London in the early 1850s, writing stories and sketches for a number of English magazines, including Dickens' *Household Words*.[1] *The Forger's Wife* tells the story of Emily Orford and her unfaithful husband Charles Roberts, a forger and imposter who is arrested in England and transported to New South Wales where his criminal habits flourish. For a moment it looks as if these two characters are the protagonists of the novel. But *The Forger's Wife* soon pushes them aside in order to introduce a powerful new figure, someone who will come to shape their destiny. "George Flower was a great character in the colony of New South Wales", the novel tells us:

> He was the son of a gamekeeper; and a handsomer lad had rarely breathed... His sagacity was on a par with his courage and personal prowess; and in many points he strikingly resembled the blood-hound. He walked about the police-office in Sydney with a swagger which spoke a consciousness of his superiority in his profession. He was a hard drinker, but liquor rarely had any effect upon him – that is to say, it never interfered with the exercise of his faculties... His word was his bond; and he never made a promise, either to do a favour for a friend, or bring about an enemy's ruin, without completing it to the very letter.[2]

The Forger's Wife is a detective novel because it takes its primary figure of law enforcement into a new realm of specialisation – and keeps him active and influential for the duration of the narrative. The first detective novel in English is often taken to be *The Notting Hill Mystery*, written under the pseudonym "Charles Felix" (possibly Charles

---

1 See Sabine Clemm, *Dickens, Journalism, and Nationhood: Mapping the World in* Household Words (New York: Routledge, 2009), 132–3.
2 John Lang, *The Forger's Wife* (London: Ward & Lock, 1855), 34–5. All subsequent references are to this edition and appear in parentheses in the text.

Warren Adams);[3] but since it was serialised in 1862-63, *The Forger's Wife* precedes it by about ten years. *The Forger's Wife*'s earlier serialisation is in fact contemporaneous with the publication of Charles Dickens' *Bleak House* (1853), which gives us the "first fully developed police detective figure to feature in a novel":[4] a character called Mr Bucket. George Flower has some character traits in common with Dickens' detective, "a sharp-eyed man – a quick keen man" who "takes in everybody's look at him, all at once, individually and collectively, in a manner that stamps him a remarkable man".[5] On the other hand, while Bucket is an opaque, rather mysterious character – appearing only occasionally, and fading out of the novel later on – George Flower is eminently tangible, a physical and striking presence with a significant role to play, retaining his centrality right to the end. The title of this novel notwithstanding, Flower is the protagonist of *The Forger's Wife*. What we see for the first time here is a detective emerging as a major character, not a minor one.

The Forger's Wife places Flower not only at the centre of the narrative but also at the core of Sydney society and its legal apparatus. He seems to be connected to everyone, everywhere: "No great man was ever more easy of access than George Flower, and no one more popular with informers, for he invariably acted 'on the square'" (34-5). At one point Flower boasts, "*I am all the police*" (106), as if he is an intensification of his type, encompassing the police and transcending them at the same time. The novel sustains this view of Flower even at this early stage in the genre's history, holding him up as an exemplary figure. He places himself right at the centre of colonial governance, eliminating bushrangers, establishing a viable future for settlers, and giving directions to local administrators: "I wish to teach you settlers, and the Gov'ment, and bushrangers, a great moral lesson", he says, towards the end of the novel; "I want to make you more independent and secure . . . and Gov'ment more economical and sensible" (113). This early colonial detective plays a crucial role in stabilising the social and fiscal realities of day-to-day life in the colonies. But his own identity is much less stable. Flower is also a transported convict, sent to Australia "for discharging, in cold blood, the contents of a double-barrelled gun into the body of a young squire who had seduced his sister" (34). A violent, forceful detective, he is nevertheless in sympathy with other convicts who live productively within the system – having "none of that vulgar prejudice which most emancipated constables entertained, against men in an *actual* state of bondage" (36). Later on, Flower disguises himself as a bushranger to infiltrate a local gang, and finds himself for a moment enjoying their adventurous, rough existence. He tells the leader Millighan, who he much admires, "Don't let us talk much, or I may forget my mission, and become a bushranger myself" (84). So this colonial law enforcer is put into predicaments that enable him to sympathise with – and even become – his opposites, the character types from which he is otherwise structurally distinguished: convicts and bushrangers. Of course, manliness and moral fibre are the things that tie these opposites together: these are the qualities that draw Flower

---

3 Kate Watson attributes the claim that *The Notting Hill Mystery* is the "first full-blown detective novel in English" to various literary commentators, including Stephen Knight, Julian Symons and Michael Cox: see *Women Writing Crime Fiction, 1860–1880: Fourteen American, British and Australian Authors* (Jefferson, NC: McFarland & Company, 2012), 18.
4 Watson, *Women Writing Crime Fiction*, 18.
5 Charles Dickens, *Bleak House* (London: Bradbury & Evans, 1853), 475. Lang was living in London and publishing in Dickens's *Household Words* in the early- to mid-1850s, and the two authors knew each other's work well.

to Millighan. By contrast, Flower is appalled by the deceitful crimes and infidelities of the transported forger Charles Roberts. When Roberts finally becomes a bushranger, Flower comes out of retirement to track him down and kill him.

Detectives vs Police

Both Stephen Knight and Kate Watson have noted that Flower was based on a "real-life policeman in Sydney", Israel Chapman.[6] Chapman was in fact another transported convict; granted a conditional pardon (like Flower) in 1821, he joined the Sydney Police and went on to become Australia's first detective. An 1831 article in the *Sydney Gazette and New South Wales Advertiser* called him "that prince of man-traps, the notorious Israel Chapman",[7] giving us a sense that this individual is already gaining momentum and definition as a specific, local character type. Little has been written on the history of colonial detectives in Australia, and it is difficult to say exactly when detectives were first appointed to local police forces. Dean Wilson and Mark Finnane have noted that "a small detective force consisting of four constables and a sergeant" was formed in colonial Victoria in 1844.[8] This is just two years, according to Dana Brand, after the establishment of the "world's first detective department" in London in 1842.[9] The fluid relationship between convict and detective is once again important in the Australian context: this early Victorian detective force was made up primarily of "emancipists – convicts who had been granted a conditional or absolute pardon before the term of their sentence had expired".[10]

Detective Branches certainly expanded across the colonies in the 1850s, an outcome of social anxieties about flourishing criminal activity fed by increasingly systematic practices of record keeping (by police) and reporting (by journalists). One of the key debates at the time was to do with whether colonial society was best served by a police force that protects citizens *from* crime, or a detective branch that investigates crimes after they have happened. The *Australian* argued for the former in 1845:

> In principle, all Police Forces ought to be Protective. When a poor man has been robbed, and his property made away with, it is but poor consolation to him to have the thief found out. Our Police are much too scanty for the requirements of the city, and we can therefore ill afford to occupy any portion of them, exclusively, to a Detective branch.[11]

---

6   Stephen Knight, *Continent of Mystery: A Thematic History of Australian Crime Fiction* (Melbourne: Melbourne University Press, 1997), 112; Watson, *Women Writing Crime Fiction*, 142.
7   "James Hardy Vaux", *Sydney Gazette and New South Wales Advertiser*, 27 October 1831, 3.
8   Dean Wilson and Mark Finnane, "From Sleuths to Technicians? Changing Images of the Detective in Victoria", in *Police Detectives in History, 1750–1950*, ed. Clive Emsley and Haia Shpayer-Makov (Aldershot, UK: Ashgate Publishing, 2006), 136.
9   Dana Brand, *The Spectator and the City in Nineteenth-Century American Literature* (Cambridge: Cambridge University Press, 1991), 94. Haia Shpayer-Makov notes that a separate detective department was establishment in London's Metropolitan Police in August 1842: "This marked the official, if tentative, start of Scotland Yard – the famous detective team stationed in the Metropolitan Police headquarters – which would become a familiar name far beyond the British borders": see Haia Shpayer-Makov, *The Ascent of the Detective: Police Sleuths in Victorian and Edwardian England* (Oxford: Oxford University Press, 2011), 33.
10 Wilson and Finnane, "From Sleuths to Technicians?", 136.
11 "The Detective Force", *Australian*, 15 May 1845, 3.

This passage already acknowledges the inability of police in the colonies to live up to the "principle" of protecting citizens and property from crime. In response to this, some senior police officers went on to prioritise criminal investigation and, in doing so, invested the detective with a unique set of qualities. A report of the Commissioner of Police published in the *South Australian Register* in 1853 asks for a special class of detectives to be exempt from normal police duties, in order to develop their investigative powers:

> In this art depends much upon individual qualifications, sagacity in drawing inferences from slight things, fertility of resource, a blood-hound tenacity of pursuit, intimate acquaintance with the habits of thieves, and their probable mode of acting in particular circumstances, and in the knack of making a cast in the right direction in search of a clue.[12]

Here, detectives are given a set of unique skills and characteristics that utterly distinguish them from ordinary police. Wilson and Finnane note that the Detective Branch in Victoria – established in the early 1850s – "remained autonomous from the general body of police, having its own rank structure and recruiting civilians directly".[13] The genre of detective fiction in colonial Australia relied precisely not only on the establishment of a detective's autonomy from the police, but also on his ability to eclipse their role. This is evident in Lang's *The Forger's Wife* through the way Flower steps outside the confines of normal police procedures and yet remains fully representative ("*I* am all the police") of everything they do. The view that police "ought to be protective" is of no use to detective fiction anyway, since the genre (as Tzvetan Todorov famously noted) depends on the fact that a crime has indeed already happened: this has to occur precisely so that the narrative itself – that is, the investigation – can proceed.[14]

In his book *Mysteries and Conspiracies* (2012), the French critic Luc Boltanski draws an important distinction between police and detectives that resonates with what we have been discussing here. As it emerges in the mid-nineteenth century, the detective novel brings the detective into focus at the expense of the police officer, who is deprived of insight and charisma and becomes minor – even though he remains, as Boltanski puts it, "a representative of the state".[15] The police officer, he writes,

> knows reality only in its officially determined form. He believes naively in its unity and its sturdiness. The detective, in contrast, possessing the same type of intelligence and the same perversity as the great criminal, also knows how to dig into the crevasses and interstices of reality so as to exploit its inconsistencies, which perhaps means also unveiling its incoherence.[16]

We can pause for a moment here to think again about a popular colonial Australian novel that, perhaps surprisingly, exactly reflects Boltanski's distinction between detectives and the police: Rolf Boldrewood's bushranger novel *Robbery Under Arms*. As we noted in

---

12 "Report of the Commissioner of Police", *South Australian Register*, 3 June 1853, 3.
13 Wilson and Finnane, "From Sleuths to Technicians", 137.
14 See Tzvetan Todorov, "The Typology of Detective Fiction", in *The Poetics of Prose*, trans. Richard Howard (Ithaca, NY: Cornell University Press, 1977), 44–6.
15 Luc Boltanksi, *Mysteries and Conspiracies: Detective Stories, Spy Novels and the Making of Modern Societies*, trans. Catherine Porter (Cambridge: Polity Press, 2014), 31.
16 Boltanski, *Mysteries and Conspiracies*, 31.

Chapter 2, this novel is set in the 1840s and 1850s, just as the colonial detective is emerging as a recognisable type. As Dick Marston, Captain Starlight and other bushrangers rob and plunder the colonies, newspapers routinely complain about the inability of the police to protect colonial wealth and property. One local journalist remarks, "We have always regarded the present system – facetiously called police protection – as a farce" (503). On the other hand, from the bushrangers' perspective "[t]he whole place seemed to be alive with police" (295) and the country is "thick with police stations" (387). When Starlight and Marston are arrested early on, the latter observes: "Detectives and constables would seem to be pretty thick in the colonies" (126). The novel's key police officer is Senior Constable Goring, an ambitious man ("he was sure to be promoted") who arrests Marston at his homestead. But there is also a detective, who follows Starlight to New Zealand, apprehends him and testifies against him in court. "My name is Stephen Stillbrook...", he begins, in the only speech he ever makes in the novel. But although he appears only briefly – rather like Mr Bucket in Dickens' *Bleak House* – Stillbrook makes an extraordinary impression on Marston, the novel's narrator:

> A quiet, oldish-looking man got up now and came forward to the witness box. I didn't know who he was; but Starlight nodded to him quite pleasant. He had a short, close trimmed beard and was one of those nothing-particular-looking old chaps. I'm blessed if I could have told what he was. He might have been a merchant, or a squatter, or a head-clerk, or a wine merchant, or a broker, or lived in the town, or lived in the country. Any of half-a-dozen trades would suit him. The only thing that was out of the common was his eyes. They had a sort of curious way of looking at you, as if he wondered whether you was speaking true, and yet seein' nothing and tellin' nothing. He regular took in Starlight (he told me afterwards) by always talking about the China Seas; he'd been there, it seems; he'd been everywhere... (169)

A police officer always represents the police, but a detective's identity is much more fluid and mutable, as if all sorts of different, unrelated (but prosperous) colonial character types could be projected onto him ("He might have been a merchant, or a squatter..."). A police officer is also local, whereas Stillbrook has apparently been "everywhere": a feature he shares with the "great criminal" Starlight, who had himself "been all over the world" (104).

Undercover Detectives

The gold rushes in Victoria in the 1850s considerably complicated local crime scenes and underscored the need for a detective with investigative powers and a certain capacity for freedom of movement – to go undercover, to infiltrate criminal communities, and so on. As Wilson and Finnane note, Detective Branches expanded rapidly during this time. Detective fiction mirrored this expansion, with new kinds of police stories from William Burrows (*Adventures of the Mounted Trooper in the Australian Constabulary*, 1859), James "Skipp" Borlase (*The Night Fossickers and Other Tales of Peril and Adventure*, 1867), and Mary Fortune: where the crimes and the investigations, as Stephen Knight notes, "all occur in Australia".[17] Under the pseudonym "Waif Wander", Fortune published over four

---

17 Knight, *Continent of Mystery*, 31.

hundred crime and detective stories in the *Australian Journal* from 1865 to 1899, and her *The Detective's Album: Tales of the Australian Police* (1871) was the first collection of detective fiction to be published locally.[18] Her earliest *Australian Journal* story, "The Stolen Specimens" (1865), begins by wryly noting the growing acceptance of the role of policing and detective work in the colonies and amongst colonial readerships: "We, members of the police force of Victoria, are, I think, a little – a very little – less despised in this year of grace, eighteen hundred and sixty-five, than we were when I first donned the uniform twelve years ago".[19] Fortune invented several detectives, including James Brooke (who also appears in Borlase's stories) and Mark Sinclair, to whom she returned again and again; but she also revelled in the detective's capacity for anonymity and transformation. A private detective in Fortune's "The Major's Case" (1895) refuses to give his name: "I have a new one for every fresh case", he says; "If you entrust your business to us you may have to make my acquaintance under half a dozen different names and disguises".[20]

Going undercover in disguise soon becomes a conventional way of expressing the colonial detective's fluidity, his capacity to move freely through different environments and social worlds. The journalist and writer Robert Percy Whitworth published a few detective stories in the 1870s and 1880s. In one of them, "The Trooper's Story of the Bank Robbery" (1872), a police inspector encourages a mounted trooper to track down a notorious Vandemonian bushranger by going undercover as a swagman: "he wanted me to be perfectly free from restraint, to act entirely on my own hook . . ."[21] The *Australian Journal* was an important venue for early Australian detective fiction, and 1865 was a particularly significant year: Mary Fortune's first detective stories were published at this time; Ellen Davitt's crime novel *Force and Fraud* was serialised;[22] and so was Whitworth's novel *Mary Summers: A Romance of the Australian Bush*, which introduces another detective protagonist, David Turner. Investigating the murders of a bush hawker and a publican, Turner also disguises himself as a swagman: "he looked the character to perfection".[23] Assisted by Bungy, an Aboriginal man who has deserted the native police but gets involved in tracking the murderer, Turner's only obstacles are the police themselves, who raid properties and interrogate settlers almost at random, carrying out "more of the nature of a lawless inquisition than the prosecution of a legitimate and cautious investigation" (47). Following up clues in Sydney, Turner – without a disguise – ventures into a "hotbed of vice and crime" where everyone seems to know him; he angrily sends the police away

---

18 For an informative discussion of Mary Fortune's literary career, see Lucy Sussex, *The Fortunes of Mary Fortune* (Melbourne: Penguin, 1989) and "The (Feminine) Eye of the Law: Mary Helena Fortune", in *Women Writers and Detectives in Nineteenth-Century Crime Fiction: The Mothers of the Mystery Genre* (London: Palgrave Macmillan, 2010).
19 "Waif Wander", "The Stolen Specimens", *Australian Journal*, 14 October 1865, 106–8; reprinted in *The Colonial Journals and the Emergence of Australian Literary Culture*, ed. Ken Gelder and Rachael Weaver (Perth: University of Western Australia Press, 2014), 159.
20 "Waif Wander", "The Major's Case", *Australian Journal*, August 1895, 683–90.
21 Robert P. Whitworth, "The Trooper's Story of the Bank Robbery", in *The Anthology of Colonial Australian Crime Fiction*, ed. Ken Gelder and Rachael Weaver (Melbourne: Melbourne University Press, 2008), 107.
22 Davitt's *Force and Fraud* is widely acknowledged as the first murder-mystery novel in Australia, but it is not a detective novel: as Kate Watson notes, "there is no holistic detecting sequence or specific detective figure in this mystery novel", *Women Writing Crime Fiction*, 169.
23 Robert P. Whitworth, *Mary Summers: A Romance of the Australian Bush* (1865; Canberra: Mulini Press, 1994), 61. All subsequent references are to this edition and appear in parentheses in the text.

and interviews Nell Brown, a once-beautiful woman who is now degraded by "gin and foul disease". Turner is a later version of Lang's George Flower, a violent but virtuous man – he punches a wife-beater in Sydney, for example – who both flatters and threatens his informants. But the murderer dies during a chase by plunging into a ravine, and Turner is not able to bring him to justice and claim the reward. "He got tired of the force", the novel tells us at the end (98). Rather like Flower, he later runs a public house, marrying the murdered publican's widow; but it is never very profitable and business doesn't improve. This is a novel that does not tie the solution of the crime to the accumulation of colonial wealth; in contrast to *The Forger's Wife*, its detective settles down in retirement but does not prosper, and the focus shifts instead to a romantic story that involves the novel's eponymous heroine, Mary Summers, who is only incidentally connected to the investigation of the murders. In comparison with the detective she is arguably a minor character.

The authenticity of one's disguise – how "perfectly" a detective can become another, different character type – is the key to investigative success in these detective narratives. Mary Fortune's story "Dandy Art's Diary" was published in the *Australian Journal* much later on, in July 1897. Here, Melbourne-based detective Mark Sinclair receives a request from an eminent squatter to go undercover to investigate a series of robberies. For various reasons, the squatter asks "for someone who could play the part of a ladies' man",[24] a request that makes the inspector in charge think not of Sinclair but of another officer, Arthur Cranbrooke. Cranbrooke is nicknamed Dandy Art, because he is quite literally a dandy. With his "slim figure, and curly, fair hair, that suited his long-lashed blue eyes", he seems "as unlike a detective as could well be imagined" (519). So this is a late colonial Australian story that raises a different question to do with the ability to replace one identity with another, a more original question: namely, who can *become* a detective?

For Cranbrooke, signing up to become a detective has meant losing his dandified sense of style and fashion: "I'm a disappointed man, that's what I am, and many a bitter hour I pass in recalling my hopes and plans when life promised me something better than the card of a 'plain clothes man'" (521). However, distracted by the women on the squatter's property, he begins to play out his undercover identity as a "ladies' man". As he does so, Cranbrooke forgets about being a detective and slips back into his earlier character type. Sinclair has also gone out to the property in disguise, as a shepherd; and as he watches the beautiful young man from a distance he becomes increasingly distracted by him:

> Dandy had never, in my eyes, looked so well as he did on that memorable morning, and I really had never given the boy credit for being so good looking. Perhaps it was because I had never before seen him so carefully dressed. His loose summer morning coat, of the latest cut, suited him, and his wavy hair looked glossier under the light straw hat, with its blue ribbon . . . He was pretty enough to be a woman – so I thought at the time – with his clear-cut, small features, long lashes, and small, slender hands. (522-3)

This is a remarkable passage, where one detective, in disguise, watches another detective – also in disguise – going about his undercover business, transforming Cranbrooke into

---

24 "Waif Wander", "Dandy Art's Diary", *Australian Journal*, 1 July 1897, 519. All subsequent references are to this edition and appear in parentheses in the text.

a feminised object of erotic attention. The conventionally masculine character of the detective is turned on its head here, with Sinclair blending surveillance and voyeurism together as he secretly monitors his colleague's movements. The story allows Cranbrooke's other identity as a dandy and "ladies' man" to flourish, almost undoing his capacity to inhabit the role of a detective in the process. On the other hand, Cranbrooke reflects carefully on his role *as* a detective, keeping a diary – Dandy Art's diary – to record his investigations. The other detectives think he is too caught up with a literary ideal, and is simply not suited to actual detective work: "Dandy Art's Diary was the occasion of many a smile among the D.'s at the Detective Office, for he was fond of talking of it as a wonderful literary production, that he intended to publish some day" (523). But unlike Sinclair, Cranbrooke manages to identify the real culprit, confronting and killing him in a struggle just before he dies from his own injuries. Mary Fortune therefore gives us a story in which a dandy can indeed become a detective, even as this character bends the parameters of the role and takes it, self-consciously, into a literary register.

"Second Wave" Colonial Detective Fiction

The late colonial Australian detective novel – what Christa Ludlow calls the "second wave of detective fiction" in Australia[25] – was well aware of the contribution it made to fashioning a literary genre that by this time (the 1880s and 1890s) was transnationally identified and all too familiar. Fergus Hume's novel *The Mystery of a Hansom Cab* (1886) sold around 20,000 copies in its first Melbourne printing, and well over 300,000 copies after the novel was republished in London the following year: "a success so startling", the *Illustrated London News* reported, "as to astonish our booksellers and even the publishers themselves".[26] Hume had been especially influenced by the French crime novelist Émile Gaboriau, using him as a model for his local take on the genre in order to capitalise on its popularity:

> I enquired of a leading Melbourne bookseller what style of book he sold most of. He replied that the detective stories of Gaboriau had a large sale; and as, at this time, I had never even heard of this author, I bought all his works and ... determined to write a book of the same class; containing a mystery, a murder, and a description of low life in Melbourne.[27]

The novel then folds a series of citations to Gaboriau and other, well-known American and European authors of detective fiction – Edgar Allan Poe, Fortuné du Boisgobey, James Payn, Anna Katharine Green – into its descriptions and dialogue. One of its local characters, Felix Rolleston, is in fact a dandy, and he is especially familiar with detective

---

[25] Christa Ludlow, "The Reader Investigates: Images of Crime in the Colonial City", *Continuum: The Australian Journal of Media and Culture* 7:2 (1994). http://wwwmcc.murdoch.edu.au/ReadingRoom/7.2/Ludlow.html.
[26] Cited in Christopher Pittard, *Purity and Contamination in Late Victorian Detective Fiction* (Farnham, UK: Ashgate Publishing, 2011), 29; see also Lucy Sussex, *Blockbuster! Fergus Hume and The Mystery of a Hansom Cab* (Melbourne: Text Publishing, 2015), 134–44.
[27] Fergus Hume, quoted in Julian Symons, *Bloody Murder: from the Detective Story to the Crime Novel* (Harmondsworth, UK: Penguin Books, 1972), 60.

fiction from abroad. "Do you know anything of the detective business?" someone asks him at one point. "Oh, dear, yes", he replies: "I've read Gaboriau, you know; awfully jolly life, 'tectives".[28] Like Mary Fortune's "Dandy Art's Diary", Hume's novel asks the question: who can become a detective? Rolleston certainly aspires to this role, based on his extensive reading across the genre; and in fact he tries to solve the crime, but without success. There are other aspiring detectives, too, like Calton, a lawyer, and Margaret or Madge, the daughter of the squatter, Frettlby. Both also try unsuccessfully to solve the crime, the murder of a man called Whyte who has been blackmailing Frettlby over his unintentionally bigamous marriage to Madge's mother. It can seem as if everyone wants to be a detective in this novel, which allows a number of characters to compete with each other for the right solution to the mystery and play out the full range of interpretive possibilities. To complicate things further, it gives us two actual detectives who would seem to be the complete opposites of each other. "Mr Gorby was a very clever detective", the novel tells us, "and got on with every one with the exception of Kilsip. The latter, on the other hand, was equally as clever in his own way, and was a favourite with every one but Gorby. One was fire and the other water, so when they came together there was sure to be trouble" (91). In fact, these two detectives have their cleverness and their popularity in common in this passage. But the novel persists in distinguishing them from one another:

> Kilsip, in his outward appearance, was quite different from Gorby, being tall and slender, whereas the other was short and stout. Kilsip was dark and clever-looking, Gorby was not, his face wearing a complacent and satisfied smile, which one would not expect to find on the features of a man who was looked upon as such a clever detective. But it was this very smile that was Mr Gorby's greatest aid in getting information, as people were more ready to tell a kindly and apparently simple man like him all they knew than a sharp-looking fellow like Kilsip, whose ears and eyes seemed always on the alert. The hearts of all went forth to Gorby's sweet smile and insinuating manner, but when Kilsip appeared every one shut up like an oyster, and each retired promptly into his or her shell like an alarmed snail. The face is not always the index of the mind, in spite of the saying to that effect, and the student of Lavater is not invariably right in his readings of character by means of the features. The only sharp thing about Mr Gorby's appearance was his keen little grey eyes, which he knew how to use so well, and a glance from which startled any unsuspecting person who had been beguiled by the complacent smile and sweet manner. Kilsip, on the contrary, had one of those hawk-like faces, which always seem seeking for prey, with brilliant black eyes, hooked nose, and small, thin-lipped mouth . . . So, taking things all round, although Kilsip was the most clever of the two, yet Gorby, owing to his physical advantages, was the most successful. (91-2)

It turns out that Gorby's attempt to solve the crime is not successful at all and he drops away from the novel about halfway through. Kilsip, on the other hand, stays to the end, insisting on the correct solution and preparing an arrest warrant long before anyone else agrees with him. The long description above looks as if it disagrees with the work of Johann Lavater, the well-known eighteenth-century Swiss physiognomist whose pseudo-

---

28 Fergus Hume, *The Mystery of a Hansom Cab* (1886; London: The Hogarth Press, 1985), 76. All subsequent references are to this edition and appear in parentheses in the text.

scientific notion that character could be read in facial features "shaped the mission of the new urban police forces and their most celebrated figure, the detective".[29] But the novel nevertheless rehearses the same physiognomic cultural logics, giving detailed descriptions of the physical appearance of the two detectives who struggle with each other for distinction. Gorby is more homely and mundane, more plodding and much more like a police officer – which limits his capacity to investigate and identify the criminal. Kilsip, on the other hand, is given a licence to freely roam the metropolis, making his way through Melbourne's underworld with confidence (rather like Robert Whitworth's David Turner), "gliding" into people's offices "like a sleek cat", driven as much by his ambition and competitive spirit as by the need to solve the crime (108). The novel rewards him at the end when Margaret's fiancé Brian Fitzgerald – whom Kilsip exonerates from the crime – gives the detective "a sum of money which made him independent for life, though he still followed his old profession of a detective from sheer love of excitement" (223), enabling him, presumably, to become a *private* detective.

It is well known that late nineteenth-century detective fiction relies on the detective's ability to read and interpret the visual signs – the "clues" – of their environment. For Arthur Conan Doyle's Sherlock Holmes, as Srdjan Smajic argues, this means that the view of the metropolis is "fixed" or "petrified": limits are placed on knowledge and information, as if these things are "finite" and a detective's account of the city is a complete one, never needing to be updated or qualified.[30] It also means that only Holmes can be the detective in the Sherlock Holmes stories: he is the only "meta-character" possessed of the appropriate resources to read *other* characters and understand their predicaments, a skill he often demonstrates before the investigation itself has even begun. This is a post-*flaneurian* view of the city; it rejects the earlier conception (drawn from Edgar Allan Poe's 1840 story, "The Man of the Crowd") of the metropolitan crowd as a site where certain identities are so opaque that they turn "illegibility... itself [into] a form of crime".[31] Kilsip, with his "hawk-like countenance", is the closest in kind to Sherlock Holmes in late or "second wave" colonial Australian detective fiction. Gorby, on the other hand, is closer to a character like Inspector Athelney Jones, the "very stout, portly man in a gray suit... [with] small twinkling eyes" who works alongside Holmes in *The Sign of Four* (1890) – and who, like Gorby, comes up with the wrong solution because, the implication is, he is more like a police officer than a detective.[32] Like Holmes, Kilsip can move freely through metropolitan underworlds and lawyers' offices alike, reading the distinctive qualities of characters and classifying them as types, that is, type-casting them. He aspires ultimately to be a "meta-character" type too, helping to stabilise a colonial economy that continually runs the risk of being fraudulent and duplicitous.

The detective's special ability is to read other characters instantly, to make them legible to readers in turn and to situate them within a complicated social hierarchy. In this sense, the detective is an agent for colonial modernity itself which, as Liz Conor

---

29 Isaac Land, "Men with the Faces of Brutes: Physiognomy, Urban Anxieties, and Police States", in *Enemies of Humanity: The Nineteen-Century War on Terrorism*, ed. Isaac Land (London: Palgrave Macmillan, 2008), 119.
30 Srdjan Smajic, *Ghost-Seers, Detectives, and Spiritualists: Theories of Vision in Victorian Literature and Science* (Cambridge: Cambridge University Press, 2010), 127.
31 Brand, *The Spectator and the City*, 88. He adds: "The opacity of the urban crowd ceases to be merely confusing; it becomes actively threatening".
32 Arthur Conan Doyle, *The Sign of Four* (1890; London: Penguin Books, 2014), 46.

notes, "was increasingly bound up in systems of standarisation and classification".[33] He can also be an agent for the nation, drafting other characters into its service. William Sylvester Walker's novel *Native Born* (1900) introduces an experienced detective called Jasper Bodribb, who tells a young cab-driver why he has recruited him into the police force as a mounted trooper: "When I first met you I saw by your face at once that you were a gentleman; secondly, as I told you, that you were a new arrival; and as I prefer a stranger in the work I am engaged upon, I selected you. Besides, I am a physiognomist, and understand character . . . "[34] This ultra-confident Lavaterian reading is then valorised by the novel when the young man goes on to become an excellent trooper and, later, a successful squatter: "There happened to be a feeling prevalent at this time", the novel tells us, "that the pioneer squatters . . . were to be the big and prosperous men of the future . . . " (102). *Native Born* is a Federation novel that enmeshes its detective in colonial economic development as Bodribb also goes on to prosper, making a fortune out of opals, and becoming even in retirement "nearly as strong and energetic as in former days" (202), rather like George Flower.

The conventional view of colonial policing in Australia is that it primarily served the interests of the squattocracy. This is Annette Pedersen's argument in "Governing Images of the Australian Police Trooper". "The initial aim of the police in Australia", she writes, "was to facilitate the establishment of a capitalist state based on land ownership".[35] We have already seen examples of colonial detectives investigating crimes on squatters' properties: Dandy Art and Mark Sinclair do this in Mary Fortune's story, and in fact many of Fortune's stories play out versions of this scenario. Kilsip in *The Mystery of the Hansom Cab* also assists in preserving the reputation and wealth of one of the richest landowners in the colonies. But the preservation of economic capital – of private property and locally accumulated wealth – is not the only task of the late colonial Australian detective. In Francis Adams' *Madeline Brown's Murderer* (1887) the focus is on *social* capital: the kind that is quickly built and rapidly circulated through a flourishing print culture that is itself an expression of colonial modernity. Madeline Brown arrives in Melbourne and soon becomes a celebrated stage performer. The newspaper society pages are fascinated by her; men are erotically drawn to her; she sets off a "perfect craze" that makes colonial Melbourne claim her as its own, as if (even though her origins are obscure) she now belongs "to everyone".[36] When the society journalist David Stuart discovers her murdered body, he finds himself obsessed both with her and with the idea of solving the crime, which means he has to turn himself into a detective. "Then the thought of the detectives occurred to him", the novel tells us, "and the need they might have of seeing things exactly as they were" (26); soon afterwards, he takes on "the dark instinct of the bloodhound" (28). When a police officer and a detective named Edward Thomas arrive at the scene, Stuart turns to the latter for help, "The detective seeming the superior of the two" (31).

---

33   Liz Conor, "Introduction: Classification and Its Discontents", *Interventions: International Journal of Postcolonial Studies* 17:2 (2014), 11.
34   William Sylvester Walker, *Native Born* (London: John Long, 1900), 19.
35   Annette Pedersen, "Governing Images of the Australian Police Trooper," in *Rethinking Law, Society and Governance: Foucault's Bequest*, ed. Gary Wickham and George Pavlich (Portland, Oreg.: Hart Publishing, 2001), 28.
36   Francis W.L. Adams, *The Murder of Madeline Brown* (1887; Melbourne: Text Publishing, 2000), 21. First published as *Madeline Brown's Murderer*. All subsequent references are to this edition and appear in parentheses in the text.

Later, the case is given to Thomas' superior, a detective called Jones; but Stuart soon loses patience with both of them and decides to pursue the case on his own. *Madeline Brown's Murderer* is a novel that turns a society pages journalist into an investigative journalist, and in doing so it makes colonial print culture the proper place for the task of detection. The novel tells us, "Stuart must constitute himself a detective and find out. Think of Poe and Gaboriau. It would be a triumph for Australian journalism – the real aboriginal product" (72). These transnational literary citations, as we have noted, are routinely found in late colonial Australian detective fiction. What changes here, however, is the insistence on giving this a national identity that draws on those citations to valorise local journalism. David Stuart is an ideal type of the colonial-born, "a young and true Australian" (68). "He had all the temperance of the true Australian", the novel adds later on; "His body had the, as it were, clean and clearly porous look of the sober and the chaste" (74). The perversity of this novel is that all this is built around the murdered body of a beautiful actress, to which Stuart is erotically attracted. This is what drives his shift from social commentary to investigation, and it eats away at the image of him as a "chaste" and "true" Australian to the extent – when he finally confronts and kills the murderer on the rocks of a Sydney beach – of making him literally dissolve away, calling out Madeline's name in a state of delirious ecstasy. It is worth noting that the fate of Adams' amateur detective is quite the opposite to that of other colonial detectives like George Flower or Kilsip or Jasper Bodribb or even David Turner, all of whom end their novels as strong, settled, self-possessed and in most cases relatively prosperous ("rewarded") figures.

Duplicitous Characters

The actress turns out to be an important character in a number of late colonial Australian detective novels, which give her an exotic, promiscuous back-story that the detectives then delicately investigate. *The Mystery of a Hansom Cab*, *Madeline Brown's Murderer* and Charles Bradley's *The Belgrave Case: A Romance of Melbourne Life* (1891) all have an actress arriving in Melbourne from overseas who then triggers off a series of inquiries into fraudulent identities in the colonies. In each case she works literally as a disturbing, and seductive, influence. In Bradley's novel, Sybil Preston, the much younger wife of a colonial property investor, is revealed to have been a "notorious" actress from Europe called May Belgrave, who had once been married to a swindler and murderer, Maurice Blackmore. The "Blackmore frauds" are well known in England; so because of his notoriety, Blackmore changes his name to Learelle and emigrates to Australia. On the ship, Learelle/Blackmore becomes acquainted with a detective sent out by Scotland Yard to track him down, a man called Hearne Abagal:

> He was merely a plain sort of fellow, whom one could not help remarking had a plentiful force of character, of rather dark complexion and greyish eyes... Every line of his face betokened intelligence, sluggish certainly, and the perceptive faculties overhung the eyes with marked development... Dogged determination; a will of iron; an unrelenting hatred of that which dared betray his confidence; a subtlety so blended with candour, that none but a skilled physiognomist could comprehend correctly. Withal, this man is the stuff that success is made of; being not particularly brilliant, but constant, and with one motto ever before him, *perserverando*.[37]

Abagal is "sluggish" enough not to recognise Learelle and drops a vital clue – a photograph identifying Blackmore – at the beginning of the novel. But his perseverance enables him, finally, to solve the mystery. Abagal offers an outsider's slightly critical view of local detectives: "I found the Melbourne detectives very smart", he tells Learelle, "and think the service here equal in most respects to that of Scotland Yard, save the disguises may not be as clever. They appear too well known to the general public to have really fair opportunities" (9). This interesting view suggests that colonial detectives are like celebrities (actresses, for example), all too easily recognised – recalling Fergus Hume's description of Kilsip as "a favourite with every one". But the question of how well disguises work folds back ironically onto Abagal who cannot see that Learelle is really Blackmore. On the other hand, Blackmore's skills in fraud and imposture are equally well known throughout the colonies, not least to a wealthy colonial entrepreneur called Rowe Haddon, who is threatening to expose Sybil's past: "According to the reports", Haddon says, "it seems that Blackmore is a genius in the art of imitation. He can copy anything, even the tone of your voice, your gesture, your gait, your facial expression, and greater than all, your penmanship" (20). The novel is a complicated story of characters in disguise and mistaken or undercover identities, with the detective doggedly trying to unravel a series of mysteries that allow him first to wrongfully arrest Sybil for Haddon's murder and then to exonerate her by tracking a group of criminals through the streets of Melbourne, finally confronting Blackmore with the crime.

Returning to England at the end of the novel, Abagal regrets that it "was not altogether through his own ingenuity" that the crime was solved: as if the English detective is almost overwhelmed by the duplicities and vicissitudes of colonial Australian life. Sybil's husband George Preston is a property investor who lives in Toorak, but his financial predicament is unstable and he owes Haddon a significant amount of money. From one perspective, Haddon's murder provides some relief to the Preston family, because as well as wanting to expose Sybil, he aims to marry Preston's daughter by ruining her lover's financial reputation. Haddon is a thriving colonial capitalist without scruples, who projects a triumphant vision of Melbourne's future success:

> It is easy to divine from the present crisis. A revolution, the city in ashes, and, phoenix like, rising from the ruins a greater and more substantial organization. Don't you think this place is destined to become the chief city of the great southern empire, that in the transition of things cannot fail to be. (15)

But the novel never realises this vision of metropolitan order and success; instead, it takes the detective into the dark, labyrinthine Melbourne slums and through the chaotic streets in pursuit of his quarry. There is a connection to be drawn here between the nature of the detective's work – as an instrumental part of the "more substantial organisation" of colonial policing – and the financial instabilities of the late colonial economy. In both cases, there are almost no moments of insight or illumination. A rare exception is in any case accidental, literally solving the crime: a photograph is taken of the murderer in the act just as lightning strikes. But for most of the time events play themselves out in the shadows, as deals are done in secret, identities are altered, people are swindled and the

---

37 Charles Bradley, *The Belgrave Case: A Romance of Melbourne Life* (Melbourne: H.W. Mills & Co., 1891), 7. All subsequent references are to this edition and appear in parentheses in the text.

ongoing "transition of things" means the legibility of the city and its characters is subject to constant revision.

It has been commonplace in crime fiction criticism to associate metropolitan detection and policing not only with character legibility but also with the capacity to read and navigate urban spaces, subjecting them to modern techniques of surveillance and regulation. In his influential book *The Novel and the Police* (1988), D.A. Miller had drawn on the work of Michel Foucault to regard the detective – Mr Bucket in *Bleak House*, for example – as a sort of localised representation of a larger system of disciplinary power in which everyone ultimately (although often naively or unwittingly) participates. From this perspective, everyone can indeed become a detective. Christa Ludlow makes a related point in her article on second wave colonial Australian crime fiction, which, she argues, also enables *readers* to get involved in "the struggle for control of the colonial city and the right to represent it".[38] In a brief discussion of Henry Fletcher's bestselling detective novel, *The North Shore Mystery* (1899), Ludlow writes:

> For the reader, the city and its inhabitants did not exist until discovered, classified and made over into forms of knowledge. The reader investigated by reading or visualising, rather than venturing into the city. Through the new genres of crime fiction and crime journalism, readers were led to believe that they participated in the investigation – in fact they were encouraged to believe that urban spaces and their inhabitants could be "read" as criminal.[39]

For Ludlow, the answer to the question *who can become a detective?* could not be any more inclusive; but second wave colonial Australian detective novels are not always so democratic. Whereas Bradley's *The Belgrave Case* brings a detective over from London's Scotland Yard, Fletcher's *The North Shore Mystery* deals "entirely with an Australian subject, without any outside aid", as a review in the *Queenslander* put it.[40] The novel tells the story of an investigation into the murder of a wealthy businessman, whose body is found in his locked bedroom, stabbed in the back. A local sensation, it does indeed draw everyone into the mystery, as a newspaper report suggests: "On train, boat or bus, or wherever men are gathered together, it forms the sole and engrossing topic of conversation. Nearly every man one meets considers himself a born detective and has a solution of the mystery at his fingers' ends".[41] But the report also sees this as a kind of everyday delusion, insisting that ordinary people lack the real detective's capacity to solve the crime: "Unfortunately, however", it continues, "hardly two of three solutions agree, either as to the personality of the criminal or the method of the crime" (35).

D.A. Miller in fact sees the detective as an "eccentric" figure, set apart from the ordinary people whose lives he scrutinises[42] – a view that is consistent with our own understanding of the colonial detective as a "meta-character", a transcendent, post-*flaneurian* figure whose task is to make citizen identities in the colonial metropolis more

---

38 Ludlow, "The Reader Investigates", n.p.
39 Ludlow, "The Reader Investigates", n.p.
40 "Publications Received", *Queenslander*, 27 May 1899, 971.
41 Henry Fletcher, *The North Shore Mystery* (London: Swan Sonnenschein & Co., 1899), 35. All subsequent references are to this edition and appear in parentheses in the text.
42 D.A. Miller, *The Novel and the Police* (Berkeley: University of California Press, 1988), 35.

legible. *The North Shore Mystery* gives us four characters who might occupy this role: an ambitious police constable called Hobbs, who wants to solve a crime so he can be rewarded and promoted; a renowned detective, Dobell; a phrenologist, Professor Norris, who is a sort of Lavaterian expert in reading character; and Soft Sam, a kind of quasi-criminal type who teaches people how to make their fortune. Fletcher's novel is very much an exploration of ways of becoming financially successful in the colonies. The murder victim was initially one of several men romantically pursuing an attractive barmaid called Bertha, who makes no secret of her own financial aspirations:

> the world is full of beautiful things, nice things, and I want to have my share. What is the good of being so virtuous in a hurry? Why be too good, and better than other people? It makes you look peculiar and odd, and they don't like it. If the world's all wrong, then I will be wrong too; at any rate, I shall have plenty of company. Of course there is a medium in all things. I don't say it's right to do what is wicked and get money. Still money will do so much, smooth so much, that it seems to me just foolishness to say I don't want it. (137)

Bertha's view – that being "virtuous" is incompatible with making money – is broadly shared by other characters in the novel, some of whom (like the murderer) turn to criminal acts to acquire wealth. When her husband is found dead, Bertha becomes a suspect and is later arrested and imprisoned by Detective Dobell. But Dobell misreads Bertha's character, relying on a stereotype (of the "barmaid-with-a-past") that the novel does not uphold: "Detective Dobell began to feel uneasy. It was contrary to all his experience that a murderess, such as Mrs Booth appeared to be, should, up to the commission of the crime, have led a blameless life . . . " (232). Alec, the murder victim (and Bertha's husband by this time), is also ruled out as an effective investigator when he tries to solve the mystery of his wife's earlier abduction: "Doubtless if Alec had been endowed with half the imagination of a French detective he would have found his clue ample for the prosecution of an immediate chase. But imagination was distinctly not his forte. He could weave no theory, spin no web of conjecture . . . " (185).

The only two characters capable of penetrating the murderer's various disguises and reading the situation correctly are Constable Hobbs and Soft Sam. Hobbs in fact mistakes Sam at one point for "some expert detective brought from Melbourne or one of the other colonies" (246). But in fact, Sam transcends even the role of the detective, which he unceremoniously dismisses: "Any one but a regular detective or a duffer should be able to find it out [that is, to solve the crime] in five minutes" (247). Soft Sam is the opposite of Miller's "localised" detective, an omniscient character who assists the circulation of money, presiding over a broad network of both legitimate and criminal activities. His advice to colonial entrepreneurs is in fact to start from nothing and go immediately into debt, underwriting every venture with borrowed money:

> If a chap's smart enough for business, he's smart enough to start without capital . . . the more you owe the *right* people the safer you are. Who will help you when you are hard pushed? Your friend? Not a bit of it. Your creditors! . . . No man ever failed for debt. It was for not owing enough!" (98)

Hobbs, on the other hand, is a plodding police officer who nurses only one ambition, to *become* a detective – rather like a successful version of Gorby in *The Mystery of a Hansom*

Cab. The novel rewards him for this ambition, but only within his "localised", immediate perspective: "He felt happy and proud of himself. At any rate, he had beaten the much-vaunted Dobell so far. So pleased was he at that moment that if some peripatetic hawker had at that time called out 'prawns' in the street, he would have lavishly treated himself to a pint..." (253). At the end of the novel, Hobbs is promoted to sergeant and Bertha – who is now wealthy from her previous marriage ("I have heaps of money") – gives him 500 pounds to buy a house. The actual detective, Dobell, is peripheral to these events: we have come a long way from the decisive centrality of George Flower. *The North Shore Mystery* is a detective novel that is at the same time sceptical about the detective's role. Dobell fails, Police Constable Hobbs fumbles his way to the solution, and it turns out that Soft Sam – a kind of anti-detective who already knows the identity of the murderer – has the most insight into what colonial life is and what it might become. Soft Sam is the novel's "meta-character", to whom other characters turn for advice and information. He simultaneously enchants (by telling stories to children, for example, or helping people to get what they want) and disenchants (by taking away people's illusions and false hopes). He is a unique figure in colonial Australian fiction, a benign character in many respects who nevertheless sees the colonial economy as defined first and foremost by swindling and duplicity: a perspective that condemns the detective to only a minor, "localised" role, unable to address the bigger picture.

Hume Nisbet's *The Swampers*

Two years before *The North Shore Mystery*, the Scottish-born colonial novelist Hume Nisbet published *The Swampers* (1897): a controversial novel that had satirised the editor of the *Bulletin*, J.F. Archibald, who then threatened to sue Nisbet, his publisher and his printer. *The Swampers* begins by presenting colonial New South Wales as a place that "has always been regarded as a kind of paradise for the genteel rogue and swindler".[43] Soon afterwards it launches into a vivid attack on "the great and disastrous Australian land boom" in the colonies, where money grabbers seek get-rich-quick "paper fortunes" and where swindling is the order of the day. "There was no limit to the game", the novel tells us, "while it was being played by the reasonless or swindling mob" (128, 131). In the midst of all this, a notorious thief called Jack Milton takes charge of a criminal gang: "They were the keenest criminals in Sydney, who had managed to escape, for six full days, the supervision of the colonial detectives" (40). When Milton shoots a man in a bungled robbery attempt, his wife Rosa betrays him to the police and he flees Sydney. Disguising himself as "a sun-tanned and full-bearded bushman of fifty" (96), he heads for the Western Australian goldfields. Camping with a hut shepherd, Jack soon realises that he is being pursued by Aboriginal trackers, and almost gives up in despair. "The escaping prisoner from Siberia", the novel writes, "has several chances of eluding his pursuers, but Australia is nothing more than a vast prison yard, for even if they let him go now that they had seen him, it would only be to warn the South and West Australian police that he was coming... There was no hope, no escape" (202).

---

43   Hume Nisbet, *The Swampers: A Romance of the Westralian Goldfields* (London: F.V. White & Co., 1897), 127. All subsequent references are to this edition and appear in parentheses in the text.

3 Colonial Australian Detectives

It would seem (as it did to the bushrangers in Boldrewood's *Robbery Under Arms*) that effective police surveillance stretches right across the country; but in fact, Jack makes it to the goldfields without being apprehended. His ex-wife Rosa has gone to the goldfields too, with a new husband, Chester, to open a public house. They employ a barmaid, Sarah Hall, who has a daughter, Alice. It turns out that Sarah is being watched carefully by a detective, Wilmore, who knows about her past as a professional pickpocket in Melbourne – where she was also Jack's lover. Wilmore is different to other colonial detectives we have seen so far. For one thing, he is not particularly competitive or ambitious: "A quiet and amiable man of about forty-six was Inspector Wilmore, with sallow skin, clear, grey eyes, and close-cropped, dark brown beard . . . He was temperate and methodical in his habits, yet could be capital company when he liked" (302). Appearing only occasionally in the novel – and mostly towards the end – Wilmore is in many respects a minor figure. But he is also a "meta-character" who produces a crucial moment of Lavaterian insight when he and Sarah recognise each other in the bar: "They were both subtle students of human nature and were reading one another in that swift mutual glance" (303). Far from typecasting the barmaid (as Dobell had done), Wilmore grasps her inner life, seeing her as a redeemed figure with a hopeful future. Going against the grain of the merciless colonial detective, he lets her escape from Australia with Jack and their daughter: "it had been part of his secret duty to look after Sarah Hall since her coming to Western Australia, and he was now giving her her freedom from surveillance, to bury her past as far as he could" (237). The novel gives us a detective who uses his expertise not to read clues but to glean a character's inner qualities, which he understands sympathetically. His momentary insight completely changes the course of the narrative, which then literally transports its characters out of the "vast prison yard" of Australia, putting them finally well beyond its reach. The detective, we might say, works against his own type (and certainly, against the relentlessness of the police and Aboriginal trackers), by removing these criminals out of the range of his surveillance to some remote place, unnamed in the novel, where "at least that bugbear of civilization, the detectives, [would] have no chance of extradition" (312).

In a certain sense, Wilmore works as a *deus ex machina*, giving characters with criminal histories their freedom, allowing them to start over again. Stephen Knight has talked about *The Swampers* as one of several colonial novels about "constabular shadows, emerging from the background only to clear up the criminal chaos that is worked out through the switchback plots of outback dramas".[44] The job of policing Australia certainly goes on and the detective is afforded real significance here. The novel tells us towards the end that Wilmore "is looking after other criminals who are constantly springing up" (311), a description that suggests continued surveillance but also, interestingly, connotes some measure of sympathy for the culprits – and even hints at the possibility of police corruption (i.e. a detective "looking after" criminals). Even so, Wilmore clears up the criminal chaos only in a "localised" way. He steps in at the end of the novel in order to allow a redeemed character and her criminal associates to leave the country and lead honest lives somewhere else. He recognises the corrupt boom-and-bust economy that the novel projects, but his only option is to work within it – and the work is endless as more and more criminals keep "springing up". He has insight into a character's true nature, but no overarching critical capacity. *The Swampers* is a novel that launches a devastating attack on the precarious financial dealings of the 1890s, in relation to which the detective is now

---

44   Knight, *Continent of Mystery*, 118.

a much-diminished figure. In Lang's *The Forger's Wife*, George Flower was a muscular presence who had seen his role as directly linked to the interests of colonial governance and prosperity: with the aim of making settlers in New South Wales "more independent and secure . . . more economical and sensible". Flower was a major character type, an agent of retribution, remorselessly pursuing his criminals to the end. But Wilmore responds morally to a woman who was once a criminal but has now redeemed herself. In relation to colonial governance, Wilmore is powerless; in contrast to Flower, he is a minor character type, appearing only occasionally. But the novel brings him in at the end to perform a single sympathetic act that also goes against the conventional logic of the detective fiction genre. The last gasp of the late colonial detective is to allow his criminals to live "comfortably and honestly" in "a little colony" elsewhere, "respected by all who supply them with the comforts of life since they can meet their responsibilities". The detective's role here is, perhaps unexpectedly, one of enchantment in relation to a colonial Australian economy that is seen as little more than a debased form of swindling, wild speculation and rapidly accumulating debt. By releasing Sarah and her family from the "vast prison yard" of Australia, this otherwise peripheral figure produces a kind of microcosmic fantasy of what that economy might otherwise have been.

4
Bush Types and Metropolitan Types

For Don Watson in *The Bush* (2014), rural Australia is literally defined by the many different character types that inhabit it. "The bush", he writes,

> is squatter, selector, solider, settler, closer settler, blockie, timber worker, tin miner, drover, drover's wife, drover's dog, poet, prophet, fettler and racehorse. It is rabbiter, herd tester, shepherd, swagman, bush lawyer, bush mechanic, bushranger, grape grower, grain grower, potato grower, Country Party and Country Women's Association.[1]

This is, of course, an idiosyncratic assortment, one that could easily be expanded or modified (the shearer, the rouseabout, the boundary rider, the bullock-driver, the bush hawker, etc.). Such lists of representative bush types are never complete; and they routinely change over time, as new types emerge and others fade away. The idea of bush types fading away is a particularly resonant one, and it can often seem as if they are continually characterised – to draw on Raymond Williams' term again – by their "residual" status. We shall note in this chapter that bush types often *anticipated* the possibility of their own passing, especially in relation to the needs of a rapidly changing colonial economy. Watson makes exactly this point: "Dozens of different bush occupations have come and gone as capital found new ways to produce more with less labour, markets rejected one thing and demanded another, and modernity advanced from the cities".[2]

The view that colonial bush types were under threat from modernity only helped further to divide them from their metropolitan counterparts, making them all the more distinctive. By the 1850s, the distance and differences between bush and city were already apparent in the delineation of character types; it is generally agreed, however, that the valorisation of bush types at the expense of the city gained new intensity in the 1890s through *Bulletin* writers such as Henry Lawson and Steele Rudd. The figure of the "bushman" emerges here as a heroic type in a perpetually agonistic relationship to the bush itself. This is the point Tom Inglis Moore makes in his ground-breaking early critical analysis, *Social Patterns in Australian Literature* (1971):

---

1 Don Watson, *The Bush: Travels in the Heart of Australia* (Melbourne: Hamish Hamilton, 2014), 85.
2 Watson, *The Bush*, 85.

To be... exact, it was not the bush itself that was celebrated, but the bushmen. Contrary to popular opinion, the writing of the nineties does *not* glorify the bush. Rather it is a glorification of the bushmen versus the bush environment... [For] the *Bulletin* writers the bush is largely the means whereby the noble qualities of the bushmen are brought out – their courage and endurance in fighting the bush, their generosity and loyalty to a mate. It is the black shadow which throws up, in a simple, stark chiaroscuro, the light of the bush hero.[3]

The revival of what came to be called "cultural nationalism" in the 1950s saw left-wing writers such as Vance Palmer, Russel Ward and A.A. Phillips turn back to the *Bulletin* to further valorise the figure of the bushman as a way of defiantly reasserting the local values of an Australian literary tradition.[4] Russel Ward's *The Australian Legend* (1958) turned its attention in particular to bush workers, offering a list of local vocational types worth comparing with Don Watson's list above: "the semi-nomadic drovers, shepherds, shearers, bullock-drivers, stockmen, boundary-riders, station-hands, and others of the pastoral industry".[5] These different occupations are then collapsed into the single (and singular) figure of the bushman who, for Ward, is significant enough to be fully representative of the "national character".[6] Ward understood the bushman as a point of origin for Australian identity as it used to be. He then argued that this character type's charismatic influence travels in two directions, from the bottom up and from the bush to the city (rather than the other way around): "outback manners and *mores*, working upwards from the lowest strata of society and outwards from the interior, subtly influenced those of the whole population".[7] Drawing on the American historian Frederick Jackson Turner's notion of the frontiersman, Ward went on to characterise the Australian bush worker as both "heroic" and anti-authoritarian – although he thought the bush worker was more "collective" in temperament than his American counterpart, and much more itinerant, less tied to property ownership and settlement. To emphasise these latter points, and to further mythologise their influence on national character, Ward talked up the "mateship" of bush workers: something Don Watson doesn't see much evidence of in his more recent account ("Not in our neck of the bush").[8]

Ward had also described bush workers as a "nomad tribe", as if they were in some way "Aboriginal".[9] It has often been noted that his account of the "heroic" bushman "served to obscure the violence, especially the interracial violence, of frontier history".[10] Ward's recognition of Aboriginal people is indeed patronising at best: they are the "master and mentor" of bush workers (and they better perform some bush occupations, like "horse-breaking and cattle-mustering"), but bush workers are also their "heirs" and supplanters.[11]

---

3   Tom Inglis Moore, *Social Patterns in Australian Literature* (Berkeley: University of California Press, 1971), 78.
4   See, for example, Vance Palmer's chapter on "The Bushman's Bible", *The Legend of the Nineties* (Melbourne: Melbourne University Press, 1954).
5   Russel Ward, *The Australian Legend* (1958; Melbourne: Oxford University Press, 1974), 2.
6   Ward, *The Australian Legend*, 1.
7   Ward, *The Australian Legend*, 13.
8   Watson, *The Bush*, 103.
9   Ward, *The Australian Legend*, 245.
10 Angela Woollacott, *Settler Society in the Australian Colonies: Self-Government and Imperial Culture* (Oxford: Oxford University Press, 2015), 153.
11 Ward, *The Australian Legend*, 201.

Ian McLean refers to Ward's bush workers as "white Aborigines", writing that "their emergence incorporated Aboriginality into the new national mythos" – but this was premised on "the presumed extinction of the Aborigines whose land it was".[12] Ward's account of the bushman as an expression of national character has been critiqued in other ways, too. Graeme Davison inverted the trajectory of influence from bush to city by suggesting that Ward's "bush legend" was in fact mostly the product of Sydney *Bulletin* writers, all of whom "lived in the coastal cities, especially Sydney and Melbourne"; their disillusionment with colonial city life led them to invent the bush characteristics they needed, as a revitalising fantasy of origins.[13] For Kay Schaffer, Ward's "Australian legend" was also part of a broader effacement of the role of colonial women, who are "absent in the bush and the nationalist bush tradition".[14] We largely agree with this view – and like Schaffer, we shall therefore turn our attention to some of those exceptional moments where women do feature significantly in bush narratives. We begin this chapter by returning to the question of colonial violence and the frontier, looking firstly at the figure of the shepherd – and we will suggest that bush workers perform quite different ideological tasks, depending on the case. Reading literary representations of these types gives us very little evidence in support of Ward's view that bush workers were a "collective"; but nor were they individualised. As our book has argued, the cultural work done by colonial Australian fiction depends entirely on the character types it mobilises and the narratives they generate. The shepherd gives us a good example. His disposition, the tasks he performs and the contributions he makes, the encounters he has, the perspectives he articulates and the ways in which others regard or value him: these things all work together to give us a narrative built specifically around the shepherd as a *type*.

The Colonial Shepherd

In Chapter 1, we drew attention to Old Jock, the Scottish shepherd in Rolf Boldrewood's *A Squatter's Dream*, who presents colonial shepherding in a positive light as an elevated, Arcadian profession that offers bush workers "a calm sense o' joy and peace unknown to the dwellers in town" (291). This novel's pastoral view of the shepherd's predicament is only possible, however, as a late colonial romantic fantasy. In much earlier accounts, the day-to-day realities of a shepherd's experiences on the Australian frontier were in fact far removed from this ideal. Richard Howitt – William Howitt's brother – came to Australia in the early 1840s, buying a farm just outside of Melbourne. His *Impressions of Australia Felix, During Four Years' Residence in that Colony* (1845) is a candid account of the difficulties of emigration and settlement, going against the grain of much of the pro-emigration literature of the time. As both a landowner and a social commentator, Howitt is interested in the experiences of bush types like the shepherd. His English background leads him to assume that shepherding is a rewarding experience, but his view is soon corrected

---

12   Ian A. McLean, *White Aborigines: Identity Politics in Australian Art* (Cambridge: Cambridge University Press, 1998), 89.
13   Graeme Davison, "Sydney and the Bush: An Urban Context for the Australian Legend", *Australian Historical Studies* 18:71 (October 1978), 208.
14   Kay Schaffer, *Women and the Bush: Forces of Desire in the Australian Cultural Tradition* (Cambridge: Cambridge University Press, 1988), xii.

by the locals: "I have observed to shepherds and hut-keepers what a pleasant kind of life they seemed to have of it; the answer was a negative shake of the head". Howitt comes to realise that the realities of colonial shepherding in the 1840s are at once more monotonous, and more brutal, than he had initially imagined: "if he does not get killed and embowelled by the natives, [he will] go down through many dull years into an unlamented, lonely Bush grave. Such is the Arcadian life of the Australian shepherd!"[15]

The colonial shepherd is important to the business of settlement because – in these early accounts – he is invariably positioned on the very edge of the frontier. The frontier is generally understood as a place; but it is also defined as a particular moment in *time* during the history of settlement. In *Out of the Silence: The History and Memory of South Australia's Frontier Wars* (2012), Robert Foster and Amanda Nettlebeck use the term "frontier" to refer to "that phase of European settlement from the time when settlers first intruded into Aboriginal country to the point when colonial authority over Aboriginal people was effectively established".[16] In colonial fiction, of course, a range of different character types are shown to be involved in the establishment of colonial authority over Aboriginal people. Some of these are prominent and central, like the squatter, who is influential enough here to be given his own genre, the *squatter novel*. Others, like the shepherd, are minor or peripheral figures in this process. There is no such thing as the *shepherd novel* in Australia: shepherds inhabit novels built around other character types (like the squatter) but they are never credited with enough importance to sustain a prolonged narrative. The short story is their designated form. Even so, this character type plays out a role that is pivotal to "the growth of the colonies".[17] Foster and Nettlebeck chart the murders of a number of South Australian shepherds by Aboriginal people in the 1840s and 1850s. "In June 1848", they write, "shepherd John Hamp, who worked on William Pinkerton's Stoney Point Station on the western extreme of this new frontier, was waddied to death. In the following month on the same station, shepherd Charles Goldsmith was attacked as he tried to defend his sheep . . . " These attacks could bring the imposition of colonial law down upon Aboriginal people (trial, imprisonment, execution). But they could also unleash "lawless" reprisals: "Wherever Aboriginal attacks occurred, settlers or their shepherds would be sure to retaliate".[18] The shepherd here is on the one hand a disposable figure, the first casualty on the front line of colonial violence. On the other hand, he is instrumental in the perpetuation of that violence, an agent for the colonial project: consistent with our understanding of the role of *minor* character types, his influence outstrips his importance.

Foster and Nettlebeck discuss an exaggerated account of the 1849 murder by Aboriginal people of a shepherd's "young and pretty wife" in the Port Lincoln district: "stories of reprisals for Annie Easton's death", they note, "have circulated ever since and remain strong in local social memory to the present day".[19] Ellen Liston had arrived in South Australia just a year after this murder. In the late 1860s she went to work as a governess at Nilkerloo Station on the west coast of Eyre Peninsula, "one of the remotest

---

15 Richard Howitt, *Impressions of Australia Felix, During Four Years' Residence in that Colony* (London: Longman, Brown, Green & Longmans, 1845), 293.
16 Robert Foster and Amanda Nettlebeck, *Out of the Silence: The History and Memory of South Australia's Frontier Wars* (Adelaide: Wakefield Press, 2012), 6.
17 John Pickard, "Shepherding in Colonial Australia", *Rural History* 19:1 (2008), 76.
18 Foster and Nettlebeck, *Out of the Silence*, 84.
19 Foster and Nettlebeck, *Out of the Silence*, 137.

edges of Britain's empire".[20] Liston subsequently published a number of stories about events in the region, one of which reimagines Annie Easton's frontier encounter. "Doctor" (1882) is a story of the early days of settlement, narrated by a young shepherd's wife, Kit, who is pregnant with her second child. She is "the first white woman of the district".[21] The emphasis here is on the remoteness of the frontier in both geographical and temporal terms. "You colonists of to-day", Kit tells us, "have very little idea, if any, of what our life as pioneers in the far bush was in those days. We were one hundred and forty miles from the most embryo township . . ." (44). The shepherd's wife and her family live right at the far edge of this frontier, their location defined only in terms of their relation to other outlying shepherds and to the squatter's station: "Our hut was quite alone, the Three Peaks were fifteen miles away; ten miles in one direction was a shepherd's hut, and five miles the opposite way was another" (44). When her husband is out with the flock, Kit senses an "uncomfortable presence" in the hut and finds herself confronted by a naked "powerful blackfellow". "I knew him", she writes; "Coomultie by name, and by report one of the worst and most brutal of his tribe" (44). Coomultie kills her sheep dog and is about to attack the shepherd's wife and her child when Doctor – a mysterious stray dog that has been hanging around – suddenly rushes in and mauls him to death.

It is worth briefly contrasting the shepherd's wife's experience here with Lawson's iconic story about a related character type, "The Drover's Wife", published ten years later in the *Bulletin* in 1892. Like Kit, the drover's wife is left at home with her children while her husband, an ex-squatter, is away with his sheep. Their hut is isolated (surrounded by bush), but it is no longer on the frontier. Even so, the story gives us an exact replication of Kit's encounter in Liston's "Doctor". The important difference here is that the threatening intruder is now not a "brutal" Aboriginal man but a large black snake, "a black brute, five feet long";[22] and it is the family dog – rather than a stray – that rushes in to maul it to death. So "The Drover's Wife" is a post-frontier story, one that seems to draw explicit attention to its residual position in the aftermath of violent encounters with Aboriginal people. It replicates (almost to the letter) the nature of that encounter, but holds it at a symbolic distance. The Aboriginal people who *do* appear in Lawson's story are now integrated into a "settled" colonial world, emasculated and no longer threatening. At one point, the drover's wife "bargained with a stray blackfellow to bring her some wood" and when he seems to do a good job she praises him "for not being lazy".[23] Lawson's throwaway comment that this Aboriginal man "was the last of his tribe and a King" helps to underscore the residual role that frontier violence plays in his story, reminding us again that "The Drover's Wife" does indeed come after that moment when (as Foster and Nettlebeck put it) "colonial authority over Aboriginal people was effectively established".

We shall now examine some short stories about shepherds on the frontier published by other mid-nineteenth–century colonial Australian authors who, rather like Liston, have long been forgotten. We mentioned Horace Earle in the Introduction, a writer who came to Australia from England in the 1850s to work on the Victorian goldfields. Earle was also

---

20 Rick Hosking, "Ellen Liston's 'Doctor' and the Elliston Incident", in *Southwords: Essays on South Australian Writing*, ed. Philip Butterss (Adelaide: Wakefield Press, 1995), 62.
21 Ellen Liston ("Ellie L..."), "Doctor", *Adelaide Observer*, 17 June 1882, 44. All subsequent references are to this edition and appear in parentheses in the text.
22 Henry Lawson, "The Drover's Wife", in *While the Billy Boils: The Original Newspaper Versions*, ed. Paul Eggert (Sydney: Sydney University Press, 2013), 70.
23 Lawson, "The Drover's Wife", 69.

in India during the 1857 rebellion, employed by the East India Company. In the 1860s he returned to Australia and settled in Brisbane; a friend of James Brunton Stephens, he was one of the founders of the local Johnsonian Club, devoted to the promotion of literary culture.[24] But Earle was also heavily invested in colonial commercial life. He became editor of the *Week: A Journal of Commerce* in the mid-1870s, serialising a number of his novels in its pages, including *The Squatter and His Protegé* and *Settlement in Full*; later on, he took over editorship of the *Queensland Mercantile Gazette* and published an important book on the region's commerce and industries in 1886. So we can see Earle as a settler who was committed to economic development in the colonial world: something that significantly colours his literary writing. His earlier collection of short stories, *Ups and Downs; or, Incidents of Australian Life* (1861), contains two accounts of shepherd experiences on the frontier. The first, "Revenge; or, Jem Dalton", gives us an embittered, menacing shepherd who clashes with his employer, the squatter Mr Wootherspoon. This story tells us that a shepherd's influence can go in two opposite directions, depending on his disposition: "A shepherd has it in his power to do much harm, from malice or negligence; or he can enhance the value of his charge to an immense extent".[25] Jem Dalton is credited with enough power to significantly damage a squatter's property: his negligence in allowing dingoes to attack the flock anticipates the squatter Gilbert's claim in Rolf Boldrewood's "The Fencing of Wanderowna" that "Shepherds are about one degree better than wild dogs – with which beasts of prey... they rather sympathise".[26] This negative view of shepherds may in fact have been a prevailing one: in his article "Shepherding in Colonial Australia", John Pickard provides a remarkable string of adjectives taken from commentary at the time which saw shepherds described as "aimless, anti-social, careless, crazy, demanding, diseased, dishonest, drunken, filthy, foul-mouthed, improvident, incompetent, indolent, lacking ambition, misanthropic, perfidious, sullen, truculent, unlettered, useless, witless".[27] In Earle's story, Dalton is also illiterate and violently abuses his wife. He takes his revenge on the squatter by deliberately infecting a large number of sheep with a virulent disease: so this is a shepherd who brings the negative commentary directed towards this type to a logical (and disastrous) conclusion.

In stark contrast, Earle's second shepherd story – "Ned White; or, The Shepherd's Hut" – binds this character type much more closely to the pastoral ideology of the squatter. A wealthy squatter's son wonders why Ned is so well remunerated. Ned then tells him the story of the station's settlement, at a time when Aboriginal people were "as thick as bees" (219). First there is the squatter's log hut; then a kitchen garden is established, with grape vines that soon produce "first-rate wine". Later on, the squatter hires more employees including an overseer ("a dandy kind of fellow"), builds a large brick homestead, and gets married (222). This is a story, then, that gives a direct account of the establishment and expansion of colonial settlement. One day, Ned and the overseer go out on horseback

---

24 See "Death of Mr H. Earle", Brisbane *Telegraph*, 3 June 1919, 5; see also Leanne Day, "'Those Ungodly Pressmen': The Early Years of the Brisbane Johnsonian Club", *Australian Literary Studies* 21:1 (2003), 92–102.
25 Horace Earle, *Ups and Downs; or, Incidents of Australian Life* (London: A.W. Bennett, 1861), 230. All subsequent references are to this edition and appear in parentheses in the text.
26 Boldrewood, "The Fencing of Wanderowna: A Tale of Australian Squatting Life" *Australian Town and Country Journal*, 7 June 1873, 18. This serialised novella was later reprinted in *A Romance of Canvas Town* (London: Macmillan & Co., 1898).
27 Pickard, "Shepherding in Colonial Australia", 73.

together, "and he showed me the limits of the governor's station, which I found was greatly enlarged" (223). Ned and his wife join the squatter and some carpenters in an outlying "log-hut" at the edge of the station. A stockman arrives to tell them that around eighty armed Aboriginal men are gathering nearby, and not long afterwards the hut is under attack and a pitched battle ensues. Doors are broken down, Ned's wife is speared; the shepherd, the squatter and the others retaliate in a frenzy of violence, killing everyone around them. "The governor", Ned tells the boy, "was soon almost up to his middle in black fellows" and "the ground all round our hut was covered with blood" (226). This is a story that relishes its moment of carnage on the frontier, presenting it as a necessary phase in the "effective establishment" of settler colonial authority. What is also interesting here is the way the shepherd is completely defined through his participation in this narrative of settler domination. "There", Ned concludes, "that's the beginnin', middle, and end of the old shepherd's story" (229). This character type is there at the inception of settlement, he is an active participant (and an "equal" to the squatter) in securing it through violent encounters on the frontier, and he reaps the benefits in the aftermath. But this is also the "end" of his story and his usefulness: as "the old shepherd" tells the squatter's son about these earlier colonial days, he already recognises his status as a residual or even "archaic" figure, his role in the narrative of settlement now complete.

Like Earle, N. Walter Swan came to Victoria in the 1850s to work on the goldfields; later on, he settled in Ararat and became editor of its local newspaper. A friend of Marcus Clarke, Swan occasionally attended the Yorick Club in Melbourne. He moved to Stawell in 1869, investing in local industry and taking over the editorship of the *Pleasant Creek News*.[28] Swan's first collection of stories, *Tales of Australian Life*, was published in London in 1875 – and dedicated to the wife of Alexander Wilson, a wealthy squatter from the Western District. Included in this collection is "Two Days at Michaelmas", which had first appeared in the *Australasian* on 2 August 1873. Hugh Hardy, the narrator, is a newly appointed hut keeper at Michaelmas Hut. This story once again takes us back to the early days of colonial settlement (probably the 1840s), and is set in Queensland. In the title of Earle's "Ned White; or, The Shepherd's Hut" we can see how closely aligned a shepherd is to his place of habitation. In Swan's story, the hut itself becomes a powerful symbol of the process of settlement in this early phase, presented here as an almost animated thing that defiantly stakes its claim on the frontier:

> I always used to think the cedar logs of Michaelmas Hut put on a bold, devil-may-care look from breakfast time till the supper hour. They appeared to gather a stimulant from the sun, and to gain courage with the warmth. At noon the house was red and confident; towards evening it glowered furiously from under the leaves of the bunya-bunya like a bloodshot eye.[29]

Hardy soon becomes deeply affected by the hut's brooding but "singularly handsome" shepherd, who comes to inhabit his thoughts: "He lived in my light sleep and among my uneasy dream through the long slow hours till the pale light that tided up against the

---

28 See Harry Heseltine, introduction to N. Walter Swan's *Luke Miver's Harvest* (Sydney: UNSW Press, 1991): http://setis.library.usyd.edu.au/ozlit/pdf/p00083.pdf.
29 N. Walter Swan, "Two Days at Michaelmas", *Australasian*, 2 August 1873, 5. All subsequent references are to this edition and appear in parentheses in the text.

stars" (5). The hut is effectively a small fort on the frontier, armed and defended; and the shepherd grimly implies that his task is to kill Aboriginal people without hesitation: "I, the shepherd", he tells Hardy, "approve of the arrangement, knowing it to be the best" (5). In contrast to Earle's story where the shepherd and squatter work side by side, here the squatter is remote from the hut and its dangers. It is the shepherd who takes charge, using his own judgement to determine how much violence he dispenses. When he returns one evening, he complains to Hardy and some fencers about "Doctor Bird", the writer, as he explains, "of *Nick of the Woods*". Robert Montgomery Bird was an American author and playwright who trained as a physician in the early 1840s. His bestselling novel *Nick of the Woods; or, The Jibbenainosay: A Tale of Kentucky* (1837) tells of a Quaker in the 1780s who – when his wife and children are killed by native Americans – takes systematic, murderous revenge and is never held legally accountable. In Swan's story this novel sets off a discussion about the ethics of violence on the colonial frontier. "It's an absurd tale", the shepherd tells the hut keeper:

> "People don't meet with the escapes of the Quaker. It's one of our cheap romances, you know, and cheapness and sensationalism go together. It's only hut literature . . . Is there any excuse for taking away life?"
> "I don't know, the law must hang sometimes".
> "But outside the law?"
> "Outside the law people call it murder".
> He [the shepherd] stepped to the centre of the floor towards me, with an ugly look in his eyes. The firm mouth, the white teeth, and a slight shifting of trouble in his look, gave him that handsome, dangerous appearance that was so eminently his.
> "It depends on the provocation, sir, whether the taking away of life can be called murder". (5)

In this exchange, a character type – the shepherd – names the genre in which he is implicated: *hut literature*. But he also criticises the genre for its "cheapness and sensationalism". Swan's story therefore plays out an ambivalent relationship to Bird's murderous Kentucky saga. The next morning, Hardy sees shapes moving outside, reflected in his shaving mirror. The shepherd returns, takes a gun and an old pistol and begins to shoot Aboriginal men who are gathering outside. Soon afterwards, the shepherd goes in search of more Aboriginal men to kill, leaving the hut keeper alone in the hut. This is where the story (in contrast to Earle's "Ned White") distances itself from the "sensationalism" of "hut literature". Hardy goes outside and finds one of the shepherd's victims, paralysed by a bullet in the spine: "the wild clouded eyes came up and rested on my face . . . as he held one open hand above his head and then the other to show me he was unarmed" (5). This momentary encounter brings the hut keeper into a kind of intimate proximity with the human cost of frontier warfare; but he, too, is paralysed, unable either to help the wounded man or to see the logic of colonial violence through to its endpoint by killing him.

The shepherd is also wounded in the skirmish, but he gets the chance to recover, and live. It turns out that the shepherd's fiancée had been killed by Aboriginal people some time before, which structurally links this character to Bird's protagonist in *Nick of the Woods*, as a vigilante figure driven by personal revenge. The story ends five years later in the squatter's lavish homestead, Peckham House, with its "far-off sounds of closing doors, the drawing-room under repressed light, the carpet under repressed footsteps" (5). This fascinating passage tells us about both the consolidation of colonial authority and the way it relies on the concealment of the violent events and processes that made it possible. Hardy is there, his name now changed; and the shepherd is now a "gentleman" with white hair and "a plain gold ring". He is a shepherd who, as Hardy notes, has given up "shepherding": an occupation that in this story works as a euphemism for killing Aboriginal people on the frontier. It only remains for this ex-shepherd to renounce this earlier vigilantism, distancing himself once and for all from Bird's vicious protagonist. "No blighted hope", he says, "though it ruins a life, excuses murder" (5). In Earle's "Ned White", the old shepherd presents us with a story that highlights "the beginnin', middle, and end" of the processes of early settlement. Swan's "Two Days at Michaelmas" ends in the same way, taking us back to Foster and Nettlebeck's notion of the frontier as something *temporal*, "that phase of European settlement . . . " The story ends by making exactly the same point, and in the process it rejects the idea that the squatter's homestead could indeed successfully "repress" the bloodshed it was founded upon: "Read the phases of colonial life", Hardy insists: "The page is open" (5).

The Swagman

The swagman emerged as a recognisable type in the 1860s, also sometimes referred to at the time as a *sundowner* or *scowbanker*. In an article in the *Argus* on 11 May 1857, Henry R. Rae thought that the term *scowbanker* derives from "skull banker", someone "who carried his purse in his skull":[30] suggesting a character type who lives by his wits, a con artist of some kind. In the late 1860s the Melbourne author, editor and publisher Donald Cameron wrote a series of articles for the *Australian Journal* under the general heading "Australian Characters". His article on "The Scowbanker" begins by noting the various sub-species of this particular type:

> The scowbanker is essentially an Australian character, brought into existence by the hospitality which the distance of settled places from each other has necessitated, and the lazy *dolce far niente* habits of pastoral life. He has a great many names besides this one; he is called a "swagman", a "schemer", a "Murrumbidgee bird", a "bloodsucker" (acquired from sucking shearer's earnings), a "Condaminer", and various other appropriate adjectives.[31]

We can see in this passage a clear distinction between the scowbanker/swagman and the shepherd: the former is now *post*-frontier, literally emerging out of "settled places", that is, *after* the "effective establishment" of settler colonial authority. The shepherd (in some accounts, at least) is crucial to the growth of a pastoral economy, killing and dispersing Aboriginal people and helping to extend the range of the squatter's station. But Cameron gives quite a different account of the scowbanker. "Whenever the plough invades the district", he writes, "the scowbanker, like the kangaroo, hastens away from the contaminated place".[32] In this interesting remark, settlement and invasion are collapsed together –

---

30 Henry R. Rae, "A Working Man on 'Popular Meetings'", *Argus*, 11 May 1857, 6.
31 Donald Cameron, "The Scowbanker", *The Australian Journal*, 9 February 1867, 375.
32 Cameron, "The Scowbanker", 375.

although, in this *post*-frontier moment, it is the scowbanker who is now dispersed. On the other hand, he continually returns to disturb the equilibrium of station life. In Cameron's narrative, a group of station workers in a shepherd's hut are alarmed when a swagman, Bill Walker, suddenly appears outside: "they beheld a nondescript figure, which they instantly recognised as belonging to the genus 'swagman'".[33] One of the shepherds contemptuously calls Walker a scowbanker. "'Now, I objec's to that name!' said Bill; 'I entirely objec's to it. I calls myself a philos'pher – a gum-tree philos'pher'".[34] The encounter between the swagman and the station workers throws *lumpenproletariat* and *proletariat* together, to recall our discussion of these terms in the Introduction to this book. Bill Walker certainly fits Henry Mayhew's description of "those who will not work" in *London Labour and the London Poor*: "I goes lookin' for work hopin' I won't find it", he brazenly tells the shepherds. Instead, he plays his concertina for them; the station workers dance and drink and finally fall asleep; they neglect their flock, which is attacked by dingoes; and the next day the swagman disappears and the workers find they have been both robbed and laid off.

The swagman soon became a colonial problem, easily demonised and generally maligned. Newspapers during the 1860s routinely commented on the question of what to do with this character type. Cameron's point that the swagman is "brought into existence by the hospitality" of bush properties comes in the wake of debate about just how generous settlers should be when this character type turns up at their door. A syndicated article from April 1864 says that "the swagman now, through our mistaken kindness, is a disgrace to our country, and I hope a united effort will be made to raise him from the ranks of a worthless and disreputable pauper to that of a respectable workman".[35] But the swagman stubbornly reaffirms his parasitical *lumpenproletarian* identity. An article in the New South Wales–based *Maitland Mercury and Hunter River General Advertiser* in August 1867 reports that: "Some few days past a migratory pest, in the shape of a huge dirty brute of a swagman, called at a cattle station upon the Barwon, and finding no person at home but the superintendent's wife, without any ceremony he helped himself to whatever he fancied, silencing all expostulations by threats".[36] The sense that a swagman can abuse bush generosity is magnified in Marcus Clarke's story "Pretty Dick" (1869), when a lost boy in the bush recalls with horror a local tale of murder, where

> two swagmen, after eating and drinking, had got up in the bright, still night, and beaten out the brains of the travelling hawker, who gave them hospitality, and how, the old man being found beside his rifled cart, with his gray hairs matted with blood, search was made for the murderers, and they were taken in a tap-room in distant Hamilton, bargaining with the landlord for the purchase of their plunder . . .[37]

In Clarke's *Long Odds* (1869), a dying swagman appears at the end of the novel and turns out to be Cyril Chatteris, a villainous schemer who – after murdering a rival – has fled to Australia. The woman he had ruthlessly pursued is now happily married to a wealthy

---

33 Cameron, "The Scowbanker", 375.
34 Cameron, "The Scowbanker", 376.
35 "Swagmen – How to Improve Their Circumstances", *Border Watch*, 22 April 1864, 2; see also *Brisbane Courier*, 23 June 1864, 2.
36 "Walgett", *Maitland Mercury and Hunter River General Advertiser*, 17 August 1867, 2.
37 Marcus Clarke, "Pretty Dick", *Australian Tales* (Melbourne: Marion Clarke, 1896), 12.

squatter; when some local workers bring the swagman to the station, the couple recognise him. Chatteris also has his own final moment of recognition, after which his previous identity completely evaporates, absorbed into the character type he has now become: "the ragged figure fell back upon the hurdle, and was in an instant nothing more than the sordid corpse of some nameless swagman".[38]

The representation of the swagman as a violent threat to settlers was fuelled by newspaper reports such as the widely circulated article about the attempted rape and murder of a farmer's wife near Echuca in central Victoria in October 1865. A farmer, Michael O'Brien, had surrendered himself to the police after pursuing and shooting dead a swagman, later identified as Thomas Dunn. It turns out that Dunn had arrived at O'Brien's farm, finding his wife Honora there, alone with her child. "The man now lying dead came to the outside fence of my hut yesterday", she later testifies,

> and asked for something to eat and a drink. I had nothing to give him to eat, but I gave him some water, which he threw away, and immediately grasped me by the neck with both hands, and nearly choked me. He tried to raise up my clothes, and threw me on the ground . . . He endeavoured to take improper liberties with me, but I resisted until my husband came.[39]

Honora O'Brien's account turns on the rapid shift from the swagman's request for bush hospitality (which she is unable to offer him) to sexual violence. Her husband hears her screams and crosses the Campaspe River to come to her aid: "I asked my wife what was the matter", he says, "and she replied that the man had been murdering her and that she was almost dead". A witness later finds Honora O'Brien "lying on the bed vomiting": "She told me that she had been ill-treated by a swagman, who had caught her by the neck, and that he was shot".[40]

It is worth comparing this attack with what is perhaps the best-known account of a menacing swagman in colonial fiction, Barbara Baynton's "The Tramp" (1896): first published in the *Bulletin* and later collected in *Bush Studies* (1902) under the revised title (and with some significant narrative changes), "The Chosen Vessel". Here – as we saw earlier in Ellen Liston's story and in Lawson's "The Drover's Wife" – a woman and her child are alone in a remote hut. Her husband, a shearer who mistreats and abuses his wife, is absent. The woman is already "terrified" of swagmen, as if this character type is now completely synonymous with predatory behaviour.[41] A swagman arrives at her door and she offers him food. But he wants more: "Then he asked for money . . . "[42] He pretends to leave but she is suspicious and – when night falls – she tries to fortify her hut from the inside to prevent him from entering. The swagman returns to the property, lurking outside with "cruel eyes, lascivious mouth, and gleaming knife" (136). When she hears a passing horseman, the woman runs out of the hut with her baby – but the swagman is waiting for her "with outstretched arms that caught her as she fell": "She knew he was offering terms if she ceased to

---

38   Marcus Clarke, *Long Odds: A Novel* (Melbourne: Clarson, Massina, 1869), 343.
39   "A Man Shot Dead near Echuca", *Leader*, 21 October 1865, 5.
40   "A Man Shot Dead near Echuca", 5.
41   Lawson's "The Drover's Wife" gives us the same gendered sense of threat: "Occasionally . . . a villainous-looking 'sundowner' comes and scares the life out of her", 67.
42   Barbara Baynton, "The Chosen Vessel", *Bush Studies* (1902; Sydney: Angus & Robertson, 1989), 133. All subsequent references are to this edition and appear in parentheses in the text.

struggle and cry for help, though louder and louder did she cry for it, but it was only when the man's hand gripped her throat, that the cry of 'Murder' came from her lips" (136-7).

Baynton's story has been important to a number of feminist reconsiderations of colonial women's experiences in the bush.[43] More recently, Nina Philadelphoff-Puren has examined Baynton's story in relation to the *Bulletin* and its hostile view towards female victims of sexual assault – especially in relation to the 1886-87 Mount Rennie rape case, in which a young domestic servant in Sydney was sexually assaulted by a city cabman and some members of "the local larrikin push".[44] The *Bulletin* had consistently characterised this young woman as sexually active and morally dubious, writing her "into the character of the prostitute" in order to discredit her account of the brutal attack.[45] The mother in Baynton's story, by contrast, is written into "the Victorian archetype of feminine virtue". Her violation and murder "unfolds the only plot-line about rape which [the *Bulletin*] was prepared to accept as 'real' – that is, the rape of a 'really virtuous woman' in the 'lonely bush'".[46] But Philadelphoff-Puren also suggests that Baynton's story relies on a "remarkable *over-writing* of the position of the perpetrator", that is, the swagman.[47] In Baynton's story, the swagman seems to actualise the absent husband's abusive disposition; the "threat of rape by strangers" is thus a displaced expression of a husband's already demonstrated sexual aggression towards his wife. Philadelphoff-Puren is right to note the general anxiety in the 1890s about the "lonely bush woman's" sexual vulnerability in relation to marauding or itinerant men; but this kind of anxiety has had a much longer colonial history, manifesting itself at least as far back as the 1860s – the time of the Echuca case we have outlined above. In December 1867, the Melbourne *Argus* editorialised:

> In the country districts of the colony women are frequently left for long periods together their own and sole protectors; and this, added to the large preponderance of the male over the female portion of the population, has wisely induced our legislators to visit with capital punishment the gravest offence which, next to murder, it is possible to commit.[48]

Amanda Kaladelfos has written extensively about debates concerning rape and capital punishment in the Australian colonies. Prior to the 1860s, the focus is primarily on Aboriginal perpetrators: "The punishment of Aboriginal men for rape", she notes, "attracted considerable public attention in frontier regions during the mid-nineteenth century".[49] This is another illustration of the "effective establishment" of settler colonial authority during the frontier phase. After this moment, however, colonial law extends its range to encompass peripheral settler types like the swagman – or, in the Mount Rennie case, the larrikin. Kaladelfos makes exactly this point: "it was . . . important that the law be seen to protect the

---

43   See, for example, Susan Sheridan, introduction to Barbara Baynton's *Bush Studies* (Sydney: Sydney University Press, 2009), v-xi; Schaffer, *Women and the Bush*, 150–70.
44   Nina Philadelphoff-Puren, "Reading Rape in Colonial Australia: Barbara Baynton's 'The Tramp', the *Bulletin* and Cultural Criticism", *JASAL: Journal of the Association for the Study of Australian Literature* 2 (2010): http://openjournals.library.usyd.edu.au/index.php/JASAL/article/view/10169.
45   Philadelphoff-Puren, "Reading Rape in Colonial Australia", 4.
46   Philadelphoff-Puren, "Reading Rape in Colonial Australia", 7.
47   Philadelphoff-Puren, "Reading Rape in Colonial Australia", 9.
48   Editorial, *Argus*, 9 December 1867, 4.
49   Amanda Kaladelfos, "The Politics of Punishment: Rape and the Death Penalty in Colonial Australia, 1841–1901", *History Australia* 9:1 (2012): 171.

beacons of 'civilisation' – virtuous white colonial women – in danger from the 'vagabonds' of Australia's penal past and Indigenous people".[50] In the Echuca case, Michael O'Brien was brought to trial for killing the swagman, but public sympathy prevailed and he was finally acquitted. Just before his trial, the *Leader* reprinted an editorial from the rural newspapers that traded on popular sentiment about the need to protect colonial women, mothers especially:

> Possibly of late no crime has been so much on the increase as outrages upon women and children, and we have little hesitation in saying that the prompt vengeance visited upon Thomas Dunn will have more effect in deterring brutes of a similar stamp from similar deeds than fear of the law. It may seem harsh to say so, and we are no advocates of a system of Lynch justice, but we cannot refrain from expressing our deliberate conviction that such is the case.[51]

This editorial aimed to influence the outcome of the trial by lending its support to O'Brien's defence. In the Echuca case, the husband protects his wife from the swagman by executing him; he goes to trial, but a prevailing sense that colonial women must be protected – alongside the popular demonisation of the swagman as a sexual threat – helps to secure his acquittal. In Baynton's "The Chosen Vessel", by contrast, the swagman is a kind of proxy for the husband. They both equally threaten the colonial mother's safety. There is no protection for the woman in this story, and there is no settler vengeance and no invocation of the law and its threat of capital punishment. "The Chosen Vessel" gives us a momentary hope when a horseman riding past the hut sees the woman as she tries to escape. But Baynton strips even this possibility of protection away from her, with the man utterly preoccupied by his Catholic faith and unable to recognise the crime as it unfolds.[52] The swagman in this case manages to evade all forms of justice (including "Lynch justice") and survives, with the story offering only a modest concluding gesture towards a moral after-effect: "the sight of blood made the man tremble" (140).

The swagman's capacity for survival is always limited, however. This character type is always dying or disappearing: a view that was made famous, of course, in Banjo Paterson's "Waltzing Matilda" (1895), where a swagman, pursued for the theft of a sheep by a squatter and a police officer on horseback, drowns himself in a water-hole. As Michael Farrell puts it, the swagman in this poem "chooses death over detention", refusing to submit himself to colonial law and risk losing his itinerant freedom.[53] Matthew Richardson suggests that Paterson had drawn on some actual local examples of drowned or suicidal swagmen for his poem: "If the swagman is a hero", he suggests, "he's hardly one to emulate – not for a listener with a future at least".[54] The dead or disappearing swagman became a readily

---

50   Kaladelfos, "The Politics of Punishment", 175.
51   "Echuca", *Leader*, 28 October 1865, 17.
52   Interestingly, this character – Peter Hennessey – turns away from the sexually abused woman and decides to vote for a political candidate who serves "the interests of the squatter". For a longer discussion of Hennessey's role in Baynton's story – and the role of colonial "masculinity" more broadly – see Schaffer's discussion in *Women and the Bush*, 163–70.
53   Michael Farrell, "Death Watch: Reading the Common Object of the Billycan in 'Waltzing Matilda'", *JASAL: Journal of the Association for the Study of Australian Literature* 10 (2010), 7.
54   Matthew Richardson, *Once a Jolly Swagman: The Ballad of Waltzing Matilda* (Melbourne: Melbourne University Press, 2006), 88.

available trope: by the 1890s, this character type is sighted only occasionally in colonial fiction, departing almost as soon as he arrives – although he also lingers on as a kind of residue, like the ghostly voice of "Waltzing Matilda's" swagman-suicide. In Henry Lawson's "Brummy Usen" (1893) – collected in *While the Billy Boils* (1896) – an "old swagman" talks about men being "reported dead" in the bush. "I've been dead a few times myself", he confesses, "and found out afterwards that my friends was so sorry about it, and that I was such a good sort of a chap, after all, when I was dead that – that I was sorry I didn't stop dead".[55] *While the Billy Boils* introduces a more iconic swagman, Jack Mitchell, who comes and goes through a number of stories here and elsewhere. In "That Swag (Enter Mitchell)", "a lot of ordinary passengers and one swagman" arrive in Sydney by train: as if this figure must immediately be distinguished from everybody else.[56] Mitchell knows he has to change his appearance in order to blend in, to lose the distinguishing features of his character type (his swag, his dog, his clothing); but the ending suggests that this is unlikely to happen. *While the Billy Boils* intermittently tracks Mitchell's itinerant trajectory, letting him speak of his predicament as a swagman first hand. The stories he features in offer fragmentary glimpses into his character: his romantic past (the failed romance in "Some Day" or his fake proposal of marriage in "A Camp-fire Yarn"), his encounters with squatters and station workers (the cunning bid for provisions from a station cook in "Mitchell: A Character Sketch"), and his empty fantasies about a settled, respectable life ("Another of Mitchell's Plans for the Future"). The accumulated effect of these glimpses is to insist that, in spite of everything, Mitchell is condemned to remain a swagman, structurally bonded to his character type and the objects that give it definition: "till your swag seems part of yourself, and you'd be lost and uneasy and light-shouldered without it".[57] In "On the Edge of a Plain", Mitchell returns home to his family after eight years' absence: "They thought at first I was a ghost", he remarks.[58] But after just a week, he leaves again to go back on the road. The stories about Mitchell are about a character type who cannot adapt or change and who is therefore irredeemable: he is chronically unable to stop being a swagman.

Joseph Furphy's Swagman

In *The Bush*, Don Watson turns to Joseph Furphy's Riverina classic *Such Is Life* (1903) to say the following about this character type: "It seems certain that Joseph Furphy meant us to conclude that our humanity can be measured by how we think about the swagman, how we treat him if he camps in our paddock or comes to our door, and he is therefore also the touchstone of Australian democracy".[59] How we "think about the swagman", however, is a matter of perspective: as we have suggested, the solitary woman in the bush (and the popular sentiments that sought to defend her honour) presented a very different view of this visiting figure. For Tom Collins, the narrator of *Such Is Life*, even the received tradition of squatter generosity towards the swagman has little truth to it. When he thinks about how squatters routinely discriminate between itinerants (favouring the "decent-looking

---

55   Henry Lawson, "Brummy Usen", *While the Billy Boils*, 190.
56   Henry Lawson, "That Swag (Enter Mitchell)", *While the Billy Boils*, 287.
57   Henry Lawson, "Some Day", *While the Billy Boils*, 149.
58   Henry Lawson, "On the Edge of a Plain", *While the Billy Boils*, 109.
59   Watson, *The Bush*, 149.

swagman" over the rest) and restrict what they provide when these figures "come to the door", he concludes: "Don't you believe the yarns your enthusiast tells of the squatter's free-and-easy hospitality toward the swagman".[60] Collins views the swagman sympathetically but, like Lawson and Paterson, he also regards him as "a futureless person" in a bush economy that is already stretched to the limit (127). *Such Is Life* is preoccupied with the spectre of redundancy, with the novel's opening sentence – "Unemployed at last!" – resonating through its pages. The swagman gives a particular shape to that spectre, habitually disappearing and yet always *there*. "The swagman", Collins philosophises – just like the unemployed (and the poor, for that matter) – "we have always with us" (128).

Andy Glover is the swagman in *Such Is Life*, a man who is almost deaf and is also nearly blinded by sandy blight. He is the complete opposite of the threatening, predatory swagman we saw earlier on. Now, it is the swagman's turn to complain – about low prospects and a lack of politeness in a pastoral economy that has become increasingly bureaucratised and instrumental. "Not much chance of a man makin' a rise the way things is now", he tells Collins. "Dunno what the country's comin' to. I don't blame people for not givin' work when they got no work to give, but they might be civil" (136). We saw that the shepherd's career corresponded with the phases of colonial settlement: as Earle's "Ned White" had told us, "that's the beginnin', middle, and end of the old shepherd's story". But the swagman is a *post*-settlement figure who is excluded from the escalating project of nation-building. When Collins first sees Andy Glover, he reflects: "That swagman had a history, highly important, at all events, to himself. He had been born; he lived; he would probably die – and if any human being wants a higher record than that, he must work for it" (126). The swagman's history here is particular to his type, not a reflection of the nation's development; and the only thing that can lift it up is the very thing he can't get, namely, work. Collins imagines he can read character types accurately, but as Carrie Dawson notes, he often "misapplies categorical knowledge"[61] – which means that he simply doesn't recognise characters for what they are or what they've become. Later on, Collins burns a haystack on a squatter's property to divert attention from an embarrassing predicament. Because the squatter had refused to give Glover work, the police assume it is the swagman who has taken his revenge. Glover is therefore blamed for the fire and sent to prison. The novel ends with Collins and some other characters sitting down to dinner in a hut on a squatter's station. Glover has also arrived, with another swagman. He then tells the story of his imprisonment and insists on his innocence. Although they had met earlier in the novel, Tom Collins doesn't seem to recognise the swagman: "Confused identity seemed to be in the air. Had I seen that weary looking figure, and that weather-worn face, before?" (423). Andy Glover is like a revenant here, almost a ghost at the table, an "apparition on the retina of my mind's eye", as Collins puts it. Don Watson had suggested that "Furphy meant us to conclude that our humanity can be measured by how we think about the swagman". This may well be true in the novel, as Collins becomes increasingly uncomfortable under Glover's blight-impaired gaze. He has sent this swagman to prison and he wants to avoid exposure. So he tries to make amends with a seeming gesture of bush generosity: "'Here, mate', said I, fearlessly removing my

---

60 Joseph Furphy, *Such Is Life* (1903; Melbourne: Text Publishing, 2013), 422. All subsequent references are to this edition and appear in parentheses in the text.
61 Carrie Dawson, "'The Slaughterman of Wagga Wagga': Imposture, National Identity, and the Tichborne Affair", in *Who's Who? Hoaxes, Imposture and Identity Crises in Australian Literature*, ed. Maggie Nolan and Carrie Dawson, special issue of *Australian Literary Studies* 21.4 (2004), 10.

clouded glasses, and handing them, with their case, to Andrew; 'you'll find the advantage of these'" (431). Julian Croft has written that the end of Furphy's novel

> has always surprised me and made me feel very uncomfortable about the moral bearings of the work: Tom's callous treatment of Andy... keeping silent about his responsibility for the crime for which the innocent Andy has been imprisoned, then capping the atrocity by handing the almost blind man his clouded glasses and addressing him as "mate".[62]

This is the gesture that brings *Such Is Life* to a close: not "fearless" at all, but directly serving Collins' interests. Contrary to Russel Ward's thesis, his expression of mateship in the bush here is pretty hollow. The swagman may indeed be a measurement of the humanity of other people; but in Furphy's novel he lingers on as a way of exposing the *limits* of that humanity in an increasingly competitive, instrumental bush economy.

The City Larrikin

In colonial metropolitan narratives the frontier is almost immediately placed at a distance, spatially and temporally, because cities in the colonies are the sites where the "effective establishment" of colonial authority is a matter of rapid and spectacular development. The first poem published in Victoria was "Melbourne", by "Coloniensis". It appeared in the *Port Phillip Gazette* in January 1839, only a few years after white settlement here had properly begun. The poem gives a narrative of the pace of the development of Melbourne that starts with the selection of a "large patch of land". This is precisely the moment that announces the end of the frontier as a "phase" in the emergent city's history:

> The swarthy
> Tribe appeas'd, remov'd; or with force of arms
> Into the Interior driven back;
> (For power, the law of right, too oft o'ercomes)
> A savage, to a civil race gives way.[63]

For the poet, colonial authority is established and asserted in the space of a couple of lines, as Melbourne lays its foundations.[64] In *The Chronicles of Early Melbourne, 1835–1852* (1888), "Garryowen" reproduces this poem and identifies its author as George Arden, the *Port Phillip Gazette*'s editor and co-founder. "Garryowen" was the writer and journalist Edmund Finn; he took his pseudonym from a place close to Limerick in Ireland where he was born, made famous in Gerald Griffin's popular novel *The Collegians: A Tale of Garryowen* (1829). The *Chronicles* reminds us that, among other things, Arden's poem was

---

62 Julian Croft, "Reading the Three as One: *Such Is Life* in 1897", *JASAL: Journal of the Association for the Study of Australian Literature* 13:1 (2013), 7.
63 "Coloniensis", "Melbourne", *Port Phillip Gazette*, 26 January 1839, 4.
64 James Boyce notes that the founding of Melbourne brought "colonial ambition, regulation and law ... finally into alignment", to the extent that it was "Melbourne's birth" – rather than Sydney's settlement – that "signaled the emergence of European control over Australia": see *1835: The Founding of Melbourne and the Conquest of Australia* (Melbourne: Black Inc., 2013), i–ii.

published around the same time as the establishment of George Augustus Robinson's failed Port Phillip Aboriginal protectorate, which systematically moved Aboriginal people out of this burgeoning metropolitan space. Finn charts Melbourne's development and increased prosperity, and populates the city with myriad character types and an extraordinary array of everyday events and anecdotes. He was especially interested in what he called "peculiarity", a trait he felt was under threat from the homogenising forces of modernity:

> There are in all communities certain units of the population who may be classified as unaffiliated or individualised "odd" fellows, in the literal acceptation of the term. In a large city like the Melbourne of to-day, the peculiarities of such people attract comparatively little attention, for they become merged in the great vortex of humanity, but in Melbourne, such as it was up to 1852, the reverse formed the rule, and some of the old townies, subjects of mild eccentricities, became notables in their own way . . . [65]

Colonial metropolitan development might "merge" people together, but it can also usher in new character types and release them into the city streets. The larrikin is a spectacular example, and the *Chronicles of Early Melbourne* devotes a chapter to this troublesome figure. "No little ingenuity has been employed in tracing the origin of the word 'larrikinism'", Finn writes, "as designating a comparatively modern human development, which has gathered into the most mischievous social ulcer of the present day, for its contagion communicates to both sexes of successive rising generations of young colonists".[66] We have seen the swagman or sundowner become residual almost to the point of extinction; by contrast, the larrikin appears as something both emergent and viral. In our introduction, we noted that the literary identification of the larrikin could be traced back to early 1870 with Marcus Clarke's declaration that "[t]he larrikin lives". Melissa Bellanta highlights a claim in the *Argus* that the term "larrikin" was in use "[b]ack in the 1860s", and she links the term to *leary*, an "old cant word meaning sharp, savvy, not easily duped".[67] But Finn also traces the etymology of the word *larrikin* to a Melbourne court case in 1850, when an Irish police sergeant, John Staunton, found it difficult to pronounce the word "larking" (a term, interestingly, that comes from the Old Norse *leika*, meaning *play*). "Staunton . . . was wont to include as 'larkers' everyone engaged in nocturnal illegalities about town", he writes; but "[t]he 'r' and the 'k' conjoined seemed too much for him, though separately he could manage them well . . . The response therefore, took this form, 'He was a lar–ri–kin, your Worship', and so was coined a word now of common use".[68] The larrikin is an emergent type here, but he is also cast as a degraded or debased version of the earlier Melbourne larker or "sky-larker". For Finn, larrikins are thus second-generation trouble-makers, much less endearing than their high-spirited precursors and much further down the class hierarchy: "The old sky-larkers", he tells us,

> were drawn from the cream instead of the scum of society, the scions of families of good blood and reputation, who came to Australia in search of fortunes – gay sparks,

---

65 "Garryowen", *The Chronicles of Early Melbourne, 1835–1852*, vol. 2 (Melbourne: Fergusson & Mitchell, 1888), 938.
66 "Garryowen", *The Chronicles of Early Melbourne*, 768.
67 Melissa Bellanta, *Larrikins: A History* (St Lucia: University of Queensland Press, 2012), 2.
68 "Garryowen", *The Chronicles of Early Melbourne*, 768–9.

some with light and few with heavy purses, the contents of which were sent flying in every direction. Some of them, at the turn of the tide, settled down quietly and amassed fortunes, afterwards enjoyed both in the colony and at home; but death made sad havoc with many, for the best and the brightest and the gayest of the frolicsome scapegraces went down before its remorseless scythe.[69]

In this section we want to look at two novels that feature larrikins and locate these character types in terms of their success or failure in a rapidly growing colonial economy. Three years after Clarke registered the birth of the larrikin, Donald Cameron published *Mysteries of Melbourne Life: A Story Founded on Fact* (1873). As Stephen Knight suggests, Cameron's novel is a colonial version of the nineteenth-century "Mysteries of the City" genre popularised across Europe and America in the early 1840s by writers like Eugène Sue (*Les Mystères de Paris*) and G.M. Reynolds (*The Mysteries of London*); but it also modernises this genre by taking it into a realm of "white-collar crime fiction".[70] *Mysteries of Melbourne Life* introduces three friends, two of whom, Harry and Robert, are clerks in a city bank, while the third – Hugh Hanlon – is initially down on his luck and needs to borrow money. A prologue to the novel also introduces "Little Billy Dawson", "the roughest of the *genus* 'larrikin'": "His apology for clothes, his shrunken form, attenuated face, and sharp eyes, told easily that he lived upon his wits, and a scanty living they afforded".[71] Billy discovers the murdered body of a woman on the banks of the Yarra; it is later revealed that she is his estranged sister, Bell. Robert is married to Linda and lives in a modest house in East St Kilda, hiring Billy as his employee. Harry takes a paternal interest in the young man, who tells him about growing up in Collingwood and joining "the boys the newspaper people call larrikins. They weren't called larrikins then" (18). The novel introduces three other members of the gang: a leader, Bob Smith; the cunning Patsy Quinlan; and Will Slabang, who informs Harry that Bell had once been married to Hugh. Hugh, in the meantime, has made a fortune "speculating in mining stocks", gambling and betting on horse races (15). When Robert finds himself in debt, Hugh encourages him to "go in on the quiet for a little speculation": "My dear boy", he says, "this is the land of rapid fortunes, of transformations ... The dashing, the adventurous, the far-sighted have every chance. It is a country where everything is increasing in value" (24). While the novel acknowledges that speculation is essential to the growth of colonial capitalism in the city, it morally distances itself from this through the more cautious, financially responsible figure of Harry – who has inherited a large amount of money, but saves rather than speculates. When Robert's debts dramatically increase, Harry takes Billy into his employ and orchestrates the larrikin's transition into respectable colonial life. Quinlan ends up in jail and Slabang dies after a larrikin brawl; but the novel rehabilitates Billy, charting his intellectual progress and even beautifying his appearance, until he becomes "handsome in body and brilliant in mind. To Harry he was a standing example of what can be done with those that the world contemptuously sets down as irreclaimable" (57).

---

69   "Garryowen", *The Chronicles of Early Melbourne*, 769.
70   Stephen Knight, *The Mysteries of the Cities: Urban Crime Fiction in the Nineteenth Century* (Jefferson, NC: McFarland & Company, 2012), 186.
71   Donald Cameron, *Mysteries of Melbourne Life: A Story Founded on Fact* (Melbourne: Mason, Firth & M'Cutcheon, 1873), 3. All subsequent references are to this edition and appear in parentheses in the text.

Hugh gambles his money away and is in any case exposed as Bell's murderer. In the meantime Harry clears Robert's debts and helps to reintegrate him into a more legitimate relationship to colonial metropolitan development. The larrikin's rehabilitation is complete when Billy joins Robert's "mercantile establishment" and becomes "his trusted confidant [*sic*]": "he is certain", the novel concludes, "to become a leading and respected citizen" (82). Cameron's novel – against the grain of public opinion about the larrikin – thus reverses the fortunes of this character type by making him an integral part of the metropolitan business establishment.

Melissa Bellanta has charted in detail the increasing "larrikin menace" in colonial cities in the 1880s and 1890s, and the various larrikin "pushes" and gangs that congregated in Melbourne suburbs like Collingwood and Fitzroy – and overran inner Sydney beach suburbs like Clontarf.[72] In *A Colonial Tramp* (1891), on the other hand, Hume Nisbet describes an encounter with a larrikin *outside* of the city, as he journeys by train to Echuca in country Victoria:

> I had only one fellow-passenger to Echuca in the carriage which I had been escorted to – a very small young man . . . and supernaturally sharp, loquacious, and inquisitive. He was very youthful; indeed, he had not yet begun to cultivate a moustache. But he was very old in experience and the ways of the world, and thoroughly self-possessed; a perfect representative of the colonial "larrikin" – i.e. the working, not the pickpocket, "larrikin".[73]

Nisbet draws a version of Henry Mayhew's distinction here, between larrikins who will work and those who will not. Bellanta suggests that "larrikinism had a profound connection to unskilled labour", noting that "[j]ob-hopping and itinerant work" were also commonplace.[74] The larrikin on the Echuca train bears out this sense of continually moving on – rather like the swagman – but he takes it into a completely different register, developing his skills in a series of creative, though poorly remunerated, trades. He consequently has some sympathy for Nisbet's own position as a struggling professional writer and illustrator in the colonies:

> A self-confident and patronising young man, he had tried art and literature, also acting, scene-painting, and the circus business, and pitied my position, for, as he remarked, they were the worst paying games he had ever been at. Indeed, I found out before we had got many miles upon our way that he had been everything that mortal man might aim at as a calling, except coach-painting; but he was now post-haste up to Echuca to add that to his general accomplishments.[75]

---

72 The *Bulletin* editors John Haynes and J.F. Archibald were famously sent to jail for libel after they published an article by W.H. Traill titled "The Larrikin Residuum", which described an "orgy" of larrikin activity in a public house in Clontarf on Boxing Day, 1880. G.D. Woods notes that Traill's article was a familiar example of an exaggerated reaction to larrikin activity, "exciting respectable citizens to outrage": *A History of Criminal Law in New South Wales: The Colonial Period 1788–1900* (Sydney: The Federation Press, 2002), 317. See also Shelagh Champion and George Champion, "The Clontarf Case", *Manly Library Local Studies*, 1992: http://bit.ly/2nl5xS4.
73 Hume Nisbet, *A Colonial Tramp: Travels and Adventures in Australia and New Guinea* (London: Ward & Downey, 1891), 168–9.
74 Bellanta, *Larrikins*, 10, 16.
75 Nisbet, *A Colonial Tramp*, 169.

The larrikin in this passage is self-interested but also remarkably enterprising and adaptable, and Nisbet's admiration for him no doubt led to a more sustained celebration of this character type's future potential in *The Bushranger's Sweetheart* – published just one year after *A Colonial Tramp*. We discussed this novel in Chapter 2, briefly mentioning a "Melbourne larrikin" known as Stringy Bark. There is a sundowner or swagman in that novel, too; and Nisbet juxtaposes these two character types (bush and city) in an interesting passage in the preface to *The Bushranger's Sweetheart* , worth quoting in full:

> The Sundowner is, I think, fast being driven away, ie., the colonials are becoming less sympathetic to the weary wanderer, and hard-hearted enough nowadays to make him work for his night's lodgings; yet I believe he still may be met with in the outlying districts. But that distinct production of Australia the Larikin [sic] is still very much to the fore, as spry, active and wicked as ever he was, perhaps rather more so. Stringy Bark and his chums are not at all scarce, although I don't think they have been made studies of before – educated by the Free State Schools, and smartened up by the generous climate until they beat the rest of creation for impish audacity – who only require the chance to become anything, from a boarding-house tout to a Member of Parliament, in that free and glorious colony, where every man, woman, and child are as near to the highest state of smart perfection as it is possible for frail humanity to reach.[76]

The sundowner here is once again a residual figure, relegated to the "outlying districts"; but the larrikin is full of colonial possibility. Stringy Bark begins the novel as a much more charismatic version of Cameron's Billy Dawson: he was, the novel tells us,

> the wickedest and most daring of boys, if he really was a boy, and the most audacious and slangy of old men, if he was an old man. He would . . . make love like an immature Rochester to the women – married or single – reaching up on his tip-toes to chuck even the stern matron under the chin . . . No subject or person was sacred to this premature little weazened fiend, for having used up life, he eclipsed the cynicism of Voltaire, and could have given that philosopher points and won. (30)

Stringy Bark is fully representative of his type, "a larikin of the larikins [sic]", as the novel puts it. The force of his personality is strong enough to preoccupy the narrator; rather like the effect of the shepherd on the narrator in Swan's "Two Days at Michaelmas", he "haunted my thoughts, waking and sleeping" (30). Stringy Bark soon takes a job with the American speculator and investor Ovinius Hardwake, who establishes a muckraking newspaper called the *Financial Diver and Undercurrent Searcher*. Later on, Stringy Bark takes over as editor and becomes increasingly prosperous and dandified:

> He had discarded the picturesque flannel suit which he once affected and was now got up to suit the tastes of the loungers who frequented the "Block" in Collins Street on Saturday, with the Athenaeum, Melbourne, and Yorick Clubs during the afternoons and evenings of other days . . . He was a toff and no mistake – a scarlet runner at the very height of its blooming. (174-5)

---

76 Hume Nisbet, *The Bushranger's Sweetheart: An Australian Romance* (London: F.V. White & Co., 1897), viii. Subsequent references are to this edition and appear in parentheses in the text.

The *Financial Diver's* unscrupulous practices inhibit the growth of the city's economy, and when the newspaper finally collapses, the economy flourishes: "a universal lightness seemed to pervade the commercial world" (249). Stringy Bark is forced to reinvent himself, selling patent medicines and managing a troupe of female dancers. "It was the same Stringy, but in a new character", the novel tells us. "He was no longer the larky larikin [sic] or the supercilious and arrogant editor or the cynical and amusing advocate. He was now the gravely suave and insinuating professor of medicine with a wonderfully impressive earnestness about him which betokened future success" (285). After the novel's closing shoot-out – when the bushrangers are killed – we finally hear that Stringy Bark has married into a wealthy Victorian family and become a Member of Parliament. "Thus this literary larikin [sic]", the novel concludes, "with his constant habit of ever looking upward, has achieved the sum total of his desires, for he can rise no higher in the colonies . . . " (312).

The Colonial Dandy

In the novels by Cameron and Nisbet, larrikins are both representative and exceptional. On the one hand, they transcend the limitations of their character type. On the other hand, the very qualities of their type (resilience, adaptability, cleverness, enterprise) are what enable them to make this transition. In *The Mysteries of Melbourne Life*, this transition is demonstrated through Billy Dawson's beautification, while Stringy Bark's success in *The Bushranger's Sweetheart* is reflected in his increasingly extravagant costumes. "I have often wondered how his tailor could fit him so perfectly", the narrator says; "he was like a rare black and white orchid, with some dewdrops trembling on the edges . . . " (195). Nisbet's notion that the larrikin-dandy can reach the "highest state of smart perfection" is reflected both in Stringy Bark's financial success and his refined, elegant appearance. It is not that far away from Charles Baudelaire's notion of the European dandy, whose sartorial brilliance reflects an "aristocratic superiority of mind".[77] Baudelaire had written about the dandy in "The Painter of Modern Life" (1863), casting him as a unique but residual type in danger of extinction under "the rising tide of bourgeois capitalist modernity".[78] "Dandyism is a setting sun", he famously lamented:

> like the declining star, it is magnificent, without heat and full of melancholy. But alas! the rising tide of democracy, which spreads everywhere and reduces everything to the same level, is daily carrying away these last champions of human pride, and submerging, in the waters of oblivion, the last traces of these remarkable myrmidons.[79]

It is interesting to note that just when the dandy begins to decline in Europe, he emerges in a kind of revitalised form in the Australian colonies. One year before Baudelaire's essay, the lawyer and traveller Robert Harrison published *Colonial Sketches: or, Five Years in*

---

77 Charles Baudelaire, *The Painter of Modern Life*, trans. P.E. Charvet (1863; London: Penguin, 2010), 37.
78 Debarati Sanyal, *The Violence of Modernity: Baudelaire, Irony, and the Politics of Form* (Baltimore: Johns Hopkins University Press, 2006), 148.
79 Baudelaire, *The Painter of Modern Life*, 39.

South Australia (1862). Notoriously critical of colonial life, he registered his impressions of people he saw on the streets of Adelaide, singling out the figure of the dandy as a notably visible type:

> I have sometimes seen the apparition of a colonial dandy; but these exotics do not flourish in "our culture", as the sun is too apt to tarnish their lustre; and it is certainly a ludicrous scene to observe a would-be exquisite, with an immense extension of collar, endeavouring to look cool on the shady side of the street, with the thermometer above one hundred degrees in the shade, and with furtive glances of dismay, contemplate the gradual decline and fall of "his beloved" appendages.[80]

For Baudelaire, dandyism in Europe is "a setting sun"; for Harrison (who was also obsessed with Adelaide's hot summer weather), the sun is too intense in the colonies for dandies to survive. Just a few years later, however, Donald Cameron gave a much more robust account of the dandy in the colonies in his *Australian Characters* series. "The Melbourne Dandy" (1866) begins by defending its subject against those, like Harrison, who might assume this figure is out of place in a colonial city. "Perhaps readers may fancy that this character is not an Australian one", he writes, "but when they have read this article, they will agree with me that it is essentially so".[81] The dandy in this sketch is given a name – Willie Gordon – and the narrative that follows turns him into the exact opposite of Baudelaire's representation of the European dandy as the last gasp of aristocratic self-fashioning, "who has no profession other than elegance" and who is disdainful of money and financial transactions.[82] In stark contrast, Willie is a thriving opportunist, a parasitical and predatory metropolitan figure who lends vigour to the commercial prospects of a colonial economy now reaping the benefits of the gold rush:

> How Willie managed to live and keep himself so primly dressed, few could tell ... His "office" evidently lay in Bourke-street, and it was here he used to spend most of his time. He lived in a great hotel, and made himself "necessary" to all new comers from the country. Willie knew a new arrival "flush" with the ready, as easily as a dog smells game ... Few rich young men came to town bent on having a "spree" but Willie would become their *chaperon*; and ere they left Melbourne, Willie was pretty sure to have made "his own" out of them ... In fact, to confess the truth, Willie had such wheedling, coaxing ways about him, that no man or woman could resist him.[83]

Willie is *faux*-aristocratic but he is also genuinely seductive, drawing in new arrivals indiscriminately, regaling them with stories and encouraging them to spend their money. He constitutes an essential part of the fabric of colonial Melbourne, highly visible and ever-present, working – albeit in a certain non-normative sense – towards the common good, performing an unconventional type of civic duty. Willie also seems to have an immense amount of erotic appeal to both sexes. So while he is "a perfect 'lady killer'", a

---

80 Robert Harrison, *Colonial Sketches: or, Five Years in South Australia, with Hints to Capitalists and Emigrants* (London: Hall, Virtue & Co., 1862), 36–7.
81 Donald Cameron, "The Melbourne Dandy", *Australian Journal*, 26 May 1866, 618.
82 Baudelaire, "The Painter of Modern Life", 36.
83 Cameron, "The Melbourne Dandy", 618.

scene also develops around a wealthy squatter who "had fallen in love with Willie at first sight".[84] Here, two conflicting colonial character types – the metropolitan dandy and the bush squatter – are drawn to each other in a way that brings them into sharper relief. Willie "fleeces" the squatter "disgracefully". But the squatter enacts a good-humoured revenge by inviting Willie into the bush to take him on a kangaroo hunt where, out of his depth, the dandy's city affectations are held to ridicule. The scene playfully exaggerates Willie's predicament as a metropolitan colonial type who is hopelessly out of place in the bush: "Oh! How can we depict Willie's utter discomfiture. Talk of a countryman being bewildered in the wilderness of London; it is nothing compared to Willie Gordon's bewilderment in the wilderness of Australia".[85] By the end of the story, Willie has returned to Melbourne and "given up his tricks", now absorbed into the legitimate world of financial exchange. But this is still not quite Baudelaire's "setting sun", since Willie still has the "impudent swagger" and fashionable tastes of the dandy, and remains a strongly realised metropolitan type – with the story of his bush experience now added to his ever-expanding repertoire.

The larrikin and the dandy can be artful in both senses of that word: crafty and cunning, but also creative, even artistic. Baudelaire's sense that European dandies "have no other status but that of cultivating the idea of beauty in their own persons" is borne out by several fictional colonial dandies; and their charisma and sheer visibility provide a sharp contrast to the vanishing swagman. We have already mentioned Felix Rolleston in Fergus Hume's *The Mystery of a Hansom Cab* (1886), "one of the best known young men in Melbourne ... [who] had an income of his own, scribbled a little for the papers, was to be seen at every house of any pretensions to fashion in Melbourne, and was always bright, happy, and full of news. Whenever any scandal occurred, Felix Rolleston was sure to know it first..."[86] Rolleston is like Stringy Bark here, a source of information and gossip who is similarly connected to the social pages of the metropolitan newspapers. He rivals Stringy Bark in terms of appearance and, unlike Harrison's dandy, he flourishes in the Australian sun: "His well-brushed top hat glittered, his varnished boots glittered, and his rings and scarf-pin glittered; in fact, so resplendent was his appearance that he looked like an animated diamond coming along in the blazing sunshine" (84). Like Stringy Bark, Rolleston marries into colonial aristocracy and, at his wife's insistence, studies politics and becomes a Member of Parliament. But the essential features of his character type – frivolity, a cultivated artfulness, self-indulgence, *ennui*, the sense of taking pleasure in distractions – persist, despite the weight of his responsibilities: "Felix had rebelled at first, but ultimately gave way, as he found that when he had a good novel concealed among his parliamentary papers time passed quite pleasantly, and he got the reputation of a hard worker at little cost" (140).

In Chapter 3 we noted that Hume Nisbet's *The Swampers* (1897) presents colonial Australia as "a kind of paradise for the genteel rogue and swindler", a speculative boom-and-bust "paper" economy that forms the background to its criminal events. Almost halfway through, the novel suddenly pauses to introduce Anthony Vandyke Jenkins, a Sydney sign writer and a "grainer"; that is, someone trained in the "art of imitating

---

84 Cameron, "The Melbourne Dandy", 618.
85 Cameron, "The Melbourne Dandy", 618.
86 Fergus Hume, *The Mystery of a Hansom Cab* (1886; London: The Hogarth Press, 1985), 38. Subsequent references are to this edition and appear in parentheses in the text.

coloured and fancy woods".[87] These trades – all to do with ornamentation or decoration, with artifice and surface imitation – seem to be the perfect provenance of the dandy. "Now as I suppose everyone here may have noticed", the novel tells us,

> house painters and paperhangers are great dandies as a rule, and aim at being very genteel and artistic in their habits. They like to curl and anoint their long tresses, and are careful about the cut of their moustaches and beards. They wear very tight and dressy boots, with high heels, and are generally a swaggering and cavalier set of beings . . . [88]

Jenkins is the only character in the novel whose appearance and dress is described in detail, as if the opportunity to lay out every component of his sartorial extravagance on the page is too enjoyable to miss:

> He was then a thin, little, withered man of about thirty, with a pot-hook nose, wearied-looking, crow-blue eyes, long auburn tresses and a highly cultivated moustache which curled over his wan cheeks like a pair of corkscrews. He always wore elastic-sided and exceedingly high-heeled boots, a size, if not more, too tight for his small feet, a Byronic shirt and collar, with a flowing necktie, brown velveteen jacket with light tweed trousers, a crimson or blue sash round his waist instead of a vest, and a broad-brimmed Alpine felt hat with puggerie attached, cocked jauntily on the side of his frizzled hair. If the weather chanced to be cool enough, he added to this picturesque costume a Spanish-shaped cloak, which, dangling carelessly from his narrow shoulders by a chain and hook, gave him, in his own estimation, that distinguished appearance which characterised the Dutch painter after whom he has condescended to name himself. (130)

We saw Marcus Clarke's comparable description of the young squatter-dandy Dudley Smooth in Chapter 1, as someone who embodies a satirised sense of success-without-content in a "brand-new-go-ahead colony". Some twenty-five years later, Nisbet transfers this character type to metropolitan Sydney, situates him in a decorative trade, and shows him working his way up through what is cast as a "boom-and-bust" economy that is now in overdrive. Jenkins begins to buy property, riding out what has been referred to as "the greatest land boom of the century" in Sydney during the 1880s.[89] He subdivides and sells, borrows more money from the banks, speculates, and continues to purchase. Soon, Jenkins becomes "the director of several land companies", and – breaking up with a dressmaker sweetheart, Mary – he sets out to marry a daughter of an "unscrupulous politician". This massive change of fortune only consolidates Jenkins' identity as a dandy. In fact, being a dandy turns out to be an advantage, as if this character type perfectly reflects the artificial inflation of rampant financial speculation: "The love of finery and ostentation which had been the weakness of Anthony in his sign-writing days, became his strength now that he was a board director and company promoter . . . " (135). All too soon, however, the 1880s land boom is followed by the collapse of major financial institutions in the colonies,

---

87   John W. Masury, *The American Grainers' Hand-Book* (New York: John W. Masury & Son, 1872), 7.
88   Hume Nisbet, *The Swampers: A Romance of the Westralian Goldfields* (London: F.V. White & Co., 1897), 128-9. Subsequent references are to this edition and appear in parentheses in the text.
89   See Maurice Daly and Patrick Malone, "Sydney: The Economic and Political Roots of Darling Harbour", in *City, Capital and Water*, ed. Patrick Malone (London: Routledge, 1996), 107, n10.

which brings "a rise in personal bankruptcies and company failures of those speculating in property and shares".⁹⁰ *The Swampers* gives a concentrated, melodramatic account of these definitive events in the early 1890s: "The catastrophe", it says, "came with the suddenness of a thunderbolt. Speculators and shareholders went to sleep, filled with confidence and security, and woke up next morning, dishonoured paupers" (142). Jenkins is ruined; but the dressmaker Mary comes "to the rescue in his hour of need" and as a result of her careful financial management they survive the crisis.

The Swampers introduces the figure of an extravagant dandy to personify the hazards of financial speculation in colonial New South Wales. When "equilibrium" is restored and financial speculation becomes restrained and normalised, the dandy literally loses his lustre: "His jauntiness was gone, his Alpine hat and velveteen coat had grown rusty and frayed, his trousers were patched and baggy, his boots heelless, and all that was left to him of his former pride were his moustache, long hair, and atheistic opinions" (145). This is the colonial version of Baudelaire's "setting sun": but here, in Australia, the dandy has never been above or separate from the marketplace. Baudelaire's dandy had belonged "to a class of individuals who were defined neither by their occupations (indeed the dandy professed none) nor by their financial situations (a dandy was happy to live on credit)".⁹¹ In *The Swampers*, however, the colonial dandy is tied to *both* these things, which gives him a certain vulgar resilience that Baudelaire's more rarefied dandy lacks. His prospects, in fact, continue to be a matter of speculation: "What he may become in the future", the narrator remarks, "I am not clairvoyant enough to prognosticate . . ." (145).

---

90   David Tolmie Merrett, "The Australian Bank Crashes of the 1890s Revisited", *Business History Review* 87:3 (Autumn 2013): 413.
91   Daniel Sipe, *Text, Image, and the Problem with Perfection in Nineteenth-Century France: Utopia and Its Afterlives* (London and New York: Routledge, 2016), 161.

5
The Australian Girl

The "Australian girl" emerged as a recognisable type in the 1860s, but she had an important predecessor in the "currency lass", who first announced her existence in New South Wales at a very precise moment: 13 September 1822. A few years earlier, the colony had commenced importing large quantities of Spanish dollars, raising concerns about how to establish and regulate monetary value. Around 40,000 Spanish dollars had arrived in 1812 and the colony's governor at the time, Lachlan Macquarie, drew on the skills of a convict forger to establish a local form of currency by cutting holes out of them to form a "Dump", valued at fifteen pence, and a Colonial or "Holey" dollar valued at five shillings. Further large-scale importations of Spanish dollars in 1822, however, risked devaluing local currency. The governor at this time, Thomas Brisbane, defended the use of Spanish dollars, "a coin", as he memorably put it, "which from the extension of its circulation over every part of the commercial globe, may justly be defined the money of the world".[1] But local free colonists, landowners and merchants protested over the use of "a foreign coin of doubtful and fluctuating value".[2] For the economist S.J. Butlin, these developments in 1822 worked to reduce the value of local currency in relation to British sterling. "The Spanish dollar", he writes, "had been devalued from 5s. 'sterling' to an uncertain value of about 4s. 2d. 'sterling' and 5s. 'currency'. Large numbers of dollars had been introduced as a basic coinage and the dual system of reckoning in 'sterling' and 'currency' was given a new lease of life".[3] Local currency was literally worth less than British sterling here, impacting on trade and importation, land value, and investment in the colony. These events generated a great deal of public commentary. A series of letters in Robert Howe's *Sydney Gazette and New South Wales Advertiser* gives us a vivid sense of the issues at stake here. Correspondents writing under portentous pseudonyms ("Mercator", "Democritus", "The Subscriber") or in the guise of colonial character types ("Old Emigrant Settler", "Old Settler of the Middle Class") – engaged in cordial, even amusing debates that carried

---

[1] Thomas Brisbane, "His Excellency's Reply", *Sydney Gazette and New South Wales Advertiser*, 30 August 1822, 2.
[2] "To His Excellency Sir Thomas Brisbane", *Sydney Gazette and New South Wales Advertiser*, 30 August 1822, 2.
[3] S.J. Butlin, *Foundations of the Australian Monetary System, 1788–1851* (Sydney: Sydney University Press, 1968), 153: http://setis.library.usyd.edu.au/ozlit/pdf/sup0003.pdf.

on right through the middle of 1822. But on 13 September, a strikingly different voice intervened. "I am a young woman, eighteen years old last birth-day", the correspondence begins,

> and arrived in this Colony about a year ago; at which time your Paper (which my mother takes in regularly) used to be very amusing with accounts of balls, marriages, dinner-parties, poetry, and other agreeable matters; of late, however, it is filled with nothing but letters about dollars, bank-notes, circulating medium, and such nonsense, which is, I declare, enough to give one the vapours.[4]

This correspondent signs herself "Lydia Languish", taking the name of a character in Richard Brinsley Sheridan's play *The Rivals* (1775), a "sentimental young Lady" who reads popular romances and values love over money. The letter promises to "unmask" each of the previous correspondents to the *Sydney Gazette* and "shew their real intentions". For example, she writes of "The Subscriber",

> I suspect it was he who brought the dollars here; or, at least, he must have a good portion of them, or he never would write so much about them. I should like to know if he be single, as I wish to marry a rich husband; though, between ourselves, Mr. Editor, I think he would make a tiresome one, if we may judge him from his stupid long letters; but I would soon cure him of that.[5]

"Lydia Languish" does not dismiss the problem of currency in the colonies altogether, however. Instead, she opens a space for a feminine mode of discretionary spending (her mother sells some sheep so that her daughters can "buy ribbands") and also advocates for a modest investment in the colony's social life (a season of balls, for example, or "agreeable amusements"). This, she suggests, is what women in the colony want: "I have shewn this letter to half-a-dozen charming *currency lasses* who are delighted with it; and who, together with [my] sister, all join me in requesting you will publish it as soon as possible".[6]

The author of this letter is not colonial-born, but she highlights her relationship to a social network of local settler women who validate and support her position. There are particular expressions of colonial femininity here that will become important later on to the way we understand the Australian girl: a bold assertiveness, a flirtatious manner that is also self-empowering, a sense of humour and a love of "amusement", and an investment in the social wellbeing of the colony at large. The following year saw other letters published in the *Sydney Gazette* wanting recognition for young women. A correspondent writing as "Fanny Flirt" complains that the newspaper "scandalously neglect[s] us poor damsels"; she also wants less focus on trade and commerce ("cargoes of this, and cargoes of that") and more on society life.[7] A recent arrival in Sydney, this correspondent criticises the way colonial men seem to think that romantic success

---

4 "Lydia Languish", "To the Editor of the *Sydney Gazette*", *Sydney Gazette and New South Wales Advertiser*, 13 September 1822, 3.
5 "Lydia Languish", "To the Editor of the *Sydney Gazette*", 3.
6 "Lydia Languish", "To the Editor of the *Sydney Gazette*", 3.
7 "Fanny Flirt", "To the Editor of the *Sydney Gazette*", *Sydney Gazette and New South Wales Advertiser*, 9 October 1823, 4. It is unclear if these correspondents are actually women; even so, they give lively expression to a significant prevailing discourse of colonial gender identification.

depends entirely on material wealth. "Young *Arable*'s wits are gone a wool gathering ever since he commenced grazing", she writes (already casting her colonial suitors as character types); "Talk of music, and ask for a song, young *Wholesale* chaunts over an invoice, 'Money is your friend, is it not?'".[8] This letter was then met by strenuous defences of the colony from a number of other correspondents. "We girls of Australia are to be put in the background", writes "Mary Merino", "as soon as these 'imported' ladies appear. They affect over us a style of superiority . . . if ['Fanny Flirt'] will only lay aside the spleen, and impart to us Australian girls those acquirements she may naturally be supposed to possess over us, we shall be very happy to hail her residence among us".[9] Another correspondent, "Betsy Bandicoot", launches a more colourful, colloquial defence, offering her cousin "Bill Kangaroo" as a suitor ("our Bill can play the flute, hunt the wild cattle, and shoot and swim with the best in the Colony") and affiliating herself to the social network of "us currency girls".[10]

These sentiments work to polarise the differences between immigrant and local girls in Sydney, within a light-hearted framework that takes pleasure in its type-casting. Peter Cunningham's popular colonial memoir, *Two Years in New South Wales* (1827) – mentioned in our introduction – gives a useful summary of the etymology of the term currency lass:

> Our colonial-born brethren are best known here by the name of *Currency*, in contradistinction to *Sterling*, or those born in the mother-country . . . the pound currency being at that time *inferior* to the pound sterling. Our Currency lads and lasses are a fine interesting race, and do honour to the country whence they originated.[11]

This account ties the currency lads and lasses to the devaluation of local currency and, by implication, a sense of cultural second-rateness. But it also racialises the colonial-born subject and anticipates its recasting as *native-born*, a term we have already briefly discussed. This transition is neatly captured in the title of Edward Geoghegan's popular play, *The Currency Lass; or, My Native Girl*, first performed at the Royal Victoria Theatre in Sydney in May 1844: the "first Australian musical with a local setting".[12] Edward Stanford has been living in Sydney and meets an old friend, the colonial-born Harry Hearty. Stanford is already planning to marry Harry's sister, Susan; but his anxious uncle, Samuel Similie, arrives in the colony, having mistakenly concluded that a "native girl" must be Aboriginal. Similie is a playwright and determined for his nephew to marry a local actress. But Susan Hearty takes charge of events ("leave it all to me"). She teasingly goes along with the uncle's misconception, allowing him to think she *is* Aboriginal while she confuses him with a series of impostures and performances – designed to show off her acting talents,

---

8 "Fanny Flirt", "To the Editor of the *Sydney Gazette*", 4.
9 "Mary Merino", "To the Editor of the *Sydney Gazette*", *Sydney Gazette and New South Wales Advertiser*, 30 October 1823, 4.
10 "Betsy Bandicoot", "To the Editor of the *Sydney Gazette*", *Sydney Gazette and New South Wales Advertiser*, 30 October 1823, 4.
11 Peter Cunningham, *Two Years in New South Wales; A Series of Letters, Comprising Sketches of the Actual State of Society in That Colony; of Its Peculiar Advantages to Emigrants; of Its Topography, Natural History, &c., &c.*, vol. 1 (London: Henry Colburn, 1827) 53.
12 Jill Dimond and Peter Kirkpatrick, *Literary Sydney: A Walking Guide to Writers' Haunts and Other Bookish and Bohemian Places* (St Lucia: University of Queensland Press, 2000), 28.

and to convince the uncle finally to agree to let his nephew marry her. At the end of the play, Edward reveals the "real" Susan to his uncle. "My dear sir", Harry explains, "you have fallen into the error of confounding the terms 'Aboriginal' and 'native'. This is my sister Susan Hearty, and I assure you that both she and I esteem it is our proudest boast to be privileged to claim our birthright as 'natives' of the soil – and children of Australia!"[13] The conundrum of this play relies on the elision of the word "born" from the phrase *native-born girl*. Susan is now a *native girl*: a term that was routinely used to refer to young Aboriginal women. We can say the same thing about the phrase "natives of the soil", which also circulated widely as a term for Aboriginal people. The play gains its racist humour from the idea that a colonial settler might marry an Aboriginal woman. But its ideological work involves replacing Aboriginal claims on land and place with a strident expression of rightful settler ownership. The currency lass – and currency lad – may have been tied to a devalued local economy, but the coming nation is already inflating its rhetorical investment in this "original" character type.[14]

The Australian Girl and England

The native-born Australian girl became more visible in colonial fiction by the middle of the nineteenth century – supplanting the currency lass, who disappeared until well after Federation, when she was rekindled as an entertaining early colonial anachronism.[15] The investment in her buoyant "native-born" femininity persisted, but the narratives this character type inhabits could often be equivocal about their commitment to the colonies and the emergent nation. A good example is Alice Brentwood in Henry Kingsley's *The Recollections of Geoffry Hamlyn* (1859). Although the term is never explicitly used here, her character traits – good health and beauty, a Sydney-based education, horse-riding skills, freely offered opinions, and affinity with wild native species as well as with domesticated garden spaces and floral abundance ("among petunias and roses, oleander and magnolia") – clearly identify her with the "Australian girl" as a type. Unlike the squatters in this novel, Alice also has a "divine compassion" for Aboriginal people: as if this kind of young woman, wrapped up in the rhetoric of the "native-born", could somehow bridge the gulf between colonial settler and Indigene. But, perhaps reflecting Kingsley's own experience as someone who only briefly resided in the colonies, Alice's ambitions are eventually directed away from Australia and towards England. "It seems like a waste of existence for a man to stay here tending sheep", she tells the emigrant squatter Sam Buckley, "when his birthright

---

13 Edward Geoghegan, *The Currency Lass; or, My Native Girl* (Sydney: Currency Methuen Drama, 1976), 66.
14 Katherine Newey notes that the "triumphant celebration of the white subject as an Australian 'native'" in Geoghegan's play "is founded on the displacement of the indigenous Australian"; and she adds, "The theatrical slipperiness and racism of this colonisation of identity was demonstrated with great wit in the Q Theatre's production of *The Currency Lass* (Penrith 1987) in which Aboriginal actor Justine Saunders played Samuel Simile, the Englishman who rushes out to Australia to stop his nephew marrying a 'native girl'": "When Is an Australian Playwright Not an Australian Playwright? The Case of May Holt", in *Playing Australia: Australian Theatre and the International Stage*, ed. Elizabeth Schafer and Susan Bradley Smith (Amsterdam: Rodopi, 2003), 94.
15 See, for example, J.H.M. Abbott, *Sally: The Tale of a Currency Lass* (Sydney: NSW Book Stall Company, 1918), or James Devaney, *The Currency Lass: A Tale of the Convict Days* (Sydney: Cornstalk, 1927).

is that of an Englishman: the right to move among his peers, and find his fit place in the greatest empire in the world".[16]

What is the relationship of a "native-born" Australian girl to the "greatest empire in the world"? This was a question that shaped so much of the colonial fiction that took this character type as its protagonist – but its outcomes could be completely different, depending on the case. To illustrate this, we can compare a relatively early novel by Ellen Davitt, "The Black Sheep: A Tale of Australian Life" (1865-66), with Rosa Praed's first published novel, *An Australian Heroine* (1880).[17] In "The Black Sheep", Isabel Drummond and her husband have settled in rural Victoria, around the time that colony separated from New South Wales and "was to have a constitution of her own": that is, in the mid-1850s.[18] Their daughter Marguerite (who arrived with her family as an infant) is now "an overgrown-looking girl, very thin, of a pale sallow complexion".[19] Raised in the colony, she is nevertheless resilient and capable and, unlike her mother, does not yearn for the familiar comforts of England: "Her young mind having developed amid scenes of danger and vicissitude, she knew nothing of the regrets that it was natural her mother should feel for former luxuries . . . "[20] When Francis Saville arrives from England, Marguerite impresses him by helping to kill a snake. Another character expresses the distinction between this colonial girl and her English mother as follows: "Miss Drummond was a heroine of the bush, if her mother had been one of the ball-room".[21] Saville becomes her suitor and composes a song about her as a national type, "The Australian Maid", which opens,

> The rose of England may be sweet,
> And France's lily fair,
> But I know a flower that blooms beneath
> The Bright Australian air.[22]

If nothing else, this verse does some significant rhetorical work: distinguishing "girls" from different nations, and tying the Australian girl to the outdoors – rather than the home – and to an invigorating Australian climate. In fact, Marguerite blossoms in this newly independent colony, inhabiting a floral, feminised realm ("inhaling the fragrance of the evening air") that reimagines the "national space not as a hostile and alien environment but as a garden".[23] Susan K. Martin notes that in late colonial fiction the garden "produced

---

16 Henry Kingsley, *The Recollections of Geoffry Hamlyn*, ed. Stanton Mellick, Patrick Morgan and Paul Eggert (1859; St Lucia: University of Queensland Press, 1996), 318.
17 The first novel to actually bear the title of "Australian girl" was Janet Carroll's *Magna: An Australian Girl*, serialised in the *Australian Journal* in 1882. The heroine is Magna Macdonald, the dutiful daughter of a Scottish store book-keeper on a squatter's station. Nothing much is known about Carroll, who was nevertheless a prolific writer of serialised fiction across a range of colonial regional newspapers and periodicals.
18 Ellen Davitt, "The Black Sheep: A Tale of Australian Life", *Australian Journal*, 9 December 1865, 230.
19 Davitt, "The Black Sheep", 229.
20 Davitt, "The Black Sheep", 230.
21 Davitt, "The Black Sheep", 231.
22 This early piece of verse is an unpolished precursor to Ethel Castilla's well-known centennial poem "An Australian Girl", first published in the *Australian Town and Country Journal* on 22 September 1888. Castilla's poem begins in a similar way: "She has a beauty of her own, / a beauty of a paler tone / Than English belles" (28).
23 Susan K. Martin, "Gardening and the Cultivation of Australian National Space: the Writings of Ethel Turner", *Australian Feminist Studies* 18:42 (2003): 285.

a different set of possibilities for the settler colonial plot": "Instead of beleaguered fighters against an unyielding wilderness, fictions figuring the nation as a garden produced a potentially more fruitful and less doomed role for the protagonist, particularly the female protagonist".[24] The association of the Australian girl with the garden (flowers, fruit, fertility and plenitude) certainly placed this character type in a narrative framework where settlement was now firmly established: this is, generically speaking, post-frontier colonial romance fiction. Even so, the wilderness as a category was still necessary in terms of shaping the Australian girl's character. It is true that the issue of violent settler-Indigenous relations rarely created tension in these narratives – in contrast, for example, to the shepherd's stories discussed in Chapter 4. Instead, the Australian girl was identified through her capacity to move freely back and forth between "wilderness" (a different category to the frontier) and its opposite, cultivation (the garden, the orchard, etc.). She was strengthened by the former, but "civilised" through the latter. The combination of these two things then determined the Australian girl's romantic trajectory and where it took her. In "The Black Sheep", Marguerite and her mother move to a small farm near Mount Macedon, a cultivated place "considered to be of some value in consequence of the rich soil and the abundant crop it yielded".[25] When her father dies, however, Marguerite's English aunt refuses to invite her to stay, fearing that this "wild Australian girl" might "become acquainted with her London cousins".[26] Whether the Australian girl is "wild" or "cultivated" is clearly a matter of perspective here. Saville himself returns to England to claim an inheritance, and there is some expectation that Marguerite will follow him. But the novel wants to insist that it is important to remain loyal to Australia:

> [A]t this period, both Melbourne and many other places in the colonies had become really pleasant residences (at least, for those who had plenty of money); indeed many old colonists were *returning from choice* . . . Such persons naturally considered that the civilisation of the settled districts in Australia was already *un fait accompli* . . .[27]

This passage does a lot of ideological work, valorising cultivation in the colonies while also linking it to settler wealth and using it as a way of expressing the successful establishment of post-frontier colonial authority: successful (and "pleasant") enough to make expatriate "old colonists" want to come back. Saville himself returns to the colony and Marguerite finally accepts his proposal of marriage. But the novel is not quite confident enough to give her an exclusively colonial future: it ends instead with Marguerite and her husband arriving in England, welcomed by Saville's family and already adjusting to the comforts of English life "*though*" (as the novel emphatically concludes) "*they had lived in Australia*".[28]

The Australian girl in fact emerged out of a struggle between colonial independence and the influence of England – a struggle that played itself out across a great deal of colonial romance fiction. The title of Rosa Praed's *An Australian Heroine* would seem to suggest an investment in the former, promising a vigorous female protagonist capable of asserting a distinctive set of national characteristics. When the novel opens, Esther Hagart

---

24   Martin, "Gardening and the Cultivation of Australian National Space", 285.
25   Ellen Davitt, "The Black Sheep", *Australian Journal*, 13 January 1866, 305.
26   Davitt, "The Black Sheep", 306.
27   Davitt, "The Black Sheep", 322.
28   Davitt, "The Black Sheep", *Australian Journal*, 27 January 1866, 344.

is sixteen and living on "Mundoolan Island", off the coast of northeast Queensland. A wild and dreamy girl, she is in one sense full of colonial possibility. But her mother has died and her father, a convicted forger and ex-convict, is now an alcoholic and is violently abusive towards her. A squatter (a "go-ahead man") and his family live nearby and welcome Esther to their thriving property – and it looks for a moment as if she might have a "cultivated" future there. As we shall see, the destiny of the Australian girl was often connected to the success of the squattocracy. But Praed's novel refuses to take this option. Instead, rather like Davitt's "The Black Sheep", it introduces an English lover and English relatives who call Esther away from the colonies, never to return. Seduced by a promiscuous young soldier, George Brand, Esther finally finds herself in a bitter, loveless marriage in London that in some respects echoes her earlier relationship on the island with her violent father: "There was a slight blue bruise upon Esther's arm which she had regarded upon discovering it with a mournful shudder . . . physical violence seems to a woman the deepest mark of degradation".[29] Fiona Giles insightfully suggests that Esther is in effect "transported back to England . . . to serve a sentence of reinsertion into English provincial society".[30] This is the opposite of colonial independence, where taking the "Australian heroine" out of the colonies is represented not as the realisation of her aspirations, but as the loss of her (potential) freedom. The novel explicitly and melodramatically articulates this predicament: Esther plaintively cries "I want to be free!" while her benefactor advises her to "be gentle and submissive to your husband" (vol. 3, 226, 244). *An Australian Heroine* effectively cancels out the implications of its own title, ending with a resigned expression of Esther's "sense of bondage" in an English marriage.

Catherine Martin's *An Australian Girl*

Praed's early novel essentially disavows the idea of the Australian girl as a type; and it does so partly because it never really invests in colonial development and the project of nation-building. Mundoolan Island is a peripheral, melancholy place, associated with Esther's dead mother and, later on, her abusive father's suicide. It is not far from "Frazerville" on the mainland: a town that was proposed as the capital of "Northern Australia", but which "has disappointed the expectations of its well-wishers, and is rather in a state of decadence than of development" (vol. 1, 12). One of the English characters in the novel tries to build a new colony on the island, but the novel has little interest in its progress. So Esther has no positive national/colonial foundation to build on. It is not until the beginning of the next decade that confidence in the emerging nation was sufficient to properly valorise the Australian girl as a representative literary type. Catherine Martin's *An Australian Girl* was first published anonymously in London in 1890 and then reprinted in abridged form in 1891. It begins in the inner city suburb of North Adelaide, where the properties are surrounded by "genuine gardens – roomy, shadowy, well planted, and well watered; rich in flowers and many fruit trees . . . "[31]

---

29 Rosa Praed, *An Australian Heroine*, vol. 3 (London: Chapman & Hall, 1880), 44. All subsequent references are to this edition and appear in parentheses in the text.
30 Fiona Giles, "Romance: An Embarrassing Subject", in *The Penguin New Literary History of Australia*, ed. Laurie Hergenhan et al. (Melbourne: Penguin, 1988), 230.
31 Catherine Martin, *An Australian Girl* (1890; Oxford: Oxford University Press, 1999), ed. Graham Tulloch, 5. All subsequent references are to this edition and appear in parentheses in the text.

This is a fully settled, cultivated and *feminised* colonial space, utterly different in kind to Esther's remote, melancholy and violently patriarchal island. The protagonist Stella Courtland is already romantically connected to a squatter, Ted Ritchie, the wealthy owner of Strathhaye Station. The novel eventually conforms to the generic expectation that an Australian girl will indeed marry a squatter; but it goes about this in a remarkably conflicted and convoluted way. Even when Stella marries Ted – about three quarters of the way through the novel – nothing seems properly settled. The Australian girl by this time was a recognisable and familiar character type; but Stella is made *exceptional*, and this complicates her predicament. A review of the novel in the *Sydney Mail* on 15 November 1890 made exactly this point when it spoke of Stella as "a new and original type of Australian heroine":

> We have met with Australian girls (in books) whose principal characteristics were a tendency to use slang on every possible occasion, a predilection for riding barebacked on unmanageable horses, and their somewhat hazy notions as the manners considered becoming in a young English lady; but never, in books or out of them, did we encounter the prototype of Stella Courtland, the "Australian girl", who had Kant's "Kritik of Pure Reason" at her fingers' ends, and spoke and wrote interminable pages of reflections on life, death, and theological doctrines.[32]

This view of Stella as a *prototype* suggests that she is in some way conspicuously "original"; on the other hand, she emerges out of a familiar field of types that were by this time already well defined. A review by William Sharp in the English journal the *Academy* in fact thought that Martin's novel had plagiarised another local novel from around the same time, "Tasma's" (Jessie Couvreur's) *In Her Earliest Youth*, serialised in the *Australasian* in the first half of 1890. For Sharp, "[t]he resemblance between the stories is sometimes startling"; both novelists, he adds, "may have been nearly simultaneously inspired by the desire to paint the dark side of matrimony under the Southern Cross".[33] Rosemary Campbell argues convincingly that Martin did not plagiarise "Tasma's" novel; even so, she notes that the heroines in both novels were so familiar to readers that they "were already being seen as stereotypes".[34] Stella Courtland, then, is a *prototype* and a *stereotype* at the same time.

These two descriptors make sense together if we understand the Australian girl as a character type defined by her unconventionality: her slang, her "wildness", her outspokenness, her commitment to "freedom", and so on. Because she was a *type*, her unconventionality was itself a matter of convention, which is why the Australian girl already seemed so familiar. But her unconventionality also always made her seem exceptional to the type she inhabited. She is an example of what Sara Ahmed calls a "wilful character", one "who 'stands out' in the force field of the social".[35] For Ted Ritchie, Stella's unconventionality is precisely what enlivens her (for him) and makes her different: "It's not because she is a lady; it's just because she's Stella, and I've known her all my life, and

---

32   "An Australian Girl", *Sydney Mail and New South Wales Advertiser*, 15 November 1890, 1089.
33   Cited in Rosemary Campbell, introduction to *An Australian Girl* by Catherine Martin, ed. Rosemary Campbell (St Lucia: University of Queensland Press, 2002), xxxiv.
34   Campbell, introduction to *An Australian Girl*, xxxv.
35   Sara Ahmed, "Wilful Parts: Problem Characters or the Problem of Character", *New Literary History* 42:2 (Spring 2011): 245.

every other girl seems common and flat beside her..." (48). Stella, on the other hand, continually refuses to commit to matrimony, imagining that marriage is incompatible with friendship – and romance. Later on, she becomes involved with an English doctor, Anselm Langdale, who, like Stella, is devoted to European literature and philosophy. The romance with Langdale offers Stella the possibility of a very different marriage trajectory; it is in this sense comparable to Rosa Praed's *Outlaw and Lawmaker*, discussed in Chapter 2, where the "flirtatious" Elsie Valliant rejects the advances of a squatter for a passionate, ill-fated affair with a bushranger. Stella is far more restrained than Elsie, but she still wonders "if she had a thread of the coquette in her" (225) – and other characters (including her rival for Ted's affections) do indeed regard her as a "perfect flirt" (196). Fiona Giles notes that although it is often considered a conservative genre, colonial romance at least "enables... the entertainment of transgressive behaviour and fantasy".[36] Tricked into thinking that Langdale has an existing marriage (to an older Italian woman), Stella finally accepts Ted's proposal. But the possibility of further romantic transgression is not laid to rest. She is physically unresponsive to Ted, still thinking of Langdale; she wears Langdale's ring after the marriage ceremony; and when she discovers that Ted drinks heavily, she almost resolves to leave him. Later on, she meets with Langdale, who rebukes her for marrying without love. When they part, she falls into a delirium. In the meantime, Ted weathers the challenges and remains loyal to Stella, gaining her admiration. It is only after the novel has almost completely derailed their relationship that it then brings the squatter and the Australian girl together with a renewed ideological force: converting Stella to the Christian values of duty and responsibility, and providing her with the resources to do the kind of charitable work that Ted himself has little interest in.

The Australian Girl vs the New Woman

Michelle J. Smith has looked at both Praed's *An Australian Heroine* and Martin's *An Australian Girl*, concluding that their heroines "lose, or unwittingly relinquish, freedoms that are associated with the Australian Girl".[37] As she puts it, these novels contribute to "the deflation of the Australian Girl's aspirations".[38] Even so, by the 1890s the Australian girl was being increasingly invested with the aspirations of the colonies themselves. There was an imperative at this time to make this character type come to life, to give her as much exuberance and energy as possible, which meant allowing her to be still more decisive and (to use Ahmed's term) "wilful". It has often been noted that colonial women were less central to 1890s Australian nationalism than men, in the same way that popular colonial romance (generally taken to be a women's genre) was supposedly less valorised than so-called bush realism.[38] This is Susan Sheridan's point in an influential early article, "'Temper, Romantic; Bias, Offensively Feminine": Australian Women Writers and Literary Nationalism" (1985). For Sheridan, the 1890s (through the *Bulletin* in particular)

---

36   Fiona Giles, *Too Far Everywhere: A Romantic Heroine in Nineteenth-Century Australia* (St Lucia: University of Queensland Press, 1998), 19.
37   Michelle J. Smith, "The 'Australian Girl' and the Domestic Ideal in Colonial Women's Fiction", in *Domestic Fiction in Colonial Australia and New Zealand*, ed. Tamara Wagner (London: Routledge, 2016), 76.
38   Smith, "The 'Australian Girl' and the Domestic Ideal in Colonial Women's Fiction", 83.
38   Smith, "The 'Australian Girl' and the Domestic Ideal in Colonial Women's Fiction", 83.

understood masculinity as "normative and positive" – a view that depended on "the projection of the deviant and the negative onto the feminine side".[39] The literary "norm" during this time is thus realist and "vernacular", which "requires as a condition of its articulation the suppressed Other – in this case, the class-bound, the romantic, the popular 'colonial' culture".[40] But colonial romance, far from being eclipsed by bush realism, *flourished* during the 1890s, and increasingly tied itself to the development of an emergent nation. In fact, while bush realism was trading on its nostalgia for character types who were already fading away (the swagman, the shepherd, etc.), colonial romance spoke directly to the dominant interests of colonial modernity. The Australian girl is a key participant in this newer formation. In *To Try Her Fortune in London*, Angela Woollacott makes exactly this point: "In contrast to the bushman, representative of Australia's older pastoral economy, 'the Australian girl' boldly stood for modernity and independence, highly desirable qualities for a new nation".[41]

To sustain these qualities, however – to make them seem all the more valuable, even necessary – the Australian girl needed her *own* "deviant and ... negative" Other. In this case, it was the so-called New Woman. The New Woman was a *fin-de-siècle*, proto-feminist figure, popularised internationally in novels by writers such as Olive Schreiner and the Irish feminist Sarah Grand – who had coined the term in an essay published in the *North American Review* in March 1894.[42] In Australia (as elsewhere), this figure could be treated with hostility, even by women writers. A few months after Grand's essay, the popular novelist Ethel Turner criticised the New Woman in her "Women's Department" column in the Sydney journal *Cosmos*:

> An exchange says the heroine of fiction is generally a type of the day. If that is so, then this year she is a clever, beautiful, bloodless creature who at twenty-two is bored to death with everything ... She is not a flirt; she is cold, indifferent – very often absolutely rude ... In spite of everything, however, she gets along all right; and when she commits suicide, it is not because she is not having a good time, but because she is not going to accept her good time with the complacency that any ordinary woman would.[43]

The New Woman here is perversely non-conformist; more importantly, she does not commit to a future, and Turner in fact goes on to treat her as a passing literary fad. The Australian girl, on the other hand, looks *forward* to the future, in particular, the future of the coming nation as Federation approaches. She is (or tries to be) normative, in other words, rather than "deviant". Michelle J. Smith similarly highlights the Australian girl's normative qualities, as a character type who generated national optimism rather than provoked national anxiety:

---

39 Susan Sheridan, "'Temper, Romantic; Bias, Offensively Feminine': Australian Women Writers and Literary Nationalism", *Kunapipi* 7:2–3 (1985), 50.
40 Sheridan, "'Temper, Romantic; Bias, Offensively Feminine', 51.
41 Angela Woollacott, *To Try Her Fortune in London: Australian Women, Colonialism, and Modernity* (Oxford: Oxford University Press, 2001), 157.
42 Sarah Grand, "The New Aspect of the Woman Question", in *The American New Woman Revisited: A Reader, 1894–1930*, ed. Martha H. Patterson (New Brunswick, NJ: Rutgers University Press, 2008), 29.
43 Ethel Turner, "Women's Department", *Cosmos*, 20 October 1894, 127.

> Unlike the New Woman ... the healthy and attractive Australian Girl was not ... defined as a threat to the gendered or sexual order and was not demonised in the periodical press. Indeed, rather than being lambasted by men, the Australian Girl was accommodated in burgeoning nationalism and in national mythologies.[44]

Tanya Dalziell makes a similar argument about the Australian girl; but she also suggests that "no consensus was reached in the colonies... with respect to the causes and consequences of the New Woman".[45]

J.D. Hennessey's *An Australian Bush Track*

The identification of the Australian girl with the prospects of the coming nation brought with it a massive ideological investment in this character type. Male authors could treat her with just as much enthusiasm as female authors; and in any case, popular romance was by no means an exclusively women's genre during this time. We want to look at a remarkable novel from the mid-1890s that gives us possibly the most vivid portrait of this character type to be found in colonial Australian fiction. Born in England, John David Hennessey arrived in Queensland in his late twenties. He went on to become a minister with the Congregational Church, as well as a prominent agricultural journalist and publisher. A popular novelist both in Australia and England, Hennessey wrote a number of murder mysteries and romances, including *An Australian Bush Track* – first serialised in early 1896 in the *Western Grazier* and several other regional newspapers and journals, and then published in book form in London by Sampson Low, Marston & Co. in the same year. *An Australian Bush Track* has usually been read as a Lemurian novel or "lost race romance",[46] a subgenre of the colonial adventure novel that presents the discovery of a lost civilisation in a remote, unmapped part of the country. H. Rider Haggard's African adventure novel *She* (1887) is an influential earlier example, and one that Hennessey draws on directly; other local Lemurian novels include George Firth Scott's *The Last Lemurian* (1896) and Rosa Praed's *Fugitive Anne* (1903). But in fact the Lemurian component occupies only the last third of Hennessey's novel. The rest of *An Australian Bush Track* is built around Dorna Stoneham, one of the daughters of Aaron Stoneham, a reclusive squatter who has staked out a property on "Smoke Island" in Moreton Bay, off the southern Queensland coast. Dorna's predicament is comparable to Esther's in Praed's *An Australian Heroine*: both girls are geographically isolated, and their fathers are violent and oppressive figures. But while Esther's island is Gothic and melancholy, Smoke Island (at least at the beginning of the novel) is fertile, abundant and *feminised*: "the very air was odorous with roses and carnations and mignonette, mingled with the perfume of tropical flowering shrubs".[47] And while Esther is never able to escape the constraints of patriarchy, Dorna is much more combative and self-determining. It helps that Dorna has three equally tenacious sisters to

---

44 Smith, "The 'Australian Girl' and the Domestic Ideal in Colonial Women's Fiction", 77.
45 Tanya Dalziell, *Settler Romances and the Australian Girl* (Perth: University of Western Australia Press, 2004), 122.
46 See, for example, Robert Dixon, *Writing the Colonial Adventure: Race, Gender and Nation in Anglo-Australian Popular Fiction, 1857–1914* (Cambridge: Cambridge University Press, 1995), 91–4.
47 J.D. Hennessey, *An Australian Bush Track* (London: Sampson Low, Marston & Company, 1896), 3. All subsequent references are to this edition and appear in parentheses in the text.

support her against Stoneham's brutality: "he found it wasn't exactly safe to knock them about much . . . there were, at any rate, four of them who were getting to be tall and fairly muscular women" (58). When Stoneham threatens one of the sisters, Marjory, with a whip, she aims a rifle at him:

"Do you mean to say you would shoot your father?"
"You put that riding-whip across my shoulders, and you will see. I'm a woman now!"
. . . He only threatened Marjory once after that with his riding-whip, and that was the day she disappeared. (59-60)

In this novel, brutalised daughters do not remain at home until a suitor comes to take them away. They walk out of their own volition, to forge a new life for themselves. Dorna is deeply affected by Marjory's absence; in the meantime, Captain Buchanan, an English relative, turns up with Sir Charles Dawson and an "adventurous and speculative" colonial, Bright Hartley (10). They are in possession of a letter, written by none other than Captain Cook, and a drawing of a boomerang inscribed with coded directions to a mysterious place called "Zoo-zoo". Buchanan is seeking revenge against Stoneham, who we later discover had murdered Buchanan's mother (Stoneham's sister). The two men fight on a remote part of the island; when Buchanan is left for dead, Dorna valiantly rescues him – a brave act that greatly impresses Hartley, who begins to fall in love with her. "He had been all his life used to society belles", the narrator remarks; "but here was a girl of nineteen, after a night's adventure which would have taxed the strength and endurance of most ordinary men, looking as fresh as a rose . . . " (75-6). We have already seen floral imagery invoked in relation to the Australian girl in Davitt's story. In Hennessey's novel, however, the emphasis is on *native* plants and flowers, which Dorna defends against Sir Charles' Anglocentric criticisms. "Now I think, Sir Charles", she says, "that I am the best judge of the beauty and fragrance of our Australian flowers, because I love them . . . " (83). When he later witnesses her horse-riding skills, the English baronet is doubly impressed: "If she's a specimen of Australian bush girls, they're simply wonders. Why, she came in without shoes or stockings, talked botany like a member of the Linnean [sic] Society, and went out over the summit of a five-barred gate" (89). The Australian girl is certainly tied to natural ("native") beauty here, but this is also cast as an example of local expertise, an *intellectual* fascination. In colonial realist fiction – Lawson's stories, for example – bush knowledge is often presented as residual, a vanishing art. In Hennessey's novel, however, it works to elevate the Australian girl *above* the "norm", to make her transcendent. "Her bringing-up had made her a speciality"; even the experienced Hartley thinks he has "made the acquaintance of something entirely new in the way of girls" (89).

Stoneham turns out to be a murderous psychopath; but he is also a kind of remnant of frontier colonial expansion, patrolling his property with a gun. When he kills an Aboriginal man, Dorna discovers the body and buries it to protect her family's reputation. But the crime is the last straw ("Crime upon crime!"), and she leaves the island to search for Marjory. Her adventure unfolds in a series of letters through the middle of the novel, taking her first to Ipswich, where she buys a whip and a revolver. "That shopman", she writes indignantly, "stared at me as though I were one of the New Women that people are talking about" (120). Her remark reminds us of the prevalence of this character type, but Dorna is keen to distinguish herself from it: she is emphatically an Australian girl. We noted earlier that the Australian girl's nation-building capacity is often realised through her marriage into the squattocracy: think, for example, of Stella Courtland and Ted Ritchie in Martin's novel. In Hennessey's novel, however, Dorna has a much more playful (even "wilful") relationship to squatter suitors. On board a train, a young squatter "evidently thought me very innocent, for he caught hold of my hand in ... [a] tunnel further on; but I drew it back, and then pushed it rapidly forward again so that it knocked against something. When we got into the light there were tears in his eyes..." (126). Later on, Dorna takes a coach, sitting beside an older squatter, Jeremiah Crumbs, who soon becomes infatuated with her. En route they encounter her father, Aaron Stoneham, with two Aboriginal offsiders, and they give chase. When Stoneham shoots at them, Dorna takes the reins of the coach and makes a daring escape, impressing Crumbs all the more with her bravery and skill. When he proposes marriage, she goes along with the idea but has no intention of seeing it through; instead, she leaves, heading out to a more remote inland property, Yarrabong Station. "I ought to tell you", she writes, "that the last hundred miles I travelled by myself" (156).

Yarrabong Station, with its quasi-Indigenous name, is a kind of throwback to the colonial frontier, "a queer place", as Dorna puts it. There are three brothers on the property, sons of a hut shepherd; they had "managed to save a hundred pounds or so shearing, and bought a hundred head of cattle, and pushed out into the Never Never country" (158). This is almost, but not quite, the *post*-frontier: "For years they carried their lives in their hands with hostile natives" (158) who are now "learning that it is best policy to leave our cattle alone" (166). The brothers use Aboriginal labour, including an Aboriginal house servant who speaks English and dresses well enough to think she is "so fine a lady that she could not be expected to do any work" (159). In Kingsley's *The Recollections of Geoffry Hamlyn*, Alice has a "divine compassion" for Aboriginal people, patronising as that may be. Here, however, Dorna treats the Aboriginal house servant with racist disdain, not least because of the latter's mimicry of white femininity. Having already adopted the identity of "native (born) girl", the Australian girl then relegates this Aboriginal woman to the edge of the frontier at precisely the moment when the frontier is (almost) over. The Australian girl here is vibrant, competent and hard-working, while the Aboriginal house servant is cast as lazy and falsely aspirational. "I stumbled over her on one of the verandahs afterwards", Dorna writes, "smoking a short pipe and playing cards with three other blacks. It is a wild, rough life on these interior stations, I can tell you ... " (159). Dorna's adventures take her to the edge of the frontier at Yarrabong, but only in order to mark out her distance her from it ("I could not bear the place"): her own ambitions in fact take her somewhere else.

The Lemurian fantasy in the novel is a different kind of adventure, unfolding in an imaginary place located spatially *beyond* the frontier. It begins when Dorna finally finds her sister Marjory on the Western Plains, now married to John Holdfast and living in an established homestead with "a tiny lawn ... and a garden, and fruit trees" (174). This is a feminised space, fronting on to some sort of vast inland lake. But it is also a space of masculine settler ascendancy, with the appropriately named Holdfast securing his grip on the frontier and trading "gold-dust" and diamonds with local Aborigines to become incredibly wealthy. He is, the novel tells us, "the ideal pioneer squatter" (190). Buchanan, Dawson and Hartley arrive soon afterwards, convincing Holdfast to join their expedition to find the path to Zoo-zoo. Dorna and Marjory accompany them part of the way; but after a certain point, the men proceed on their own. The refusal to allow women to participate in the Lemurian adventure has been noted in earlier critical commentary on the novel. For Robert Dixon, Dorna "is now brushed aside", while for Tanya Dalziell she is "explicitly excluded" from a journey undertaken only by men.[48] In the event, however, it is only Holdfast who ventures into the lost world – to discover "a far superior race to the ordinary aboriginals, being taller in stature and more intelligent, and seemingly stronger limbed" (267). It turns out that a "half-crazed Scotchman" is the tribal priest, and he gives Holdfast gold and diamonds, urging him never to return. Generically speaking, the Lemurian novel stages a collision between the archaic and the modern; the former is there precisely to be effaced or left behind so that the latter can triumph. For Melissa Bellanta, the Lemurian novel creates a "vision of a fabulous modernity" out of the traces of the archaic, which is already shown to be compromised.[49] The lost race in Hennessey's novel is in any case not Indigenous, having come from a "great nation" on "the mainland of Asia"; it is "superior" and eccentric at the same time. Sumanthi Ramaswamy has talked about Lemurian imaginative worlds in precisely this way, as peculiar, "out of the way" places, remote from "power centres, conspicuously undermining the status quo, the normative, and the normalising".[50] The world of Zoo-zoo in *An Australian Bush Track* is indeed out of the way and eccentric. But far from undermining the project of settler colonialism, it dutifully provides the wealth it needs to thrive. As Tanya Dalziell notes, the Lemurian episode in Hennessey's novel is "important in imaginatively securing settler capitalism in colonial Australia", where natives appear to give up their resources "without struggle".[51] As they wait for Holdfast to return laden with treasure, Dawson and Hartley plan their future investments in the interior, calculating exactly how much they will earn when they float their newly established gold mine on the London stock exchange. Dawson is worried about losses, but Hartley reassures him: "that's where the speculative element comes in, which must be connected with all mining ventures . . . But it's a splendid scheme, is it not?" (262)

Hennessey's Lemurian novel encourages us to fully absorb the double meaning of "speculation": firstly, as a way of "transforming Australia into a realm of the fabulous", as Melissa Bellanta puts it;[52] and secondly, as a way of capturing the "speculative element" of financial investment so necessary to the development of the colonies. Financial speculation is itself a kind of fantasy here, but it is tied to the future, not the past: "It is wonderful how bright and fanciful the visions of the future become to men with newly found mineral treasures sparkling in their hands by the light of a bush fire!" (279). In the meantime, the men find themselves trapped by a flood and under attack from Aboriginal people. The Lemurian fantasy closes at this point, as the narrative recreates the scene of a frontier battle. Things seem hopeless for the men, until Dorna and Marjory suddenly arrive on a boat and rescue them. The Australian girl(s) thus provide the escape route that allows the settler-explorers to survive and ultimately prosper. Hartley realises that the men "owed their lives" to Dorna's "skill and daring" (305); it makes him even more devoted to her. Back at the Western Plains homestead, he proposes to Dorna just as Aboriginal people attack once again. Dorna shoots an Aboriginal warrior, saving Hartley's life, and as they ride away together she agrees to marry him. If the Lemurian fantasy guarantees the prosperity of this settler romance, it is frontier violence that provides the impetus for

---

48 Dixon, *Writing the Colonial Adventure*, 93; Dalziell, *Settler Romances and the Australian Girl*, 69.
49 Melissa Bellanta, "Fabulating the Australian Desert: Australia's Lost Race Romances, 1890–1908", *Philament* 3 (April 2004): http://bit.ly/2hxTpOx.
50 Sumanthi Ramaswamy, *The Lost Land of Lemuria: Fabulous Geographies, Catastrophic Histories* (Berkeley: University of California Press, 2004), 17.
51 Dalziell, *Settler Romance and the Australian Girl*, 51.
52 Bellanta, "Fabulating the Australian Desert".

its consolidation. As Dawson later relates, "I believe that Mrs. Hartley tells her friends that blacks are always troublesome creatures, and that but for them she never would have married" (313). Tanya Dalziell has noted that the Australian girl's development as a settler type is "adjacent to the evolutionary notion of the 'dying Aboriginal race'".[53] But Hennessey's novel takes this much further: Dorna actively participates in the colonial project of Aboriginal extermination ("Crime upon crime!"). She takes charge of everything she does: leaving her brutal father, finding her sister, arming herself, rescuing the imperilled expedition party, choosing a husband, accumulating wealth – and driving off Aboriginal assailants. She is undeniably, as John Docker vividly expresses it, a "colonial Woman on Top".[54]

The Australian Girl and the Problem of the National Type

But the Australian girl aims higher than the colonies: she aspires to be a *national* type. Stella makes exactly this point in Martin's *An Australian Girl*, in a fervently patriotic speech that (even in 1890) makes the idea of a set of separate colonies seem backward-looking, something that modernity ought to leave behind:

> Well, a colony – does it not suggest a handful of men ploughing scraps of land in an insignificant little state or island, or, at any rate, the first scattered handful of pioneers who have an uncertain footing in an alien land? Australia is not a colony; it is a continent, a great country where generations have already lived and died – the birthplace of thousands upon thousands who love it more dearly than any other spot in the whole world. (133)

The Australian girl is cast here as the spokesperson – and exemplar – of the nation-to-come: no longer part of a fractured pastoral economy, she connects herself instead to a maturing nation that can confidently compare itself to the rest of the world. As the colonies move closer to Federation, it might seem as if the Australian girl is at last poised to become a nationally representative figure, a clear example of an undifferentiated national type. But let us consider one more incarnation of this figure before coming to the end of our book. Miles Franklin's *My Brilliant Career* was written in the late 1890s and published in London by William Blackwood in 1901. It is a novel that anticipated Federation, and was published directly after Federation was achieved. For Jill Roe, *My Brilliant Career* was "undoubtedly the literary event of 1901, the only significant Australian novel in the year of Federation".[55] This is a novel that seemed to put the fractured colonies behind it, speaking, at last, to a unified nation. A.G. Stephens had also emphasised the forward-looking national vigour of *My Brilliant Career* in his review of the novel in the *Bulletin*: it is, he wrote, "Australian through and through", the "only Australian novel published", "fresh, natural, sincere".[56] But the novel's narrator and protagonist, Sybylla

---

53 Dalziell, *Settler Romances and the Australian Girl*, 22.
54 John Docker, *The Nervous Nineties: Australian Cultural Life in the 1890s* (Oxford: Oxford University Press, 1991), 212.
55 Jill Roe, *Her Brilliant Career: The Life of Stella Miles Franklin* (Cambridge, Mass.: Harvard University Press, 2009), 75.
56 A.G. Stephens, "Red Page", *Bulletin*, 28 September 1901.

Melvyn, posed an interpretative problem. In many respects, she shares the familiar attributes of the Australian girl: "fresh", confident, unconventional, assertive, and so on. But as Ian Henderson notes, Sybylla "has troubled readers from the start". "The 'trouble' with Sybylla", he writes, "is that she refuses to endorse any stable and unified model of identity".[57] Emerging at a time of national consolidation, this Australian girl nonetheless turns out to be strikingly unpredictable and contradictory. To draw on the terms we have been using here, she is normative and "deviant" at the same time.

We can see this polarity most obviously from the perspective of genre in the novel. To return to Susan Sheridan's distinction, noted above: is *My Brilliant Career* a woman's romance, or a "masculine" work of vernacular bush realism? In Henry Lawson's famous preface to the novel, it somehow manages to be both, but in a kind of schizophrenic way that, for him, renders the woman's romance part of the book opaque: "I don't know about the girlishly emotional parts of the book", he writes, "I leave that to girl readers to judge; but the descriptions of bush life and scenery came startlingly, painfully real to me".[58] Sybylla begins by connecting her novel explicitly to Lawsonian bush realism: "This is not a romance", she insists; "I have too often faced the music of life to the tune of hardship to waste time in snivelling and gushing over fancies and dreams; neither is it a novel, but simply a yarn – a *real* yarn".[59] Her early predicament does indeed have more in common with bush realism than with the Australian girl romance. Her father is a failed squatter who loses money and has to sell his family properties; he ends up a "broken-down farmer-cockatoo" (154), drinking heavily; and Sybylla, far from being able to realise her aspirations, feels a "bitter disappointment" at her class predicament ("from swelldom to peasantism", 23). For the moment, at least, Sybylla seems like an Australian girl *without* a future, a type stranded in the wrong genre: not speculative romance/adventure, but a localised, disillusioned settler narrative defined by "long toil-laden days" and "agonising monotony" (3). So when she remarks, "[m]y sphere in life is not congenial to me" (3), she is expressing a type's complaint. This is an Australian girl who cannot be contained by the expected paradigms of character and genre. "I certainly was utterly different to any girl I had seen or known", she tells us. "What was the hot wild spirit which surged within me? . . . Why was I not like other girls?" (36). The unconventionality (the "hot wild spirit") of the Australian girl is often framed positively in colonial romance, as we have seen with Stella and Dorna. But in Sybylla's case, it works to estrange her from the genre she ought to comfortably inhabit. At one point she confesses to have written a woman's romance herself, "in which a full-fledged hero and heroine performed the duties of a hero and heroine in the orthodox manner" (37). Deriding the genre as functional and unimaginative, she casts it aside and turns instead to a masculine canon of Australian literary realists, including Lawson himself. On the other hand, *My Brilliant Career* is about Sybylla's romantic prospects, her relationships to various suitors, and her class aspirations – which persist, despite her family's financial hardship. It has all the attributes of colonial women's romance, in other words; but it also complicates them, self-consciously placing a series of obstacles in their way. Ian Henderson perceptively remarks that "Sybylla . . . can never settle comfortably or decisively into 'male' realism or 'female' romance": as if neither genre can

---

57   Ian Henderson, "Gender, Genre, and Sybylla's Performative Identity in Miles Franklin's *My Brilliant Career*", *Australian Literary Studies* 18:2 (October 1997): 165.
58   Henry Lawson, preface to Miles Franklin's *My Brilliant Career* (Melbourne: Penguin, 2007), n.p.
59   Miles Franklin, *My Brilliant Career* (1901; Melbourne: Penguin, 2007), 3. All subsequent references are to this edition and appear in parentheses in the text.

adequately accommodate her.[60] Interestingly, she is given a copy of Hennessey's *An Australian Bush Track*, by one of her suitors: offering her the chance to read about an Australian girl whose trajectory is the complete opposite of her own.

Sybylla has three suitors in the novel: the aristocratic English barrister Everard Grey, the jackeroo Frank Hawden (who will also inherit English property), and the squatter Harold Beecham. Her interest in Everard Grey is short-lived and flatly contradicts the kind of colonial romance we have already seen in which a wealthy Englishman seduces and marries an Australian girl (e.g. Praed's *An Australian Heroine*). "Such a beau of beaux", Sybylla writes, as she rejects his advances; "no doubt he was annoyed that an insignificant little country bumpkin should not be flattered by his patronage ..." (81). Frank Hawden is smitten with her, but she takes every opportunity to humiliate him. When he angrily grasps her wrist, she strikes him a "vigorous blow on the nose": "my motto with men", she tells him, "is touch-me-not, and it is your own fault if I'm fierce" (83). Sybylla is a bit like Marjory in Hennessey's novel here: except her aggression is directed at a frustrated suitor, not a violent father. With Harold Beecham, however, a more complicated power struggle plays itself out. Beecham is a wealthy squatter, the owner of a number of large properties across several colonies. He is also known for his hot temper. When he first meets Sybylla, he thinks she is a servant girl and attempts to kiss her. After she protests, he decides instead to test her with his whip:

> "Don't be frightened, sissy, I never kiss girls, and I'm not going to start at this time of day, and against their will to boot. You haven't been long here, have you? I haven't seen you before. Stand out there till I see if you've got any grit in you, and then I am done with you".
>
> I stood in the middle of the yard, the spot he indicated, while he uncurled his long heavy stock-whip with its big lash and scented myall handle. He cracked it round and round my head and arms, but I did not feel the least afraid, as I saw at a glance that he was exceedingly dexterous in the bushman's art of handling a stock-whip, and knew, if I kept perfectly still, I was quite safe. (89)

In this remarkable scene, a squatter threatens to kiss and then to whip a young girl: but she emerges unhurt, and untouched ("touch-me-not"). The whip becomes a playfully obvious symbol of the squatter's phallic power: "Now you had better be civil", he tells Sybylla later on, "for I have got the big end of the whip" (121). Soon afterwards, Beecham proposes to her and is surprised when she accepts: "I never dreamt you would say yes so easily", he tells her, "just like any other girl" (140). But Sybylla is *not* like any other girl: or rather, she is representative (as an "Australian girl") but at the same time obstinately different. We can return to Sara Ahmed's notion of the wilful character here: "Wilfulness for women in particular ... might describe the costs of *not becoming background*".[61] When Beecham stoops to kiss her to seal the arrangement, Sybylla picks up his whip and strikes him across the face. "It left a great weal on the healthy sun-tanned skin ... [and] had blinded the left eye ... He made a gesture toward me. I half expected and fervently wished he would strike. The enormity of what I had done paralysed me ... Oh, that Harold would thrash me severely! It would have infinitely relieved me" (141).

---

60 Henderson, "Gender, Genre, and Sybylla's Performative Identity", 165.
61 Ahmed, "Wilful Parts", 245.

The two scenes of courtship with Beecham are therefore also whipping scenes: the first is a literal demonstration of masculine power, although it never actually touches Sybylla; while the second sees her grabbing the whip for herself and drawing a squatter's blood. We might recall Dorna in Hennessey's novel here, forcibly reducing a young squatter to tears in a train carriage. But Sybylla's use of the whip is more complex: a violent reaction to almost being kissed, an attack on patriarchal power (and squatter liberties), and – after the event – an abject expression of remorse that also triggers masochistic desire ("thrash me severely!"). What Beecham calls her "touch-me-not style" (142) might be thought about as an expression of "frigidity", a term increasingly pathologised in medical writing in the second half of the nineteenth century, with its use "intensifying" during the *fin-de-siècle*.[62] Alison Moore connects frigidity and female masochism around this time as "perverse exaggeration[s] of a gendered order of normalcy" for women.[63] Frigidity in particular was also often associated with the figure of the New Woman. The character of Sue Bridehead in Thomas Hardy's *Jude the Obscure* (1895) is a noted example: Kate Millet, in *Sexual Politics* (1969), had famously called her both a New Woman and a "Frigid Woman".[64] The accusation of frigidity has been one way of casting the New Woman as "deviant" – linking her to other, related character types such as the single woman or spinster, and the lesbian. This is the point that Richard Dellamora makes, when he suggests that Hardy only gives Sue Bridehead "two alternatives" in his novel, "a disabling normalcy or degrees of deviance".[65] But frigidity can also be read more positively. Simone de Beauvoir does exactly this in *The Second Sex* (1949): "the [frigid] woman", she writes, "makes the male pay for all the affronts she considers she has been subjected to by an insulting coldness".[66] In an article on de Beauvoir and frigidity, Suzanne Laba Cataldi argues that the frigid woman enacts "an active, voluntary rejection of dominance in heterosexual relationships": frigidity should therefore be viewed "as a means or method of resistance, or as a harm that women suffer in a culturally oppressive or sexist environment".[67]

We can certainly understand Sybylla's "touch-me-not style" in this way, as a mode of resistance to masculine domination – and to the generic expectations of women's romance. In another article on *My Brilliant Career*, Ian Henderson argues that Franklin stages "an internal debate about national literary style" through "the flux of Sybylla's body".[68] For Henderson, Sybylla's sexual contradictions – her "curious combination of frankness and reticence, of carnal knowledge and sexual self-denial"[69] – are symptomatic of the novel's generic inconsistency. He turns in particular to a kind of *sado*-masochistic tendency in

---

62 See Alison Moore, "Pathologising Female Sexual Frigidity in *Fin-de-Siècle* France, or How Absence Was Made into a Thing", in *Pleasure and Pain in Nineteenth-Century French Literature and Culture*, ed. David Evans and Kate Griffiths (Amsterdam: Rodopi, 2008), 187.
63 Alison Moore, *Sexual Myths of Modernity: Sadism, Masochism, and Historical Teleology* (Lanham Md.: Lexington Books, 2016), 36.
64 Kate Millet, *Sexual Politics* (New York: Columbia University Press, 2016), 130.
65 Richard Dellamora, *Masculine Desire: The Sexual Politics of Victorian Aestheticism* (Chapel Hill: University of North Carolina Press, 1990), 215.
66 Simone de Beauvoir, *The Second Sex*, trans. H.H. Parshley (1949; New York: Vintage, 1974), 439.
67 Suzanne Laba Cataldi, "Sexuality Situated: Beauvoir on 'Frigidity'", in *The Philosophy of Simone de Beauvoir: Critical Essays*, ed. Margaret A. Simons (Bloomington: Indiana University Press, 2006), 163.
68 Ian Henderson, "The Body of an Australian Girl: Sexuality and Style in Miles Franklin's *My Brilliant Career*", in *Feminism and the Body: Interdisciplinary Perspectives*, ed. Catherine Kevin (Newcastle upon Tyne: Cambridge Scholars Publishing, 2009), 117.
69 Henderson, "The Body of an Australian Girl", 117.

Sybylla's character, something already apparent in the second whipping scene. Later on, at Caddagat, her wealthy grandmother's station, Sybylla finds herself alone with Beecham in a fruit orchard: an ideal setting for the Australian girl's romantic liaison. Sybylla has been deliberately flirting with other men to provoke Beecham's jealousy. The squatter reacts angrily, grabbing her forcibly by the wrist:

> "Unhand me, sir!" I said shortly, attempting to wrench myself free . . .
>
> For answer he took a firmer hold, in one hand seizing my arm above the elbow, and gripping my shoulder with the other so tightly that, through my flimsy covering, his strong fingers bruised me so severely that in a calmer moment I would have squirmed and cried out with pain. (158-9)

This is another "touch-me-not" moment in the novel that elicits the opposite outcome, the effects of which Sybylla seems to enjoy. "I had led him on", she confesses, "because his perpetually calm demeanour had excited in me a desire to test if it were possible to disturb him" (161). Here, Sybylla is both "frigid" and flirtatious; she puts a "method of resistance" into play with Beecham, but she also takes pleasure in his expressions of masculine dominance ("I wish you would get in a rage again"). She rejects his proposal of marriage, wanting instead to throw herself into a passionate, even "violent", love affair: to not be touched, and to be (violently) touched.

That evening, undressing in her room, Sybylla remarks: "I discovered on my soft white shoulders and arms – so susceptible to bruises – many marks, and black"; "It had been a very happy day for me", she concludes (165). We have seen the bruised Australian girl before, with Esther in Praed's *An Australian Heroine* ("physical violence seems to a woman the deepest mark of degradation"). But Sybylla's bruises are framed quite differently. They caught the attention of the prominent British sexologist Havelock Ellis, who had in fact reviewed *My Brilliant Career* in September 1903, regarding the novel as "of psychological interest but painfully crude, too crude to impress as literature".[70] In volume three of his *Studies in the Psychology of Sex* – first published in the same year – Ellis invokes the second whipping scene and the orchard scene in *My Brilliant Career* as moments that demonstrate an "attraction to violence" experienced by a certain kind of woman. He is talking, of course, about the masochistic woman – and the sadistic man. These scenes typify, as he puts it, "the feminine tendency to delight in submission" in relation to male domination.[71] Sybylla may very well "delight in submission"; but as we have noted, she can also be dominant and dominating, resistant and assertive, and physically violent. Ian Henderson notes precisely this contradiction when he concludes that Sybylla has "embarked upon a sadistic search for masochistic submission".[72]

---

70   Cited in Roe, *Her Brilliant Career*, 71.
71   Havelock Ellis, *Studies in the Psychology of Sex*, vol. 3, second edition (Philadelphia, Penn.: A. Davis Company, 1921), 81–2.
72   Henderson, "The Body of an Australian Girl", 121.

The Limits of a National Type

In 1895 Alfred Deakin had famously described Federation as a matter of "entering the bonds of permanent matrimony" by bringing the colonies together.[73] Indeed, as Helen Irving notes, the "image of marriage was evoked" over and over in the late 1890s, "sometimes to reinforce the appeal of Federation, but just as often to warn that it was permanent and had to be entered into carefully".[74] The matrimonial pressure on a representative national type like the Australian girl was considerable by this time, and in fact this is the expected outcome for Sybylla in *My Brilliant Career*. But she increasingly disappoints her suitors, and her relatives: she refuses marriage as the final option, ultimately returning to "the sodden round of daily tasks" on the local family farm – much more in keeping with the secular disillusionment of vernacular bush realism (which took little interest in Federation) than the speculative ambitions of women's romance. Angela Woollacott had suggested above that the Australian girl "boldly stood for modernity and independence": but Sybylla's return to the family farm negates both of these outcomes. The view of Federation as the "marriage" of the colonies and the realisation of the new nation's independence was in any case never definitive. The constitutional lawyer George Winterton has noted that "if 'independence' is taken to mean freedom from external constraint, Australia was not independent in 1901".[75] It is as if Sybylla's predicament at the end of *My Brilliant Career* is a reaction against the promise of Federation on two levels: she refuses to marry, but neither does she achieve independence. We have come back to Michelle Smith's earlier point about the novels of Praed and Martin and "the deflation of the Australian girl's aspirations": except that *My Brilliant Career* emerges *out* of Federation, the moment when one might imagine the Australian girl should be poised to fulfil her potential.

We began this book by talking about minor character types in colonial Australia, where national identity can never be understood in monolithic, representative terms. National types (the Australian girl, the "native-born", and so on) always fragment into differentiated "species", each of which is identified in a particular way, generating its own narrative trajectory. We argued that – as we think more carefully about the specificity of colonial character types – it becomes increasingly difficult to maintain any coherent sense of a type who could properly be said to be representative of the colonies at large. The Australian girl might seem to provide an exception to this claim, as an expression of the ambitions and longings of a nation-to-come. But she remains problematic in a variety of ways, often refusing outright to conform to conventional expectations: such as marriage, or a "bold" independence. Even the heroic Dorna in Hennessey's novel is resistant to marriage most of the time – and when she *does* agree to wed, the novel taints the optimism of this event by tying it to her complicity in colonial frontier violence. The Australian girl operates along a spectrum of normativity that entirely depends on the narrative's ideological investment in the type. It is perhaps worth recalling Richard Dellamora's view above of the options offered to the New Woman at the end of the nineteenth century, "a

---

73 Cited in Helen Irving, *To Constitute a Nation: A Cultural History of Australia's Constitution* (Cambridge: Cambridge University Press, 1999), 7.
74 Irving, *To Constitute a Nation*, 7.
75 George Winterton, "The Acquisition of Independence", in *Reflections on the Australian Constitution*, ed. Robert French, Geoffrey Lindell and Cheryl Saunders (Sydney: The Federation Press, 2003), 32.

disabling normalcy or degrees of deviance". The same kinds of options seem to apply to the Australian girl: think, for example, of Esther's grim acceptance of her "disabling" marriage at the end of Praed's *An Australian Heroine*.

In fact, these options apply whenever the nation itself is invoked in a representative way. It is precisely because national identity requires "normalcy" (sameness, self-recognition, a *status quo*) that it also therefore inevitably generates "degrees of deviance". A national commitment to normalcy – or normativity – in any case sets limits and expectations that can never actually be realised, even in narrative form. And that commitment always sees others excluded from the national paradigm. At the end of *My Brilliant Career* – at the point where Sybylla's identity as an Australian girl has almost completely collapsed – she addresses the nation in one final, curious attempt at patriotic optimism. "Now for a lilt of another theme", she writes: "I am proud that I am an Australian, a daughter of the Southern Cross, a child of the mighty bush. I am thankful I am a peasant, a part of the bone and muscle of my nation . . . " (252). But as her address unfolds, she begins to distinguish herself from this kind of imagined national community, as if it is somehow beyond her: "Would that I were more worthy to be one of you – more a typical Australian peasant – cheerful, honest, brave!" (252). Here, an Australian girl's patriotism envisions another national type to which she aspires – the "typical Australian peasant" – but only in order, finally, to distinguish herself from it. This is precisely the predicament of the national type, normative and "deviant" at the same time: I want to belong, but I don't (want to) belong.

Works Cited

Adams, Francis W.L. *The Murder of Madeline Brown*. (1887) Melbourne: Text Publishing, 2000.
Ahmed, Sara. "Wilful Parts: Problem Characters or the Problem of Character". *New Literary History*. 42:2 (Spring 2011): 231–53.
Appadurai, Arjun, ed. *The Social Life of Things: Commodities in Cultural Perspective*. New York: Cambridge University Press, 1986.
Barnard, Edwin. *Emporium: Selling the Dream in Colonial Australia*. Canberra: National Library of Australia, 2015.
Barrell, John. "Putting Down the Rising". In *Scotland and the Borders of Romanticism*, edited by Leith Davis, Ian Duncan and Janet Sorensen. Cambridge: Cambridge University Press, 2004.
Baudelaire, Charles. *The Painter of Modern Life*. (1863) Translated by P.E. Charvet. London: Penguin, 2010.
Baynton, Barbara. *Bush Studies*. (1902) Sydney: Angus & Robertson, 1989.
Beer, Gillian. *Open Fields: Science in Cultural Encounter*. Cambridge: Cambridge University Press, 1996.
Bellanta, Melissa. *Larrikins: A History*. St Lucia: University of Queensland Press, 2012.
——. "Fabulating the Australian Desert: Australia's Lost Race Romances, 1890–1908". *Philament* 3 (April 2004). http://bit.ly/2hxTpOx.
Bivona, Daniel and Roger B. Henkle. *The Imagination of Class: Masculinity and the Victorian Urban Poor*. Columbus: Ohio State University Press, 2006.
Boldrewood, Rolf. *A Romance of Canvas Town*. London: Macmillan & Co., 1898.
——. *Old Melbourne Memories*. London: Macmillan & Co., Ltd.: 1896.
——. *The Squatter's Dream: A Story of Australian Life*. London: Macmillan & Co., 1891.
——. *Robbery Under Arms*. (1888) Edited by Paul Eggert and Elizabeth Webby. St Lucia: University of Queensland Press, 2006.
Boltanski, Luc. *Mysteries and Conspiracies: Detective Stories, Spy Novels and the Making of Modern Societies*. Translated by Catherine Porter. Cambridge: Polity Press, 2014.
Bonwick, James. *The Bushrangers; Illustrating the Early Days of Van Diemen's Land*. Melbourne: George Robertson, 1856.
Borlase, James Skipp. *The Night Fossickers, and Other Australian Tales of Peril and Adventure*. London: Frederick Warne & Co., 1867.
Bourdieu, Pierre. *The Rules of Art: Genesis and Structure of the Literary Field*. Translated by Susan Emanuel. Stanford, Calif.: Stanford University Press, 1996.
——. *The Field of Cultural Production*. Translated by Randal Johnson. Oxford: Polity Press, 1993.
Boyce, James. *1835: The Founding of Melbourne and the Conquest of Australia*. Melbourne: Black Inc., 2013.
——. *Van Diemen's Land: A History*. Melbourne: Black Inc., 2008.

Works Cited

Bradley, Charles. *The Belgrave Case: A Romance of Melbourne Life.* Melbourne: H.W. Mills & Co., 1891.

Brand, Dana. *The Spectator and the City in Nineteenth-Century American Literature.* Cambridge: Cambridge University Press, 1991.

Briggs, Jo. "Flaneurs, Commodities, and the Working Body in Louis Huart's *Physiologie du Flaneur* and Albert Smith's *Natural History of the Idler Upon Town*". In *The Flaneur Abroad: Historical and International Perspectives*, edited by Richard Wrigley. Newcastle upon Tyne, UK: Cambridge Scholars Publishing, 2014.

Bulfin, Ailise. "Guy Boothby's 'Bid for Fortune': Constructing an Anglo-Australian Colonial Identity for the *Fin-de-Siècle* London Literary Marketplace". In *Changing the Victorian Subject*, edited by Maggie Tonkin et al. (Adelaide: University of Adelaide Press, 2014).

Butlin, Noel. *Forming a Colonial Economy: Australia 1810–1850.* Cambridge: Cambridge University Press, 1994.

Butlin, S.J. *Foundations of the Australian Monetary System, 1788–1851.* Sydney: Sydney University Press, 1968. http://setis.library.usyd.edu.au/ozlit/pdf/sup0003.pdf.

Butterss, Philip, ed. *Southwords: Essays on South Australian Writing.* Adelaide: Wakefield Press, 1995.

Calhoun, Craig, ed. *Habermas and the Public Sphere.* Cambridge, Mass.: MIT Press, 1992.

Cameron, Donald. *Mysteries of Melbourne Life: A Story Founded on Fact.* Melbourne: Mason, Firth & M'Cutcheon, 1873.

——. "The Scowbanker". *The Australian Journal*, 9 February 1867.

——. "The Adventures of a Squatter". Serialised in the *Australian Journal*, October–December 1866.

——. "The Melbourne Dandy". *Australian Journal*, 26 May 1866.

Campbell, Rosemary. Introduction to Catherine Martin's *An Australian Girl*. St Lucia: University of Queensland Press, 2002.

Carey, Jane and Jane Lydon, eds. *Indigenous Networks: Mobility, Connections and Exchange.* London and New York: Routledge, 2014.

Cataldi, Suzanne Laba. "Sexuality Situated: Beauvoir on 'Frigidity'". In *The Philosophy of Simone de Beauvoir: Critical Essays*, edited by Margaret A. Simons. Bloomington: Indiana University Press, 2006.

Champion, Shelagh and George Champion. "The Clontarf Case". Manly: *Manly Library Local Studies*, 1992. http://bit.ly/2nl5xS4.

Clacy, Ellen. *A Lady's Visit to the Gold Diggings in Australia in 1852–53.* Auckland: The Floating Press, 2010.

Clarke, Marcus. *A Colonial City: High and Low Life: Selected Journalism of Marcus Clarke*, edited by L.T. Hergenhan. St Lucia: University of Queensland Press, 1972.

——. *Australian Tales.* Melbourne: Marion Clarke, 1896.

——. *The Future Australian Race.* Melbourne: A.H. Massina & Co., 1877.

——. "Squatters – Old Style and New". *Brisbane Courier*, 10 March 1870.

——. *Long Odds: A Novel.* Melbourne: Clarson, Massina, 1869.

Clarke, Philip A. *Aboriginal Plant Collectors: Botanists and Australian Aboriginal People in the Nineteenth Century.* Kenthurst, NSW: Rosenberg Publishing, 2008.

Clemm, Sabine. *Dickens, Journalism, and Nationhood: Mapping the World in* Household Words. New York: Routledge, 2009.

Cochrane, Peter. *Colonial Ambition: Foundations of Australian Democracy.* Melbourne: Melbourne University Press, 2006.

Conan Doyle, Arthur. *The Sign of Four.* (1890) London: Penguin Books, 2014.

Conor, Liz. "Introduction: Classification and Its Discontents". *Interventions: International Journal of Postcolonial Studies* 17:2 (2014): 155–73.

Critchett, Jan. *Untold Stories: Memories and Lives of Victorian Kooris.* Carlton, Vic.: Melbourne University Press, 1998.

Croft, Julian. "Reading the Three as One: *Such Is Life* in 1897". *Journal of the Association for the Study of Australian Literature* 13:1 (2013). http://bit.ly/2gGgE99.

Cunningham, Peter. *Two Years in New South Wales; A Series of Letters, Comprising Sketches of the Actual State of Society in that Colony; of Its Peculiar Advantages to Emigrants; of Its Topography, Natural History, &c., &c.*, vol. 1. London: Henry Colburn, 1827.

Daly, Maurice Daly and Patrick Malone. "Sydney: The Economic and Political Roots of Darling Harbour". In *City, Capital and Water*, edited by Patrick Malone. London: Routledge, 1996.

Dalziell, Tanya. *Settler Romances and the Australian Girl*. Perth: University of Western Australia Press, 2004.

Davis, Leith, Ian Duncan and Janet Sorensen, eds. *Scotland and the Borders of Romanticism*. Cambridge: Cambridge University Press, 2004.

Davison, Graeme. "Sydney and the Bush: An Urban Context for the Australian Legend". *Australian Historical Studies* 18:71 (October 1978): 191–209.

———. "Gold-Rush Melbourne". In *Gold: Forgotten Histories and Lost Objects of Australia*, edited by Iain McCalman et al. Cambridge: Cambridge University Press, 2001.

Davitt, Ellen. "The Black Sheep: A Tale of Australian Life". *Australian Journal,* 9 December 1865.

Dawson, Carrie. "'The Slaughterman of Wagga Wagga': Imposture, National Identity, and the Tichborne Affair". In *Who's Who? Hoaxes, Imposture and Identity Crises in Australian Literature*, edited by Maggie Nolan and Carrie Dawson, special issue of *Australian Literary Studies* 21.4 (2004): 1–13.

Day, Leanne. "'Those Ungodly Pressmen': The Early Years of the Brisbane Johnsonian Club". *Australian Literary Studies* 21:1 (2003), 92–102.

de Beauvoir, Simone. *The Second Sex*, trans. H.H. Parshley. (1949) New York: Vintage, 1974.

de Serville, Paul. *Rolf Boldrewood: A Life*. Melbourne: Miegunyah Press, 2000.

———. *Port Phillip Gentlemen, and Good Society in Melbourne before the Gold Rushes*. Melbourne: Oxford University Press, 1980.

Dellamora, Richard. *Masculine Desire: The Sexual Politics of Victorian Aestheticism*. Chapel Hill: University of North Carolina Press, 1990.

Dickens, Charles. *Bleak House*. London: Bradbury & Evans, 1853.

Dimond, Jill and Peter Kirkpatrick. *Literary Sydney: A Walking Guide to Writers' Haunts and Other Bookish and Bohemian Places*. St Lucia: University of Queensland Press, 2000.

Dixon, Robert. *Photography, Early Cinema, and Colonial Modernity: Frank Hurley's Synchronised Lecture Entertainments*. London: Anthem Press, 2011.

———. *Writing the Colonial Adventure: Race, Gender and Nation in Anglo-Australian Popular Fiction, 1875–1914*. Cambridge: Cambridge University Press, 1995.

Dixon, Robert and Nicholas Birns, eds. *Reading Across the Pacific: Australia–United States Intellectual Histories*. Sydney: Sydney University Press, 2010.

Docker, John. *The Nervous Nineties: Australian Cultural Life in the 1890s*. Oxford: Oxford University Press, 1991.

Doggett, Anne. "Crying in the Colonies: The Bellmen of Early Australia". *Journal of Australian Colonial History* 14 (2012): 49–68.

Dudley, Edward and Maximillian E. Novak, eds. *The Wild Man Within: An Image in Western Thought from the Renaissance to Romanticism*. Pittsburgh, Penn.: University of Pittsburgh Press, 1972.

Dyos, Jim and Michael Wolff, eds. *The Victorian City*, vol. 2. London: Routledge, 2002.

Earle, Horace. *Ups and Downs, or, Incidents of Australian Life*. London: A.W. Bennett, 1861.

Eggert, Paul. "Textual Criticism and Folklore: The Ned Kelly Story and *Robbery Under Arms*". *Script and Print* 31:2 (2007): 69–80.

Ellis, Havelock. *Studies in the Psychology of Sex*, vol. 3. Second edition. Philadelphia, Penn.: A. Davis Company, 1921.

Emsley, Clive and Haia Shpayer-Makov, ed. *Police Detectives in History, 1750–1950*. Aldershot, UK: Ashgate, 2006.

Evans, David and Kate Griffiths, ed. *Pleasure and Pain in Nineteenth-Century French Literature and Culture*. Amsterdam: Rodopi, 2008.

Falconer, Delia. *Sydney*. Sydney: NewSouth Books, 2010.

Works Cited

Farjeon, B.J. "In Australian Wilds". In *The Anthology of Colonial Australian Crime Fiction*, edited by Ken Gelder and Rachael Weaver. Melbourne: Melbourne University Press, 2008.

Farrell, Michael. "Death Watch: Reading the Common Object of the Billycan in 'Waltzing Matilda'". *Journal of the Association for the Study of Australian Literature* 10 (2010). http://bit.ly/2huSRWI.

Ferres, Kay. "Shrouded Histories: *Outlaw and Lawmaker*, Republican Politics and Women's Interests". *Australian Literary Studies* 21:1 (2003): 32–42.

Fletcher, Henry. *The North Shore Mystery*. London: Swan Sonnenschein & Co., 1899.

Foster, Robert and Amanda Nettlebeck. *Out of the Silence: The History and Memory of South Australia's Frontier Wars*. Adelaide: Wakefield Press, 2012.

Fotheringham, Richard, ed. *Australian Plays for the Colonial Stage, 1834–1899*. St Lucia: University of Queensland Press, 2006.

Fowler, Elizabeth. *Literary Character: The Human Figure in Early English Writing*. Ithaca, NY: Cornell University Press, 2003.

Fowler, Frank. *Southern Lights and Shadows*. (1859) Sydney: Sydney University Press, 1975.

Franklin, Miles. *My Brilliant Career*. (1901) Melbourne: Penguin, 2007.

Fraser, Nancy. "Rethinking the Public Sphere: A Contribution to the Critique of Actually Existing Democracy". In *Habermas and the Public Sphere*, edited by Craig Calhoun. Cambridge, Mass.: MIT Press, 1992.

Freeman, John. *Lights and Shadows of Melbourne Life*. London: Sampson Low, Marston, Searle, & Rivington, 1888.

French, Robert, Geoffrey Lindell and Cheryl Saunders, eds. *Reflections on the Australian Constitution*. Sydney: The Federation Press, 2003.

Frow, John. *Character and Person*. Oxford: Oxford University Press, 2014.

Furphy, Joseph. *Such Is Life*. (1903) Melbourne: Text Publishing, 2013.

"Garryowen". *The Chronicles of Early Melbourne, 1835–1852*, vol. 2. Melbourne: Fergusson & Mitchell, 1888.

Gelder, Ken and Rachael Weaver, eds. *The Colonial Journals, and the Emergence of Australian Literary Culture*. Perth: University of Western Australia Press, 2014.

——. *The Anthology of Colonial Australian Adventure Fiction*. Melbourne: Melbourne University Press, 2011.

——. *The Anthology of Colonial Australian Crime Fiction*. Melbourne: Melbourne University Press, 2008.

Geoghegan, Edward. *The Currency Lass; or, My Native Girl*. Sydney: Currency Methuen Drama, 1976.

Giles, Fiona. *Too Far Everywhere: A Romantic Heroine in Nineteenth-Century Australia*. St Lucia: University of Queensland Press, 1998.

——. "Romance: An Embarrassing Subject". In *The Penguin New Literary History of Australia*, edited by Laurie Hergenhan et al. Melbourne: Penguin, 1988.

Giles, Paul. *Antipodean Australia: Australasia and the Constitution of US Literature*. Oxford: Oxford University Press, 2013.

Glover, David. *Literature, Immigration and Diaspora in Fin-de-Siècle England: A Cultural History of the 1905 Aliens Act*. Cambridge: Cambridge University Press, 2012.

Gluck, Mary. *Popular Bohemia: Modernism and Urban Culture in Nineteenth-Century Paris*. Cambridge: Harvard University Press, 2005.

Goldstein, Jan. *Console and Classify: The French Psychiatric Profession in the Nineteenth Century*. Chicago: University of Chicago Press, 2001.

Goodman, David. *Gold Seeking: Victoria and California in the 1850s*. Stanford, Calif.: Stanford University Press, 1994.

Grand, Sarah. "The New Aspect of the Woman Question". In *The American New Woman Revisited: A Reader, 1894–1930*, edited by Martha H. Patterson. New Brunswick, NJ: Rutgers University Press, 2008.

Griffiths, Tom. *Hunters and Collectors: The Antiquarian Imagination in Australia*. Cambridge: Cambridge University Press, 1996.

Works Cited

Halasz, Judith R. *The Bohemian Ethos: Questioning Work and Making a Scene on the Lower East Side*. New York and London: Routledge, 2015.

Hall, Catherine. "The Slave Owner and the Settler". In *Indigenous Networks: Mobility, Connections and Exchange*, edited by Jane Carey and Jane Lydon. London and New York: Routledge, 2014.

Hall, N. John, ed. *The Letters of Anthony Trollope, Volume 2, 1871–1882*. Stanford, Calif.: Stanford University Press, 1983.

Hare, Francis Augustus. *The Last of the Bushrangers: An Account of the Capture of the Kelly Gang*. London: Hurst & Blackett, 1895.

Harrison, Robert. *Colonial Sketches: or, Five Years in South Australia, with Hints to Capitalists and Emigrants*. London: Hall, Virtue & Co., 1862.

Harrison, Rodney. *Shared Landscapes: Archaeologies of Attachment and the Pastoral Industry in New South Wales*. Sydney: UNSW Press, 2004.

Hassan, Andrew. *Sailing to Australia: Shipboard Diaries by Nineteenth-Century British Emigrants*. Manchester: Manchester University Press, 1994.

Henderson, Ian. "The Body of an Australian Girl: Sexuality and Style in Miles Franklin's *My Brilliant Career*". In *Feminism and the Body: Interdisciplinary Perspectives*, edited by Catherine Kevin. Newcastle upon Tyne, UK: Cambridge Scholars Publishing, 2009.

——. "Gender, Genre, and Sybylla's Performative Identity in Miles Franklin's *My Brilliant Career*". *Australian Literary Studies* 18:2 (October 1997): 165–73.

Hennessey, J.D. *An Australian Bush Track*. London: Sampson Low, Marston & Company, 1896.

Hergenhan, L.T. (Laurie), ed. *A Colonial City: High and Low Life: Selected Journalism of Marcus Clarke*. St Lucia: University of Queensland Press, 1972.

Hergenhan, L.T. (Laurie), eds. *The Penguin New Literary History of Australia*. Melbourne: Penguin, 1988.

Herron, Jerry et al., eds. *The Ends of Theory*. Detroit, Mich.: Wayne State University Press, 1996.

Heseltine, Harry. Introduction to N. Walter Swan's *Luke Miver's Harvest*. Sydney: UNSW Press, 1991. http://setis.library.usyd.edu.au/ozlit/pdf/p00083.pdf.

Himmelfarb, Gertrude. "The Culture of Poverty". In *The Victorian City*, vol. 2, edited by Jim Dyos and Michael Wolff. London: Routledge, 2002.

Hoffenberg, Peter H. *An Empire on Display: English, Indian, and Australian Exhibitions from the Crystal Palace to the Great War*. Berkeley and Los Angeles: University of California Press, 2001.

Hosking, Rick. "Ellen Liston's 'Doctor' and the Elliston Incident". In *Southwords: Essays on South Australian Writing*, edited by Philip Butterss. Adelaide: Wakefield Press, 1995.

Howitt, Richard. *Impressions of Australia Felix, During Four Years' Residence in that Colony*. London: Longman, Brown, Green & Longmans, 1845.

——. *Tallangetta, the Squatter's Home: A Story of Australian Life*, vol. 1. London: Longman, Brown, Green, Longmans & Roberts, 1857.

Howitt, William. *Land, Labour, and Gold: Two Years in Victoria: with Visits to Sydney and Van Diemen's Land*. (1855) Cambridge: Cambridge University Press, 2010.

Hume, Fergus. *The Mystery of a Hansom Cab*. (1886) London: The Hogarth Press, 1985.

Irving, Helen. *To Constitute a Nation: A Cultural History of Australia's Constitution*. Cambridge: Cambridge University Press, 1999.

Janin, Jules. *An American in Paris*. London: Longman, Brown, Green & Longmans, 1843.

Johnson, Murray. "Australian Bushrangers: Law, Retribution and the Public Imagination". In *Crime Over Time: Temporal Perspectives on Crime and Punishment in Australia*, edited by Robyn Lincoln and Shirleene Robinson. Newcastle upon Tyne: Cambridge Scholars Publishing, 2010.

Johnson-Woods, Toni. "'Adventures of a Squatter': A Colonial Male Romance". *Southerly* 70:2 (2010): 138–9.

Jordens, Ann-Mari. *The Stenhouse Circle: Literary Life in Mid-Nineteenth Century Sydney*. Carlton, Vic.: Melbourne University Press, 1979.

Kaladelfos, Amanda. "The Politics of Punishment: Rape and the Death Penalty in Colonial Australia, 1841–1901". *History Australia* 9:1 (2012): 155–75.

Works Cited

Keal, Paul. *European Conquest and the Rights of Indigenous Peoples: The Moral Backwardness of International Society*. Cambridge: Cambridge University Press, 2003.

Kelly, Ned. The Jerilderie Letter. 1879. Transcribed by the National Museum of Australia. http://www.nma.gov.au/collections/collection_interactives/jerilderie_letter.

Kern, Stephen. *A Cultural History of Causality: Science, Murder Novels, and Systems of Thought*. Princeton, NJ: Princeton University Press, 2004.

Kevin, Catherine, ed. *Feminism and the Body: Interdisciplinary Perspectives*. Newcastle upon Tyne, UK: Cambridge Scholars Publishing, 2009.

Kingsley, Henry. *The Hillyars and the Burtons: A Story of Two Families*. Boston, Mass.: Ticknor & Fields, 1865.

——. *The Recollections of Geoffry Hamlyn*. (1859) St Lucia: University of Queensland Press, 1996.

Knight, Stephen. *The Mysteries of the Cities: Urban Crime Fiction in the Nineteenth Century*. Jefferson, NC: McFarland & Company, 2012.

——. *Continent of Mystery: A Thematic History of Australian Crime Fiction*. Melbourne: Melbourne University Press, 1997.

Lake, Marilyn. "Historical Reconsiderations IV: The Politics of Respectability: Identifying the Masculinist Context". *Historical Studies* 22.86 (1986).

Land, Isaac. "Men with the Faces of Brutes: Physiognomy, Urban Anxieties, and Police States". In *Enemies of Humanity: The Nineteen-Century War on Terrorism*, edited by Isaac Land. London: Palgrave Macmillan, 2008.

Lang, John. *The Forger's Wife*. London: Ward & Lock, 1855.

Lawson, Henry. *While the Billy Boils: The Original Newspaper Versions*. Edited by Paul Eggert. Sydney: Sydney University Press, 2013.

Lester, Alan and Fae Dussart. *Colonisation and the Origins of Humanitarian Governance: Protecting Aborigines across the Nineteenth-Century British Empire*. Cambridge: Cambridge University Press, 2014.

Lincoln, Robyn and Shirleene Robinson, eds. *Crime Over Time: Temporal Perspectives on Crime and Punishment in Australia*. Newcastle upon Tyne, UK: Cambridge Scholars Publishing, 2010.

Liston, Ellen. "Doctor". *Adelaide Observer*, 17 June 1882.

Ludlow, Christa. "The Reader Investigates: Images of Crime in the Colonial City". *Continuum: The Australian Journal of Media and Culture* 7:2 (1994). http://wwwmcc.murdoch.edu.au/ReadingRoom/7.2/Ludlow.html.

Lynch, Deirdre Shauna. *The Economy of Character: Novels, Market Culture, and the Business of Inner Meaning*. Chicago: University of Chicago Press, 1998.

Magarey, Susan. *Unbridling the Tongues of Women: A Biography of Catherine Helen Spence*. (1985) Adelaide: University of Adelaide Press, 2010.

Malone, Patrick, ed. *City, Capital and Water*. London: Routledge, 1996.

Martin, Catherine. *An Australian Girl*. (1890) Edited by Graham Tulloch. Oxford: Oxford University Press, 1999.

Martin, Susan K. "Gardening and the Cultivation of Australian National Space: The Writings of Ethel Turner". *Australian Feminist Studies* 18:42 (2003): 285–98.

Marx, Karl. *Capital: A Critique of Political Economy*, vol. 1, book 1. Edited by Frederick Engels. Translated by Samuel Moore and Edward Aveling. https://www.marxists.org/archive/marx/works/download/pdf/Capital-Volume-I.pdf.

Masury, John W. *The American Grainers' Hand-Book*. New York: John W. Masury & Son, 1872.

Mayhew, Henry. *London Labour and the London Poor*, vol. 1. New York: Dover Publications, 1968.

McCalman, Ian et al., eds. *Gold: Forgotten Histories and Lost Objects of Australia*. Cambridge: Cambridge University Press, 2001.

McCann, Andrew. *Marcus Clarke's Bohemia: Literature and Modernity in Colonial Melbourne*. Melbourne: Melbourne University Press, 2004.

Works Cited

McCombie, Thomas. *Australian Sketches: The Gold Discovery, Bush Graves, &c., &c.* London: Sampson Low, Son & Co., 1861.

———. *Adventures of a Colonist; or, Godfrey Arabin, the Settler.* London: John & Daniel A. Darling, 1845.

McLean, Ian A. *White Aborigines: Identity Politics in Australian Art.* Cambridge: Cambridge University Press, 1998.

McLean, Ian W. *Why Australia Prospered: The Shifting Sources of Economic Growth.* Princeton, NJ: Princeton University Press, 2013.

McMichael, Philip. *Settlers and the Agrarian Question: Foundations of Capitalism in Colonial Australia.* Cambridge: Cambridge University Press, 1984.

Meadows, Kenny. *Heads of the People, or, Portraits of the English.* Philadelphia: Carey & Hart, 1841.

Mellick, Stanton, Patrick Morgan and Paul Eggert. Introduction to Henry Kingsley's *The Recollections of Geoffry Hamlyn*. St Lucia: University of Queensland Press, 1996.

Merrett, David Tolmie. "The Australian Bank Crashes of the 1890s Revisited". *Business History Review* 87:3 (Autumn 2013): 407–29.

Miller, D.A. *The Novel and the Police.* Berkeley: University of California Press, 1988.

Millet, Kate. *Sexual Politics.* New York: Columbia University Press, 2016.

Mitchell, Thomas Livingstone. *Three Expeditions into the Interior of Eastern Australia*, vol. 1. London: T. & W. Boone, 1839.

Moore, Alison. *Sexual Myths of Modernity: Sadism, Masochism, and Historical Teleology.* Lanham, Md: Lexington Books, 2016.

———. "Pathologising Female Sexual Frigidity in *Fin-de-Siècle* France, or How Absence Was Made into a Thing". In *Pleasure and Pain in Nineteenth-Century French Literature and Culture*, edited by David Evans and Kate Griffiths. Amsterdam: Rodopi, 2008.

Moore, Tom Inglis. *Social Patterns in Australian Literature.* Berkeley: University of California Press, 1971.

Morris, E.E. *Austral English: An Australasian Dictionary of Words, Phrases and Usages.* (1898) Cambridge: Cambridge University Press, 2011.

Mundy, Godfrey Charles. *Our Antipodes: or, Residence and Rambles in the Australasian Colonies.* London: Richard Bentley, 1852.

Newey, Katherine. "When Is an Australian Playwright Not an Australian Playwright? The Case of May Holt". In *Playing Australia: Australian Theatre and the International Stage*, edited by Elizabeth Schafer and Susan Bradley Smith. Amsterdam: Rodopi, 2003.

Nisbet, Hume. *The Swampers: A Romance of the Westralian Goldfields.* London: F.V. White & Co., 1897.

———. *A Bush Girl's Romance.* London: F.V. White & Co., 1894.

———. *The Bushranger's Sweetheart: An Australian Romance.* London: F.V. White & Co., 1892.

———. *A Colonial Tramp: Travels and Adventures in Australia and New Guinea.* London: Ward & Downey, 1891.

———. *Bail Up! A Romance of Bushrangers and Blacks.* London: Chatto & Windus, 1890.

———. *The Land of the Hibiscus Blossom: A Yarn of the Papuan Gulf.* London: Ward & Downey, 1888.

O'Reilly, John Boyle. *Moondyne: A Story of Life in Western Australia.* (1879) Sydney: Sydney University Press, 2003.

Ouyang, Yu. *The Chinese in Australian Fiction, 1888–1988.* Amherst, NY: Cambria Press, 2008.

Palmer, Vance. *The Legend of the Nineties.* Melbourne: Melbourne University Press, 1954.

Patterson, Martha H. *The American New Woman Revisited: A Reader, 1894–1930.* Brunswick, NJ: Rutgers University Press, 2008.

Pedersen, Annette. "Governing Images of the Australian Police Trooper". In *Rethinking Law, Society and Governance: Foucault's Bequest*, edited by Gary Wickham and George Pavlich. Portland, Oreg.: Hart Publishing, 2001.

Perelman, Bob. "Parataxis and Narrative: The New Sentence in Theory and Practice". In *The Ends of Theory*, edited by Jerry Herron et al. Detroit, Mich.: Wayne State University Press, 1996.

Works Cited

Philadelphoff-Puren, Nina. "Reading Rape in Colonial Australia: Barbara Baynton's 'The Tramp', the *Bulletin* and Cultural Criticism". *Journal of the Association for the Study of Australian Literature* 2 (2010). http://bit.ly/2gGmib8.

Pickard, John. "Shepherding in Colonial Australia". *Rural History* 19:1 (2008): 55–80.

Pittard, Christopher. *Purity and Contamination in Late Victorian Detective Fiction*. Farnham, UK: Ashgate Publishing, 2011.

Praed, Rosa. *Outlaw and Lawmaker*. London: Chatto & Windus, 1893.

——. *An Australian Heroine*. London: Chapman & Hall, 1880.

Pybus, Cassandra. *Epic Journeys of Freedom: Runaway Slaves of the American Revolution and Their Global Quest for Liberty*. Boston, Mass.: Beacon Press, 2006.

Ramaswamy, Sumanthi. *The Lost Land of Lemuria: Fabulous Geographies, Catastrophic Histories*. Berkeley: University of California Press, 2004.

Richardson, Matthew. *Once a Jolly Swagman: The Ballad of Waltzing Matilda*. Melbourne: Melbourne University Press, 2006.

Roe, Jill. *Her Brilliant Career: The Life of Stella Miles Franklin*. Cambridge, Mass.: Harvard University Press, 2009.

Rowcroft, Charles. *The Bushranger of Van Diemen's Land*. London: Smith, Elder & Co., 1846.

——. *Tales of the Colonies; or, the Adventures of an Emigrant*. London: Saunders & Otley, 1843.

Sanyal, Debarati. *The Violence of Modernity: Baudelaire, Irony, and the Politics of Form*. Baltimore: Johns Hopkins University Press, 2006.

Schafer, Elizabeth and Susan Bradley Smith, eds. *Playing Australia: Australian Theatre and the International Stage*. Amsterdam: Rodopi, 2003.

Schaffer, Kay. *Women and the Bush: Forces of Desire in the Australian Cultural Tradition*. Cambridge: Cambridge University Press, 1988.

Shannon, Mary L. *Dickens, Reynolds, and Mayhew on Wellington Street: The Print Culture of a Victorian Street*. Farnham, UK: Ashgate Publishing, 2015.

Sheridan, Susan. Introduction to Barbara Baynton's *Bush Studies*. Sydney: Sydney University Press, 2009.

——. "'Temper, Romantic; Bias, Offensively Feminine': Australian Women Writers and Literary Nationalism". *Kunapipi* 7:2–3 (1985): 49–58.

Shpayer-Makov, Haia. *The Ascent of the Detective: Police Sleuths in Victorian and Edwardian England*. Oxford: Oxford University Press, 2011.

Sidney, Samuel. *Gallops and Gossips in the Bush of Australia, or, Passages in the Life of Alfred Barnard*. London: Longman, Brown, Green & Longmans, 1854.

——. *The Three Colonies of Australia: New South Wales, Victoria, South Australia; Their Pastures, Copper Mines, and Gold Fields*. Second edition. London: Ingram, Cooke & Co., 1853.

Simons, Margaret A., ed. *The Philosophy of Simone de Beauvoir: Critical Essays*. Bloomington: Indiana University Press, 2006.

Sinclair, Jenny. *A Walking Shadow: The Remarkable Double Life of Edward Oxford*. Melbourne: Arcade Publications, 2012.

Sinnett, Frederick. "The Fiction Fields of Australia". *Illustrated Journal of Australasia*, November 1856.

Sipe, Daniel. *Text, Image, and the Problem with Perfection in Nineteenth-Century France: Utopia and Its Afterlives*. London and New York: Routledge, 2016.

Smajic, Srdjan. *Ghost-Seers, Detectives, and Spiritualists: Theories of Vision in Victorian Literature and Science*. Cambridge: Cambridge University Press, 2010.

Smith, Albert. *The Natural History of the Ballet-Girl*. London: David Bogue, 1847.

——. *The Natural History of the Gent*. London: David Bogue, 1847.

Smith, Michelle J. "The 'Australian Girl' and the Domestic Ideal in Colonial Women's Fiction". In *Domestic Fiction in Colonial Australia and New Zealand*, edited by Tamara Wagner. London: Routledge, 2016.

Spence, Catherine Helen. *Clara Morison: A Tale of South Australia During the Gold Fever*. London: John W. Parker & Son, 1854.

Works Cited

Stewart, Ken. "Transcendentalism, Emerson and Nineteenth-Century Australian Literary Culture". In *Reading Across the Pacific: Australia–United States Intellectual Histories*, edited by Robert Dixon and Nicholas Birns. Sydney: Sydney University Press, 2010.

Sussex, Lucy. *Blockbuster! Fergus Hume and The Mystery of a Hansom Cab*. Melbourne: Text Publishing, 2015.

———. *Women Writers and Detectives in Nineteenth-Century Crime Fiction: The Mothers of the Mystery Genre*. London: Palgrave Macmillan, 2010.

———. *The Fortunes of Mary Fortune*. Melbourne: Penguin, 1989.

Swan, N. Walter. *Luke Miver's Harvest*. (1879) Sydney: UNSW Press, 1991. http://setis.library.usyd.edu.au/ozlit/pdf/p00083.pdf.

———. "Two Days at Michaelmas". *Australasian*, 2 August 1873.

Symons, Julian. *Bloody Murder: From the Detective Story to the Crime Novel*. Harmondsworth, UK: Penguin Books, 1972.

Todorov, Tzvetan. *The Poetics of Prose*, trans. Richard Howard. Ithaca, NY: Cornell University Press, 1977.

Travers, Martin, ed. *European Literature from Romanticism to Postmodernism: A Reader in Aesthetic Practice*. London: Bloomsbury, 2001.

Trollope, Anthony. *Harry Heathcote of Gangoil: A Tale of Australian Bush Life*. (1874) Edited by P.D. Edwards. London: The Trollope Society, 1998.

———. *Australia and New Zealand*. (1873) Cambridge: Cambridge University Press, 2013.

Tucker, Robert C., ed. *The Marx-Engels Reader*. New York: W.W. Norton, 1972.

Twopeny, R.E.N. *Town Life in Australia*. Harmondsworth: Penguin, 1973.

Wagner, Tamara, ed. *Domestic Fiction in Colonial Australia and New Zealand*. London: Routledge, 2016.

Wakefield, E.G. *A Letter from Sydney, the Principal Town of Australasia*. London: Joseph Cross, 1829.

Walker, William Sylvester. *Native Born*. London: John Long, 1900.

Ward, Russel. *The Australian Legend*. (1958) Melbourne: Oxford University Press, 1974.

Watson, Don. *The Bush: Travels in the Heart of Australia*. Melbourne: Hamish Hamilton, 2014.

Watson, Kate. *Women Writing Crime Fiction, 1860–1880: Fourteen American, British and Australian Authors*. Jefferson, NC: McFarland & Company, 2012.

Wells, Thomas. *Michael Howe: The Last and Worst of the Bushrangers of Van Diemen's Land*. Hobart: Andrew Bent, 1818.

White, Hayden. "The Forms of Wildness". In *The Wild Man Within: An Image in Western Thought from the Renaissance to Romanticism*, edited by Edward Dudley and Maximillian E. Novak. Pittsburgh, Penn.: University of Pittsburgh Press, 1972.

Whitworth, Robert P. "The Trooper's Story of the Bank Robbery". (1872) In *The Anthology of Colonial Australian Crime Fiction*, edited by Ken Gelder and Rachael Weaver. Melbourne: Melbourne University Press, 2008.

———. *Mary Summers: A Romance of the Australian Bush*. (1865) Canberra: Mulini Press, 1994.

Wickham, Gary and George Pavlich, eds. *Rethinking Law, Society and Governance: Foucault's Bequest*. Portland, Oreg.: Hart Publishing, 2001.

Williams, Raymond. *Marxism and Literature*. Oxford: Oxford University Press, 1977.

Wilson, Dean and Mark Finnane. "From Sleuths to Technicians? Changing Images of the Detective in Victoria". In *Police Detectives in History, 1750–1950*, edited by Clive Emsley and Haia Shpayer-Makov. Aldershot, UK: Ashgate Publishing, 2006.

Winterton, George. "The Acquisition of Independence". In *Reflections on the Australian Constitution*, edited by Robert French, Geoffrey Lindell and Cheryl Saunders. Sydney: The Federation Press, 2003.

Woollacott, Angela. *Settler Society in the Australian Colonies: Self-Government and Imperial Culture*. Oxford: Oxford University Press, 2015.

———. *To Try Her Fortune in London: Australian Women, Colonialism, and Modernity*. Oxford: Oxford University Press, 2001.

Works Cited

Woloch, Alex. *The One vs the Many: Minor Characters and the Space of the Protagonist in the Novel.* Princeton, NJ: Princeton University Press, 2003.

Woods, G.D. *A History of Criminal Law in New South Wales: The Colonial Period 1788–1900.* Sydney: The Federation Press, 2002.

Wright, Claire. *The Forgotten Rebels of Eureka.* Melbourne: Text Publishing, 2013.

Wrigley, Richard, ed. *The Flaneur Abroad: Historical and International Perspectives.* Newcastle upon Tyne, UK: Cambridge Scholars Publishing, 2014.

Index

Aboriginal people *see* Indigenous Australians
Adams, Francis 83
   Madeline Brown's Murderer 83
Adelaide 18, 112, 123
adventure fiction 15, 62, 65
Ahmed, Sara 124, 133
Appadurai, Arjun 6
Archibald, J.F. 88
Australian boy, the 2, 20, 20
Australian girl, the 2, 27, 63–64, 117–137

Baker, William 4–12
Balzac, Honoré de 2–4, 10, 23
Barnard, Edwin 7
Barrell, John 50
Baudelaire, Charles 111–113, 115
Baynton, Barbara 101–103
   "The Chosen Vessel" 101, 103
Beer, Gillian 46
Bellanta, Melissa 22, 107, 109
"Betsy Bandicoot" 119
Bird, Robert Montgomery 98–99
   Nick of the Woods 98
Bivona, Daniel 9
bohemian, the 64, 68–72
Boldrewood, Rolf 25, 46–50, 58–70, 96
   Old Melbourne Memories 46
   Robbery Under Arms 53, 58–63, 64, 66, 69, 76, 89
   "The Fencing of Wanderowna" 30, 49, 96
   The Squatter's Dream 30, 47–48, 50
Boltanski, Luc 76
Bonwick, James 54
   The Bushrangers 54
Borlase, James Skipp 15, 77
   The Night Fossickers 15, 77

Bourdieu, Pierre 69–71
Boyce, James 53, 55, 106
Bradley, Charles
   The Belgrave Case 84, 86
Brand, Dana 75, 82
Briggs, Jo 2
Brisbane, Thomas 117
Bulfin, Ailise 25
Burrows, William 77
bush hawker, the 57, 78, 91, 100
bush realism 125, 132, 136
bushman, the 48, 63, 88, 91–93, 126
bushranger, the 53–72, 74, 76, 111, 125
Butlin, Noel 1
Butlin, S.J. 117

Cameron, Donald 33, 99–100, 108–112
   Mysteries of Melbourne Life 108, 111
   "The Melbourne Dandy" 112
   "The Scowbanker" 99
Campbell, Rosemary 124
Carroll, Janet 121
   Magna 121
Castilla, Ethel
   "An Australian Girl" 121
Cataldi, Suzanne Laba 134
Champion, George 109
Champion, Shelagh 109
character types, minor 10–13, 25, 90, 94
Clacy, Ellen 16
   A Lady's Visit to the Gold Diggings of Australia 16
Clarke, Marcus 23–26, 37, 40, 66, 69, 97, 100, 114
   Long Odds 40, 100
   "Pretty Dick" 100
   The Future Australian Race 25

Index

The Peripatetic Philosopher 23
Clarke, Philip A. 57
Clemm, Sabine 73
Cochrane, Peter 34
colonial-born 2, 19–22, 61, 66, 84, 119; *see also* native-born
colonial detective fiction 10, 73–90
colonial economy 1, 5, 6, 8, 31, 58, 59, 62, 67, 82, 85, 88, 108, 112
"Coloniensis" 106
  "Melbourne" 106
"Coming Man", the 25–26
Conan Doyle, Arthur 82
  The Sign of Four 82
Conor, Liz 82
convict, the 12–16, 20, 26, 55, 56, 74
"cornstalk", the 20, 21, 26, 66
"Crayon" 19
  "Sketches in Sydney" 19
Critchett, Jan 47
Croft, Julian 106
Cunningham, Peter 20, 119
  Two Years in New South Wales 20, 119
currency lad, the 119
currency lass, the 117, 119–120

Daly, Maurice 114
Dalziell, Tanya 127, 129–131
dandy, the 27, 36, 79–80, 111–115
Davison, Graeme 13, 93
Davitt, Ellen 78, 121–123, 128
  Force and Fraud 78
  "The Black Sheep" 121–123
Dawson, Carrie 105
Day, Leanne 96
de Beauvoir, Simone 134
Dellamora, Richard 134, 136
detective, the 74–90
Dickens, Charles 10, 23, 37, 74
  Bleak House 74, 77
  Dombey and Son 4
  Household Words 32, 38, 73
digger, the 13–19, 66
Dimond, Jill 119
Dixon, Robert 14, 58, 62, 64, 127
Docker, John 131
Doggett, Anne 7
Duncan, William 34

Earle, Horace 19, 95–99, 105
  Ups and Downs 19, 96

Echuca 101–103, 109
Edwards, P.D. 44
Eggert, Paul 38, 39, 59, 95
Ellis, Havelock 135
Esquirol, Jean-Étienne 70

Falconer, Delia 8
"Fanny Flirt" 118
Farjeon, Benjamin 16, 19
Farrell, Michael 103
Federation 21, 83, 126, 131, 136
"Felix, Charles" 73
  The Notting Hill Mystery 73
Ferres, Kay 63–64
Finnane, Mark 75, 76, 77
Fletcher, Henry 86
  The North Shore Mystery 86
Fortune, Mary 77–81, 83
  "Dandy Art's Diary" 79–81
  The Detective's Album 78
Foster, Robert 94–95, 99
Fotheringham, Richard 8
Fowler, Elizabeth 1
Fowler, Frank 2, 19–20, 22
  Southern Lights and Shadows 19
Franklin, Miles 131, 134
  My Brilliant Career 131, 132
Fraser, Nancy 6
Freeman, John 22
  Lights and Shadows of Melbourne Life 22
frontier violence 41, 42, 51, 92, 94, 98, 130, 136
frontier, the 29, 49, 92–100, 102, 106, 128–130
Frow, John 9
Furphy, Joseph 40, 104–106
  Such Is Life 40, 104–106

Gaboriau, Émile 22, 84
"Garryowen" (Edmund Finn) 106–108
  The Chronicles of Early Melbourne 106–107
genre 10, 33, 41, 49–51, 58, 74, 76, 80, 94, 98, 108, 125, 132–132
Geoghegan, Edward 119
  The Currency Lass 119
Giles, Fiona 123, 125
Giles, Paul 41
Gipps, Sir George 32, 34–35, 42
Glover, David 72
Gluck, Mary 3
gold rush, the 13–16, 18, 59, 77
Goldstein, Jan 71
Goodman, David 13

Index

Gothic, the 33, 37, 38, 50
Grand, Sarah 126
Griffiths, Tom 47

Haggard, H. Rider 127
Halasz, Judith R. 69
Hall, Catherine 40
Hardy, Thomas 134
Hare, Francis Augustus 58
   The Last of the Bushrangers 58
Harpur, Charles 19, 34–35
   "Squatter Songs" 35
Harrison, Robert 111
   Colonial Sketches 111
Harrison, Rodney 43
Hassan, Andrew 32
Haynes, John 109
Heads of the People 4–12
Henderson, Ian 132-132, 134–135
Henkle, Roger B. 9
Hennessey, J.D. 127–131, 133, 136
   An Australian Bush Track 127, 130, 133
Hergenhan, L.T. 24, 123
Heseltine, Harry 97
Himmelfarb, Gertrude 13
Hobart 53
Hofenberg, Peter H. 21
Hogg, James 50
Hosking, Rick 95
Howe, Michael 53–57, 60, 62, 68, 72
Howe, Robert 117
Howitt, Richard 93
   Impressions of Australia Felix 93
Howitt, William 4, 14–16, 36–39, 50, 65, 93
   Land, Labour, and Gold 14
   Tallangetta 36, 38
Huart, Louis 2
Hume, Fergus 80–81, 85
   The Mystery of a Hansom Cab 80, 84, 87
"hut literature" 98
hut-keeper, the 97, 98

India 47, 67, 96
Indigenous Australians 12, 33, 40, 41, 47, 48, 49, 55–57, 71, 94–99, 130
Inglis Moore, Tom 91
Irving, Helen 21, 136

Janin, Jules 3–4, 24
Johnson-Woods, Toni 33
Johnson, Murray 57

Jordens, Ann-Mari 19

Kaladelfos, Amanda 102
Keal, Paul 54
Kelly, Ned 57–58, 60, 63, 67, 72
   Jerilderie Letter 57
Kendall, Henry 19
Kern, Stephen 71
King, William Francis 7–8
Kingsley, Henry 7, 39–43, 47, 50, 120
   The Hillyars and the Burtons 39, 42
   The Recollections of Geoffry Hamlyn 7, 39–43, 47, 120, 129
Kirkpatrick, Peter 119
Knight, Stephen 75, 77, 89, 108

labour 11, 13, 16, 29–32, 42, 109
Land, Isaac 82
Lang, John 73, 74, 79
   The Forger's Wife 73–74, 76, 79
larrikin, the 22–23, 106–111, 113
Lawson, Henry 66, 91, 95, 101, 104, 128, 132
   "Brummy Usen" 104
   "On the Edge of a Plain" 104
   "The Drover's Wife" 95, 101
   "That Swag (Enter Mitchell)" 104
   While the Billy Boils 104
Lemurian novel, the 127, 129–130
Linnaeus, Carl 2, 53
Liston, Ellen 94–95, 101
   "Doctor" 95
Lowe, Robert 33
   "Songs of the Squatters" 33
Ludlow, Christa 80, 86
lumpenproletariat, the 11, 12–16, 20, 22, 25, 46, 100
"Lydia Languish" 118
Lynch, Deirdre Shauna 5

Magarey, Susan 17
Malone, Patrick 114
Martin, Catherine 123–125, 129
   An Australian Girl 123–131
Martin, Susan K. 121
Marx, Karl 11, 31
   Capital 11, 31
   Eighteenth Brumaire of Louis Napoleon 11
"Mary Merino" 119
Masury, John W. 114
Mayhew, Henry 8–13, 45, 100, 109

Index

London Labour and the London Poor 8–13, 23, 45, 100
McCann, Andrew 23, 69
McCombie, Thomas 3, 12–14, 20, 27, 31, 35, 50
　Adventures of a Colonist 3, 31, 35, 53
　Australian Sketches 12–14
McLean, Ian W. 1
McLean, Ian A. 93
McMichael, Philip 1, 29, 45
Melbourne 14–24, 38, 67, 80, 83–85, 106–113
Merrett, David Tolmie 115
Miller, D.A. 86–87
Millet, Kate 134
Mitchell, Thomas 49, 56
　Three Expeditions into the Interior of Eastern Australia 56
modernity 14, 82, 91, 107, 111, 126, 130, 136
Moore, Alison 134
Morris, E.E. 23, 29
　Austral English 23, 29
Mundy, Godfrey 21
　Our Antipodes 21

national character 92–93
national identity 84, 136, 137
native-born 19, 20–21, 38, 43, 119–121, 136; *see also* colonial-born
native police 78
Nettlebeck, Amanda 94–95, 99
new chum, the 14, 19–20, 22, 24–25
New South Wales 17, 19, 20, 40, 43, 60, 73, 88, 117
New Woman 125–127, 134, 136
Newey, Katherine 120
night auctioneer 4–6, 8
Nisbet, Hume 11, 57, 64–72, 88, 109–111, 113
　A Colonial Tramp 109–110
　Bail Up! 64–66, 70, 71
　The Bush Girl's Romance 64
　The Bushranger's Sweetheart 64–70
　The Savage Queen 65
　The Swampers 11, 67, 88–89, 113, 115

O'Reilly, John Boyle 62
　Moondyne 63
old chum, the 22

Palmer, Vance 92
Parramatta 7, 8
Paterson, Banjo 103, 105
　"Waltzing Matilda" 103
Pedersen, Annette 83

Perelman, Bob 5
Philadelphoff-Puren, Nina 102
Phillips, A.A. 92
Pickard, John 94, 96
pieman, the 4, 7–9
Pittard, Christopher 80
Poe, Edgar Allan 24, 80, 82, 84
police, the 26, 74–78, 83, 88–89
Praed, Rosa 62–64, 67, 71, 121, 122–125, 127, 135, 136
　An Australian Heroine 121, 122, 125, 127, 133, 135, 137
　Fugitive Anne 127
　Outlaw and Lawmaker 62–64, 68, 69, 71
Prichard, James 45
proletariat, the 11, 13, 22, 25, 100
Pybus, Cassandra 56, 60, 63, 65, 70

Queensland 44, 62, 67, 97, 123, 127

Rae, Henry R. 99
Ramaswamy, Sumanthi 130
Richardson, Matthew 103
Roe, Jill 131
romance, fiction 10, 43, 50, 58, 65, 122–133
Rowcroft, Charles 55–56, 61, 61
　Tales of the Colonies 55, 61
　The Bushranger of Van Diemen's Land 55, 61, 69
Rudd, Steele 91

Sanyal, Debarati 111
Schaffer, Kay 93, 102, 103
Schreiner, Olive 126
Scott, George Firth 127
Scott, Sir Walter 30, 31, 46, 71
scowbanker, the 99–100
selector, the 26, 43–46, 91
Serville, Paul de 46, 60
settler, the 1, 3, 12, 18–21, 31, 36, 40, 45, 55–56, 74, 91, 94, 97, 99, 102, 120, 122, 129–132
Shannon, Mary L. 23
Sharp, William 124
shepherd, the 2, 10, 26, 49–50, 91, 92–100
Sheridan, Richard Brinsley 118
Sheridan, Susan 102, 125, 132
Shpayer-Makov, Haia 75
Sidney 32–36, 48
　Gallops and Gossips in the Bush of Australia 32, 48
　The Three Colonies of Australia 32
Sinclair, Jenny 22

Index

Sinnett, Frederick 17
Sipe, Daniel 115
Smajic, Srdjan 82
Smith, Adam 11
Smith, Albert 2–4, 20
Smith, Michelle J. 125–126
social zoology 2, 23
South Australia 17–18, 38, 94
Spence, Catherine Helen 17–18, 39
  Clara Morison 15, 17–18, 39
squatter novel 10, 26, 30, 31–33, 35, 39, 41, 43, 48–51, 94
squatter, the 29–51, 60–72, 96–99
Stephens, A.G. 131
Stewart, Ken 35, 38, 40
sundowner 99, 107, 110
Sussex, Lucy 80
swagman 78, 91, 99–107, 110
Swan, N. Walter 97
  Tales of Australian Life 97
Sydney 4–10, 19–21, 30, 74, 93, 114, 118
Symons, Julian 74, 80

Tasmania *see* Van Diemen's Land

"Tasma" (Jessie Couvreur) 124
"Telemachus" (Francis Myers) 59, 61, 71
Todorov, Tzvetan 76
Traill, W.H. 109
tracker, the 41, 56, 88
Trollope, Anthony 21, 25, 43–47, 50, 70
  Australia and New Zealand 21, 44
  Harry Heathcote of Gangoil 43, 44, 46, 47, 70
Trollope, Frederick 43, 46
Turner, Ethel 121, 126
Twopeny, Richard 21–23
  Town Life in Australia 21

vagabond, the 12, 45, 49
Van Diemen's Land 15, 53–56
"Vaux, James Hardy" 75
Victoria 12–20, 39, 75, 77

Wakefield, Edward Gibbon 30–32, 35, 38, 44
  A Letter from Sydney 30
  A View of the Art of Colonisation 31
Walker, William Sylvester 83
  Native Born 83
Ward, Russell 92–93, 106

www.ingramcontent.com/pod-product-compliance
Lightning Source LLC
Chambersburg PA
CBHW081827230426
43668CB00017B/2397